A JOURNALIST

To *the publisher, editors, and staff of* The Oklahoman, *a vital part of the Sooner State's history.*

THE MIND OF A JOURNALIST

HOW REPORTERS VIEW THEMSELVES, THEIR WORLD, AND THEIR CRAFT

Jim Willis

Azusa Pacific University

Epilogue by Marilyn Thomsen

La Sierra University

Los Angeles | London | New Delhi
Singapore | Washington DC

For information:

SAGE Publications, Inc.
2455 Teller Road
Thousand Oaks,
   California 91320
E-mail: order@sagepub.com

SAGE Publications India Pvt. Ltd.
B 1/I 1 Mohan Cooperative
   Industrial Area
Mathura Road, New Delhi 110 044
India

SAGE Publications Ltd.
1 Oliver's Yard
55 City Road
London EC1Y 1SP
United Kingdom

SAGE Publications Asia-Pacific Pte. Ltd.
33 Pekin Street #02-01
Far East Square
Singapore 048763

Printed in the United States of America

Library of Congress Cataloging-in-Publication Data

Willis, Jim.
The mind of a journalist: how reporters view themselves, their world, and their craft/Jim Willis.
   p. cm.
Includes bibliographical references and index.
ISBN 978-1-4129-5457-0 (pbk.)
   1. Journalism—United States—History—21st century. 2. Reporters and reporting—United States—History—21st century. 3. Television broadcasting of news—United States—History—21st century. I. Title.

PN4867.2W55 2010
071'.3—dc22   2009011941

This book is printed on acid-free paper.

09   10   11   12   13   10   9   8   7   6   5   4   3   2   1

Acquisitions Editor:	Todd R. Armstrong
Editorial Assistant:	Aja Baker
Production Editor:	Brittany Bauhaus
Copy Editor:	Karen E. Taylor
Typesetter:	C&M Digitals (P) Ltd.
Proofreader:	Sue Irwin
Cover Designer:	Gail Buschman
Marketing Manager:	Jennifer Reed Banando

Contents

Chapter 8: Questions Vexing Journalists   123

Epilogue: Reporting From Iraq: Journalists Talk About Covering War   137

Dr. Marilyn Thomsen of the Claremont Graduate University and La Sierra University interviews several front-line journalists on how reporting on the war in Iraq has affected them on both professional and personal levels.

Afterword: A Personal Odyssey   161

The author explores the personal impact of covering the bombing of the Alfred P. Murrah Federal Building in Oklahoma City.

Appendix 1: Covering Katrina: On Taking It Personally   167

Journalist Michael Perlstein examines the coverage of Hurricane Katrina and the effect the tragedy had on reporters writing about it.

Appendix 2: Thirteen Unique Journalists   173

The author presents a series of personality profiles on the panel of journalists who provided much of the insight in this book. The journalists profiled, and their affiliations when the interviews were conducted, are

Barry Bearak, Foreign Correspondent, *The New York Times*

Jim Redmond, Former Anchor/Reporter, KUSA-TV, Denver

Arlene Notoro Morgan, Former Assistant Managing Editor, *The Philadelphia Inquirer*

Peter Bhatia, Executive Editor, *The Oregonian*

Penny Owen, Features Reporter, *The Oklahoman*

Michael Walker, Author of *Laurel Canyon* and Former Reporter, the *Los Angeles Times* and *The New York Times*

Jim Robertson, Managing Editor, *Columbia Daily Tribune*

Gretchen Dworznik, Former Reporter, WNWO-TV, Toledo

Michael Perlstein, *The Times-Picayune*

Terry Mattingly, Religion Columnist, Scripps Howard News Service

Otis Sanford, Editor for Opinions and Editorials and Former Managing Editor, *The Commercial Appeal*

Joe Hight, Director of Information and Development, *The Oklahoman*

David Waters, *The Washington Post*

Foreword

The Thinking Journalist

Contrary to what many critics of the news media believe, journalists do a lot of thinking about what they do, whether they do it right, how they might do it better the next time around, and what can and cannot be changed about the problems of the media organizations for which they work. In a nutshell, their responses to these and other questions form the focus of this book.

Many journalism books provide good instruction in the art and craft of reporting and writing news and feature stories. There are other books that plumb the ethical dilemmas in which journalists often find themselves. Even more books exist that analyze the role of the news media in our world and the impact of journalism on American society. There are also some fine biographies of individual, high-profile journalists, texts that trace their personal and professional histories. What *The Mind of a Journalist* does is to examine how a cross section of print, broadcast, and online journalists perceive themselves, their world, and their craft. And, in large measure, it lets thirteen of these talented journalists put these perceptions into their own words. The reflections and observations of this nucleus of journalists are joined in the text by many additional observations made by many other journalists over the years. So this text is a combination of both primary and secondary research.

Among the issues the journalists examine are the lure of journalism, the stance journalists take toward the world they are assigned to cover, the ethical challenges journalists face, how close to get to a story or how far to distance themselves from it, journalists and politics, and even journalists and religion. The last issue is interesting because, although I wanted to cover this topic for this book, I wasn't sure there would be enough interest among journalists in discussing it. I discovered just the opposite: that, although many mainstream media are reluctant to cover religion, journalists think about matters of faith a lot. As a result, the chapter "The Journalist and Faith" became the longest chapter by far in this book.

The observations that the journalists make come from their many years of experience in the news business. Some of these comments are philosophical, but many are anecdotal. Although the remarks may occasionally present ideas often heard about journalism, they are not stereotypes. Veteran journalists know their field better than anyone else because they live and breathe it and often treat it as more of a mission than a job.

I chose a dozen current and former American journalists whom I knew, or knew of, to interview. I asked them about their thoughts regarding the status of journalism and the things about the business they like and dislike. A thirteenth journalist, whom I met later and who had been a key member of the Pulitzer Prize-winning team covering Hurricane Katrina for *The Times-Picayune* in New Orleans, was added in January of 2008. These are journalists I respect, and they have received the accolades of their peers in the news business. Each responded to a range of questions addressing issues such as their motivation to enter the profession; their stance in the debate about attached vs. detached reporting; their thoughts on journalists and politics, journalists and religion, and the ethical dilemmas in the business; their frustrations as well as gratifications; and so on. These journalists and their observations serve as the foundation for this book, and each of the journalists is profiled in Appendix 2. To their thoughts, I have added observations from other journalists gleaned from a variety of sources; all reflections are arranged thematically in chapters 1–8. In the afterword, I have added my own observations on some of these issues—observations accumulated from my own years as a journalist, which were capped by my experience of covering one of America's great tragedies, the 1995 bombing of the Alfred P. Murrah Federal Building in Oklahoma City.

In am indebted to Dr. Marilyn Thomsen, whose work at the Claremont Graduate University in Claremont, California, culminated in the interviews of several front-line journalists who covered the war in Iraq. Although these journalists are separate from the thirteen whose comments are spread through chapters 1–8, I chose to include Thomsen's report on these interviews because it adds an important, contemporary element to how journalists approach their work and the effects that work has on them, both professionally and personally. The subject of how traumatic stories affect journalists who do the reporting is a growing issue, and no story is more traumatic than war.

The book winds up with two appendices, the first of which is a personal look by journalist Michael Perlstein at the coverage of Hurricane Katrina in New Orleans. The second appendix is a series of personality profiles on the panel of thirteen journalists selected to form the backbone of this book.

I hope that, taken together, all these observations will provide current and future journalists with added insight into the various perspectives that reporters and editors take into this very vital business of covering the day's news in this American democracy.

The thirteen journalists interviewed for this book represent large and small news operations in the print, broadcast, and online media worlds. The group is comprised of both male and female journalists. It includes journalists who have reported from around the world and some who are committed to community journalism. There are Pulitzer Prize winners in the group, managing editors, a foreign correspondent, television news anchors, beat reporters, a past president of the American Society of Newspaper Editors, and a future president of the Associated Press Managing Editors organization. Some are still in the business, decades after beginning; some have left and moved on to other careers. It is interesting, however, that those who have left have moved on to universities, where they teach journalism. Such is my own case, and it speaks to the desire of these journalists to take time to reflect on journalism, discover ways it can be done better, and then pass that knowledge on to students who are majoring in the field.

In the order in which they were interviewed, here are the journalists who form the foundational panel for this study, the news organizations for which they work or worked, and what they do now if they have moved on:

Barry Bearak, Pulitzer Prize-winning foreign correspondent for *The New York Times* and a former national correspondent for the *Los Angeles Times.*

Jim Redmond, longtime news anchor and reporter for KUSA-TV in Denver and professor of journalism at the University of Memphis, where he chaired the Department of Journalism until the summer of 2008.

Gretchen Dworznik, former reporter for WNWO-TV in Toledo and now an assistant professor of communication arts at Ashland University.

Joe Hight, managing editor for features for *The Oklahoman* and former two-term president of the Dart Center for Trauma and Journalism.

Arlene Notoro Morgan, veteran reporter and assistant managing editor for *The Philadelphia Inquirer,* who is now associate dean of the Columbia University Graduate School of Journalism in New York City.

Otis Sanford, managing editor of *The Commercial Appeal* in Memphis and on the leadership team of the Associated Press Managing Editors group, over which he will preside in 2011. Sanford is also the first African American managing editor of *The Commercial Appeal.*

David Waters, producer of the On Faith Web site project of *The Washington Post* and its sister publication *Newsweek* and a veteran religion editor and award-winning religion writer for *The Commercial Appeal.*

Penny Owen, veteran police and feature reporter for *The Oklahoman,* who helped lead that newspaper's award-winning coverage of the bombing of the

Alfred P. Murrah Federal Building in 1995 and who stayed on that story for some six years afterwards. She was also an Associated Press reporter in Dallas.

Jim Robertson, managing editor of the *Columbia Daily Tribune* in Columbia, Missouri, long recognized as one of the best community dailies in America.

Peter Bhatia, executive editor of the Pulitzer Prize-winning newspaper *The Oregonian,* in Portland. Bhatia is a former managing editor of the *Sacramento Bee* and a past president of the American Society of Newspaper Editors.

Terry Mattingly, syndicated religion columnist for the Scripps Howard News Service, editor of the GetReligion.org Web site, and director of the Washington Journalism Center, a training program for college journalism majors sponsored by the Council of Christian Colleges and Universities.

Michael Walker, former reporter for both *The New York Times* and the *Los Angeles Times,* who now is author of the best-selling book *Laurel Canyon: The Inside History of Rock and Roll's Legendary Neighborhood.*

Michael Perlstein, veteran reporter for *The Times-Picayune* in New Orleans who was instrumental in the Pulitzer Prize-winning team coverage of Hurricane Katrina in 2005. Perlstein is now visiting professor of journalism at Loyola University in New Orleans.

The observations of these gifted and dedicated journalists are found in two forms within the pages that follow. First, their insights are woven throughout each chapter as they address the focal points found in those chapters. Second, each of the thirteen journalists is profiled in Appendix 2 of the book. When their observations appear in the main chapters, they are not footnoted, although their comments are attributed to them. Their quoted insights all come from the series of interviews I conducted with them either in person, over the phone, or online in the summer of 2007. Michael Perlstein's comments were made in a January 2008 interview, and some of his observations are reproduced with permission from the alumni magazine of his alma mater, Reed College. The full text of the article "Covering Katrina: On Taking It Personally," which he wrote for that magazine in 2006, forms Appendix 1.

My heartfelt thanks go out to each of these journalists, not just for agreeing to contribute to this project but mostly for the talent, wisdom, and dedication they have brought to the profession of journalism over the decades in which they have produced some amazing pieces of American reporting. I would also like to thank the other journalists, from whose wisdom I have borrowed to round out this study of how reporters and editors view themselves, their world, and the craft of journalism. As always, I also want to thank my wonderful wife Anne for her constant love and support and my colleagues at Azusa Pacific University for letting their department chair divert his focus to his publishing ventures yet again.

The author and SAGE gratefully acknowledge the contributions of the following reviewers:

Berrin A. Beasley, *University of North Florida*

Ceres Birkhead, *University of Utah*

David C. Craig, *University of Oklahoma*

Charles Fountain, *Northeastern University*

John F. Greenman, *University of Georgia*

Harry Kloman, *University of Pittsburgh*

Thomas P. Oates, *Penn State University, New Kensington*

Mark Popovich, *Ball State University*

Bill Reader, *Ohio University*

Richard C. Ward, *Columbia University, Graduate School of Journalism*

1

The Lure of Journalism

What motivates a young person to become a journalist? This is a very competitive profession that primarily takes college graduates who are highly literate and who have high levels of intellectual curiosity. Yet these young journalists received average starting salaries of only $30,000 in 2006.[1] Why make the effort? Why would a college student, active in student life and in the plethora of organizations that come with it, turn to a profession that tends to isolate its members from socializing with others? Journalism does not rate that high in popularity among the general public, and many parents worry that their children will not be able to make much of a living if they become journalists. Additionally, the newspaper industry is facing serious threats to its survival with readers and advertisers turning to other media platforms such as television and the Internet. Finally, although the average daily newspaper in America is still highly profitable, much of that profit comes from cutbacks in departments seen as "non-revenue producing," and several media companies perceive the newsroom as one of these departments. Therefore, even as the number of daily newspapers has shrunk from two or three in every major city to one in all but a few cities, the number of reporting and editing jobs on many newspapers has also decreased. The profession is now more competitive than ever. So we return to the question: What motivates a young person to become a journalist?

The Love of Reading and Writing

One of the most common traits found among aspiring journalists is that they simply love to read and they love to write. Part of this love springs from their insatiable curiosity, but part of it is their love affair with the written word and their artistic desire to create something profound and beautiful. Here's what author Michael Walker, formerly of *The New York Times* and the *Los Angeles Times*, says about this passion: "What got me interested in journalism was good writing," Walker explains.

> My father used to read my brother and me James Thurber short stories as bedtime stories; plus both parents were avid readers of the *Chicago Daily News* in the 70s when it still had Mike Royko and others. Also I was deeply influenced by *Rolling Stone* and the writings of Joe Eszterhas, Hunter Thompson, and Timothy Crouse.

> They were such good writers; they made me want to write and report as well as they did. So I took the shortest route I could think of, and, since I liked rock and played in a band, I started writing concert reviews for my high school paper. Stuff like Jethro Tull, Elton John, the Faces, etc. All the big shows that came through Chicago.[2]

Walker combined those passions of reading, writing, and music and wound up as an arts and entertainment writer for the *Los Angeles Times* and then as author of *Laurel Canyon: An Inside History of Rock and Roll's Legendary Neighborhood*.

Jim Robertson, managing editor of the *Columbia Daily Tribune*, found he could weld his love of writing to newspaper journalism.

"I got my first byline in our community weekly paper at about age 10," Robertson says. "It was an account of a 4-H camping trip, and I instinctively used storytelling technique. The positive feedback was a revelation. I led a team in high school that established a weekly community alternative newspaper. During that time in the late 1960s and early 1970s, the power of newspaper journalism took on a new tone for me as I read reports from Vietnam and Watergate—unprecedented war coverage."

What he discovered was there is a kind of unwritten contract existing between the journalist and the reader when it comes to newspaper journalism.

"I started to understand the intimate connection between readers and their newspapers," he explains, "and the fact that readers expect not only information but leadership. Tremendous potential to be a progressive force. The mix of ego and altruism hooked me early and sustained me through high school and college."

And one Illinois reporter said in response to a nationwide survey on reporter motivations:

> Reporters most enjoy the creative process that goes into writing a good story, being able to choose the correct words, organization and mood without the interference of someone else.[3]

Journalists are, by nature, voracious readers. Walk into most journalists' homes or apartments and you will be greeted by full bookcases and other books scattered about, both nonfiction and fiction. Journalists love to devour information and get a lot of their story ideas and observational clues from other writers' works. They also pick up ideas on writing itself. Many journalists are born or cultivated editors who read not just for pleasure and information but also to see how the author writes. Is there anything about this style that I like or dislike? Can I incorporate it into my own writing style, or even change my style to read more like this? These are questions that haunt journalists as they read, and, consciously or subconsciously, they are believers in the saying that "to write well, you have to read a lot and write a lot." So journalism becomes a favored choice for a profession because reading and writing are what journalists do on a daily basis as they research and report their stories.

As for writing itself, journalists find a lot of creative possibilities existing within the framework of journalistic style because that framework evolves to make room for the best writers and reporters. The traditional "inverted pyramid" format has given way to more narrative storytelling that is nearly identical in form to the narrative style that fiction writers use. But even within the inverted pyramid (summary lead, amplification paragraph, followed by details in descending order of importance), many journalists find creative territory and work with a wide range of creative analogies, similes, and individual words and combinations of them to create beautifully descriptive passages. Ever since Truman Capote shook the journalistic world with his new style of "nonfiction novel" when he wrote *In Cold Blood* nearly five decades ago, other journalists have continued to open what had been a formulaic journalistic structure, to adapt this structure to the styles of many different writers.

An Intense Curiosity

Closely associated with their passion for reading is the insatiable curiosity that journalists have about what is going on. Journalists must determine whether the surface action is as it seems or whether there is something else going on beneath the surface and why. A nationwide survey of reporters revealed the following areas related to curiosity as prime positives of the profession for these responders: learning new things every day, meeting newsmakers, covering a variety of stories, and having a status as an insider.[4] Journalists, probably since childhood, have wanted to know how things work and have been unsatisfied with pat answers. Frequently, journalists will say that one of the best things about their jobs is getting to learn new things every day. If a newspaper is the classroom of its readers, then the world is a classroom for journalists—or at least that portion of the world the journalist covers.

One television journalist turned college professor, Gretchen Dworznik, described her motivation this way: "Even as a child I'd always loved the news, and I got most of it from television news shows. Also, Mom was a magazine freak, and I'd read her *Time* and *Newsweek* magazines and even cut out articles on major stories like the Challenger disaster and Pan Am 103. Not out of morbidity, but just out of interest." Her story is not unlike that of many other current and former journalists. If people are interested in slaking their curiosity about the world, then journalism is the career for them.

A Desire to Contribute

The love of reading and writing and an intense curiosity about the world can help drive a person into journalism, but the desire to contribute to society— to right the wrongs and make things better—is often what keeps them there. And, for many, this embodiment of near-missionary zeal is the prime motivator for entering the profession. Listen to what a couple of journalists have to say about this. Here is what Peter Bhatia, executive editor of *The Oregonian*, says about his motivation:

> It is the same today as it was when I was a teenager. I loved writing stories, I loved being the eyes and ears for others, and I very much wanted the opportunity to do something that had a social purpose. Working in newspapers has fulfilled my career expectations. I wanted to do meaningful work, have the opportunity to be a witness to history, have an opportunity to make a difference through the work we do in newsrooms.

A deep concern for helping others was a prime motivation for Joe Hight's becoming a journalist in the first place, and he discovered that many people could be helped simply by learning the truth about situations in the world. He majored in journalism at the University of Central Oklahoma and has spent nearly 30 years in the profession since. He is managing editor for features and newsroom training at *The Oklahoman*, the Oklahoma City newspaper that led the coverage of the 1995 bombing of the Alfred P. Murrah Federal Building.

"Idealistically, I wanted to make a difference in people's lives," Hight says. "Early on when I worked at a campus newspaper I learned that the media have a significant effect on people and how they react to news and events that affect their lives. I also found that, because of the First Amendment, journalists were vital to our democracy. Those two factors, and my instructors and fellow journalism students in college, motivated me."

The Grady College of Journalism at the University of Georgia conducts an annual, nationwide survey of recent graduates in journalism and mass communication. Among the questions asked are ones related to what new journalists like about their jobs. Every year, these recent grads report a high level of satisfaction derived from feeling they are making a difference in society.[5]

The Independence Factor

Most writers love the independence that comes with this creative craft. Writing or reporting is often an individual effort, although much less so when one reports for a television station, where reporters, videographers, and editors usually work as a team. A newspaper reporter generally pursues a story on her own, however, possibly after initial consultation with the editor and any photographer or graphic artist assigned to do supplements to the story. Reporters love blending into the woodwork of the events they cover. Again, that is harder to do for television reporters because they are on-air talent who are easily recognized by many on the street. Even so, television reporters enjoy the same ideal of independence that newspaper reporters do when it comes to actually reporting and crafting the text of their stories. Few other professions allow their practitioners to enjoy the kind of independence that journalists enjoy, and that is a big draw for many who go into journalism. Even with the ever-present reality of editors, some of whom are prone to make changes to reporters' copy without first consulting them, reporters seem to feel they have more independence than those in most other professions.

Like other aspects of the business, however, independence is not an absolute. There are pressures and organizational requirements, and the team aspect of television news is one, as has been noted. But there are several other potential restrictions to a reporter's independence. Among them are the following:

• *Available resources.* Some stories are just too time consuming or expensive for a newspaper or television station to cover. For example, a reporter wanting to do a story requiring expensive travel to another region might discover that the project is too expensive. The story, if done at all, will have to be done from home base. A more common example of a resource restriction is lack of time. A story that would take a reporter a long time to research and produce is rarely pursued. Most daily news operations require their reporters to produce at least one story a day, if not more. One reason investigative projects have been curtailed at many news outlets is that these stories just take too long, take the reporter out of the daily rotation of stories, and are deemed too expensive.

• *Editors and their expectations.* When a reporter wants to do a story that his editor doesn't define as news or when he wants to take a different angle on the story than the editor wants, friction can arise, and the story may not be done at all. At least not by that reporter. Getting approval of the reporter's version depends on how flexible the editor is and how well the reporter can sell the story and its angle to the editor.

• *The marketing department.* In newsrooms across the nation, walls have come down between the newsroom and the marketing department. More and more, stories are being judged as interesting (or not) to those who live in areas of the city where the newspaper wants to concentrate its efforts to secure subscribers and advertisers. To the dismay of many reporters and editors, that means more suburban, middle-class coverage and less coverage of those in need in the inner city. The disenfranchised don't usually subscribe to newspapers, and advertisers don't target them as buyers. So the marketing goals of the newspaper or TV station may emerge as paramount in some decisions on what areas of town to cover the most. This potential restriction varies from one news company to the next, depending on how much independence the company grants its news operation.

• *Public journalism.* This concept of news, which has been in existence for a couple of decades and which gains more favor with some news companies than with others, is controversial in the profession. Some see it simply as paying more legitimate attention to the news consumers by asking them what they would like to see covered. Others see it as abdicating the editorial responsibilities of the newsroom to untrained and self-interested groups and individuals. Public journalism is an effort to connect more with news consumers, getting them more involved in the selection of news stories, seeking more feedback from them, and setting up forums that look for solutions to the problems covered. Some news media set up editorial advisory boards of readers or viewers; other news operations do readership or viewership surveys and use the results to help them define news for that market.

• *Consultants.* Television news operations have used consultants for many years to guide them in their selection of what news to cover and in the ways of packaging those stories. One of the jobs of these consultants is to monitor the kinds of stories and "sweeps" series that are working in other markets around the country and to inform news directors at client stations about these results. Some of these consulting companies are national in scope, and they include Frank N. Magid Associates, Inc., as well as Audience Research & Development. Many journalists dislike the influence these consultants have over their own newsrooms and over the kinds of stories they are assigned to cover.

- *The "chilling effect" of libel.* Another reason that some news media have backed off from doing investigative stories is that they often result in allegations of wrongdoing that can result in libel suits filed against the newspaper or television station. Even though the news operation may feel it can win the case, the cost of fighting a libel suit can be extreme in and of itself. It is out of the question for some smaller news operations to respond to lawsuits, and it is an unwanted hassle for many larger news media. So the threat of libel itself can cool a story down if the editors, news directors, or publishers and general managers decide it's not worth it. This threat is felt by even the largest news media. CBS decided to back off airing the full interview with Jeffrey Wigand, former head of research for Brown & Williamson Tobacco Corporation, who was alleging nicotine boosting by the company. The reason was the threat of a lawsuit (in this case because of "tortuous interference") posed by B&W and treated seriously by the legal division and top management of CBS-TV. The interview aired at a later date, but only after other media had published and aired the same story first. The whole episode, which tarnished the CBS reputation for a while, was the subject of the film, *The Insider.*

At first glance, it would seem there are several threats to journalistic independence, but many daily news reporters never encounter these potential restrictions and, when they do, don't run into them often. Journalism is still a job with a great deal of creative independence.

Being on the Inside

Journalists love being on the inside of things. They love meeting newsmakers and getting to know them, and they love being the first to know things. This motivation is related to the one previously discussed, curiosity, but it extends that motivation to being able to rub shoulders with newsmakers on a regular basis. This desire can also compromise a reporter, however, so journalists know they must be vigilant in keeping the line drawn between friendships and professional relationships. In the real world, that line gets crossed a lot, and it falls to the reporter to keep her integrity as a journalist intact, even though a friendship with a source or government official may exist. It's not easy to mix the two kinds of relationships, especially when events call for the reporter to do a harsh story on a friend.

Both journalists and government officials know they need each other to achieve their own goals. It's a symbiotic relationship in which the source needs the journalist to get a particular side of the story out, and the journalist needs the source in order to provide the story in the first place. The journalist-source manipulation can go both ways. The film *Capote* depicted the relationship that writer Truman Capote had with the convicted murderer Perry Smith following the 1959 brutal slaying of Herbert Clutter's family on a quiet Kansas farm. This was a complicated relationship wherein Smith and Capote needed one another, and each tried to manipulate the other for his own individual ends. Capote was working on what would become the classic nonfiction novel, *In Cold Blood,* and he needed everything Perry could tell him. Perry wanted to stay alive and needed Capote to help him gain appeals. Beyond the self-interest and manipulation, however, there seemed to exist a real friendship and caring between the two men, who found themselves to be more alike than many would assume. At one point in the film, while talking with Perry in his death-row prison cell, Capote tells Perry, "We came from the same house; I came out the front door, and you went out the back." In crossing the line between friend and professional journalist, Capote created difficulties both for himself and for Perry. Others noted the closeness between the writer and his source. One could make an argument that, in cases like this, the lure of journalism can also be the writer's quest to understand himself or herself better. Here is how one writer viewed Capote and Perry Smith:

> After "In Cold Blood" was published, Capote's friends and detractors (and he had plenty of both) would remark on the parallels between the author and Perry Smith, the more sensitive and guilt-ridden of the two killers (Richard Hickock was the other). Possibly, Capote felt a physical kinship to Smith: His body, as one of his "swans" would later recount in George Plimpton's "Truman Capote," combined a boyish face and torso with "the legs of a truck driver." More likely he simply understood that what separated him from Smith, more than anything, was luck. Capote, like Smith, had been born to absent, unreliable parents. Both had suicide and alcoholism in the family. Both were desperate for acceptance, but they also had ironclad estimations of their own importance— Perry, in his words, was "special"; Capote, in his own, "a genius." Were it not for his mother's second marriage and his own considerable charms and angelic good looks (and his keen ability to ingratiate himself to his benefactors), Capote might have ended up as alone and desperate as Smith did. Like Smith,

Capote knew exactly what he wanted to be, and he constructed himself accordingly. Capote's ambitions were realized; Smith's weren't.[6]

Another journalist has written about how being so close to the intensity of stories can lead a writer to a deeper understanding of himself or herself. He is Anderson Cooper of CNN's popular news show *AC 360°*. About this phenomenon, which for him is a lure in journalism, he writes about his mother's advice to him when he asked her, following the pain of his brother's suicide, what she thought he should do after graduating from Yale:

> "Follow your bliss," she said, quoting Joseph Campbell. I was hoping for something more specific—"Plastics," for instance. I worried I couldn't "follow my bliss" because I couldn't feel my bliss. I couldn't feel anything at all. I wanted to be someplace where emotions were palpable, where the pain outside matched the pain I was feeling inside. I needed balance, equilibrium, or as close to it as I could get. I also wanted to survive, and I thought I could learn from others who had. War seemed like my only option.[7]

So Cooper headed to the war zones of the world as a freelance journalist, quickly parlaying his stories into jobs with the networks, winding up at CNN. Discussing one particular harrowing moment in Croatia, he reveals what he saw in himself in a near-death moment:

> I'd just set up my tripod when I heard a loud crack. I turned and saw a tile fall off a nearby column. But the time it hit the ground, I realized that it had been struck by a bullet. Someone had taken a shot . . . I captured some of it on camera, and narrated what I was seeing. I was white as a corpse. When I looked at the tape recently, though, I saw something I hadn't remembered. I noticed the faint hint of a smile on my face.[8]

Being on the inside of news in the making is an alluring thing for journalists, but it can also cause trouble when they try to separate themselves out personally and professionally from the people and events they cover. Former Toledo television reporter Gretchen Dworznik put her dilemma this way: "My decision to leave the news business had a lot to do with the issue of detachment," she says. "I didn't like to be too detached, but it became hard to handle the attachment as well after the fact. So I was in a kind of Catch-22 situation. Do I care? Do I not care? So I told myself maybe this dilemma is telling me perhaps I should get out now."

The lure to be on the inside of major news events or within the inner circle of newsmakers is tempting, but also potentially co-opting. In the case of Washington DC reporters, this lure is at once both promising and problematic.

High-profile journalists are often on the invitation lists of Washington's best and brightest. There might be a hope of co-opting a reporter to a particular side of an issue; sometimes, a network journalist just adds cachet to the guest list. But journalists might also be invited because a politician or bureaucrat wants to leak information to them or—sometimes—to find out what they know. If the reason is to leak information, it is a planned leak, generally authorized up the line. This information is usually off the record and often to be used for background purposes only. Veteran reporters understand all this and must filter the information they receive through that prism as well as recognize the attempts on the part of their host to persuade them to see things their host's way. Understanding the nature of the invitation, reporters often attend these events gladly because it gets them closer to the newsmakers and the issues they are covering and may allow them to pick up on some unplanned leaks that could advance their stories.

This cat-and-mouse game of Washington invitations is one of the most obvious examples of the symbiotic relationship that exists between journalists and politicians. Just as in the case of Truman Capote and Perry Smith, Washington reporters and politicians desperately need each other to further their own goals.

The Challenges of Going Deeper

Sometimes, the lure of journalism is simply to tell a story better and in more detail than it has been told so far. And, sometimes, the hurdles to telling that story act as a catalyst for writers addicted to their mission. The reminisces of writers are strewn with tales of how they saw a story about an interesting event, thought it was underdeveloped, and felt a compelling urge to go deeper into that story. They knew that the story deserved more than it got, that the reaction of the friends and loved ones of the victims was missing. Here is how writer Sebastian Junger describes the origins of his book *The Perfect Storm*:

> My own experience in the storm was limited to standing on Gloucester's Back Shore watching thirty-foot swells advance on Cape Ann, but that was all it took. The next day I read in the paper that a Gloucester boat was feared lost at sea, and I clipped the article and stuck it in a drawer. Without even knowing it, I had begun to write *The Perfect Storm*.[9]

Simply having the desire to tell a deeper story, however, does not guarantee that a reporter can get access to that story easily or that other challenges do not await. Yet these challenges often act as added bait to a writer hungry to tell that untold story. It was that way with Junger, who overcame his own doubts about his ability to get to the heart of this story and who describes many initial challenges when confronting his sources in a Gloucester fisherman's bar:

> The first time I'd ever gone into the Crow's Nest, it had taken me half an hour to work up the nerve . . . I was going in there to ask a woman about the death of her son. I wasn't a fisherman, I wasn't from Gloucester, and I wasn't a journalist, at least by my own definition of the word. I was just a guy with a pen and paper and an idea for a book. I slid a steno pad under my belt against the small of my back . . . Then I took a long breath and I got out of the car and walked across the street. The front door was heavier than I expected. . . . There were a dozen men clutching beers in the indoor gloom. Every single one turned and looked at me when I walked in. I ignored their looks.[10]

From that improbable start, Junger made friends with the bar's owner, Ethel Shatford, who had lost her son Bobby in the storm. With her on his side, the others in the bar gradually opened up to him, and a book was born. Anyone who has reported a tough story knows what the adrenaline rush must have felt like to Junger when he succeeded in getting people to talk.

Truman Capote's experience was similar to Junger's. He had read a brief 300-word story in the back of the *New York Times* about the Clutter family murder in Kansas. The story was done in journalism's classic inverted pyramid style, summarizing the act but never getting to the why of it or its impact. The lead read simply:

> Holcomb, Kan., Nov. 15 [1959] (UPI)—A wealthy wheat farmer, his wife and their two young children were found shot to death today in their home. They had been killed by shotgun blasts at close range after being bound and gagged . . . There were no signs of a struggle, and nothing had been stolen. The telephone lines had been cut.[11]

Capote immediately called his editor at *The New Yorker* and told him this was the story he wanted to write next, envisioning it first as probably a magazine piece. When asked why he wanted to cover a story about a murder in Kansas, Capote responded that he wanted to write about more than the murder itself; he wanted to write about how people in this quiet, heartland community dealt with such a senseless tragedy as the slaying of an entire farm family for no apparent reason. He envisioned the story as a collision of two different worlds, and it was a story that eventually took him six years to write before his groundbreaking book, *In Cold Blood,* was published in 1965.

Notes

1. "Salary Survey Report for Job: Journalist," *PayScale*, http://www.payscale.com/research/US/Job=Journalist/Salary (accessed April 22, 2008).

2. This quotation and all future quotations without corresponding endnotes are from personal interviews that the author has conducted with eminent journalists. Attribution is in the text of this book.

3. Jim Willis, "Good and Bad of Reporting and Editing," *Editor & Publisher*, February 27, 1982, 44.

4. Willis, "Good and Bad," 44.

5. Lee B. Becker, Tudor Vlad, Megan Vogel, Stephanie Hanisak, and Donna Wilcox, eds., 2007 *Annual Survey of Mass Communication Graduates* (Athens, GA: Grady College of Journalism & Mass Communication, 2007), 17.

6. Amy Standen, "In Cold Blood," *Salon*, January 22, 2002, http://dir.salon.com/story/ent/masterpiece/2002/01/22/cold_blood/index.html (accessed October 20, 2007), 1–2.

7. Anderson Cooper, *Dispatches from the Edge: A Memoir of War, Disasters, and Survival* (New York: Harper Collins, 2006), 46.

8. Cooper, 55.

9. Sebastian Junger, *The Perfect Storm* (New York: Harper Collins, 1997), x.

10. Junger, 227–228.

11. "Wealthy Farmer, 3 of Family Slain," *The New York Times*, Nov. 16, 1959, 39.

2

The Priesthood of Journalists

Many journalists call their work a profession, while others call it a craft. Increasingly, the more jaded reporters see it mainly as a highly profitable business built largely on newsroom cutbacks. But there is one way in which many journalists see themselves, although this perception may not arise until after they have been practicing the craft for some time: Journalists see journalism as a kind of *professional priesthood* in which they, much like the clergy or even police officers, surrender to the higher calling of serving others. Theorists might refer to two theories in describing this priesthood: *hegemony* theory (directed at what journalists believe and comprising the social, cultural, and ideological beliefs of journalists) and *news work* (directed at what journalists learn and experience on the job.) New York University researcher Jay Rosen notes that this priesthood "creates and maintains its authority over what counts as serious journalism" and has a well-developed sense of duty. He even goes on to describe what he calls the "god terms and faith objects in journalism." In sum, he calls it a "high church in journalism, with high ceremonies, like awarding of a Pulitzer Prize, joining the panel on 'Meet the Press,'" and so on.[1]

While this coming together as a unique work group may be a helpful stance for journalists to take in separating themselves from the stories they cover, it is also a stance that suggests arrogance to many news consumers. One common criticism of the news media is that editors and reporters are the ones who decide what is important for the world to know, and they are the ones who decide how that information should be used and framed, if they choose to use it at all. Critics deride reporters and editors for appearing to shut the public out of the loop when it comes to deciding what is news, and that often is defined as arrogance on the part of an elite community of journalists. Some have referred to journalists as a clan whose members carry out their responsibilities according to the rules of the clan in order to get validation from others within the clan. The kind of clan that journalists comprise is discussed in the next chapter, specifically under the heading of "Socialization of Journalists." That socialization process is one of the factors leading to the worldviews that journalists hold.

Some criticize journalists for myopia, which critics perceive to be induced by the news industry, as a later chapter will show when it discusses former MIT linguist Noam Chomsky, who proposed that journalists work for news media that are in the grip of powerful corporations run by individuals in league with powerful government officials. The information that comes through the media pipeline is controlled by the power elite in America, which uses it as a weapon to sell specific ideologies and keep the masses in line.

These critiques of the media have not gone unnoticed by media managers, who have tried to bring readers and viewers more into the loop over the years in deciding which kinds of stories should be covered more often. This consumer feedback is the crux of the concept known as "public journalism" or "civic journalism," which intentionally promotes more interactivity with the market's public. Critics within the journalistic community perceive that as a cop-out, turning over a big portion of the editorial function to untrained people who don't understand the nature of journalism. But the news media are all in a fight for survival and larger market shares in an age of intense media competition. The day of editors standing on Mount Olympus and dictating to the people what they should and shouldn't know is, to a large degree, over. In its place has come more attention to audience research and readership studies, along with more public forums hosted by newspapers and television stations to let the public have more of a say about what the news should be for them.

Journalism as the Fourth Estate

This "higher calling" is typified by the classical description of journalism as the "fourth estate," a term generally attributed to Thomas Carlyle, a noted historian of the nineteenth century. Carlyle, however, attributed its genesis back to English writer Edmond Burke, who said that the press gallery in Parliament was more important than any of the three official branches of British government the press covered. To Carlyle, the British press was a powerful, unofficial branch of government, as important as the priesthood, the aristocracy, and the House of Commons.[2] Other commentators and philosophers have used the term "fourth estate" to signify the media as the fourth power that provides counterbalances and checks on the executive, legislative, and judicial branches of American government. Other uses and interpretations of the term refer to the mediation role of the press between government and society, its translating of government policy and decisions for the American public, for example, and to the so-called "watchdog" function of the media in free societies, where the press serves as a guardian of public welfare. Later, this chapter provides an illustration of this watchdog role when it outlines the role some journalists interpret for themselves as giving voice to the powerless.

The concept of the fourth estate is not voiced as much today in daily conversations about journalism, but the meanings attached to the concept remain intact in the minds of serious journalists serving free societies everywhere. It is a big part of the lure that draws many idealistic young people into the world of journalism in the first place—and that keeps them in the business as a career—as later discussions with journalists will show.

Learning the Ropes

A second aspect of this *priesthood* is that the norms and ethics of the calling are a product of a kind of journalistic inbreeding. In other words, a journalist learns what is acceptable and unacceptable behavior from other journalists who learned it from other journalists, etc. There are also the various ethical codes published by journalistic organizations such as the Society of Professional Journalists and the American Society of Newspaper Editors, along with standards and practices laid down by individual media operations. Although a formal hierarchy, like that of the Catholic Church, is missing, there is a more informal—yet very real—set of in-profession (and often in-house) standards that guide the work of individual journalists. This socialization aspect will be the focus of a later chapter.

The term "professional priesthood" has been applied to the journalism profession by many people over many years. Even a casual survey of those keywords on the World Wide Web will underscore that. Here is an interesting interpretation of the concept:

> Today's news is created, packaged, and delivered by a priesthood of journalists, trained by editors who hired them because they had the right "instincts," that is, they had the same set of cultural expectations and values as the editors themselves. The news is delivered, take it or leave it, to a passive audience. The public has little ability to add anything to the news agenda or to correct errors

of interpretation or omission. Theoretically, both the news production process and the product are protected from outside influence in order to preserve journalists' ability to tell the truth, without fear or favor. Traditional news organizations seldom offer information about their reporters' qualifications, how they choose what becomes news, or what citizens can do to affect the news agenda. In fact, inquiries into the political affiliations of journalists are viewed as inappropriate, and many reporters do not disclose even their outside income from interest group speeches.[3]

Aside from socialization, the issue of journalists detaching themselves from the community is a subject of debate within the journalistic community. Often, the decision of how attached or detached reporters and editors should be is left up to the newspaper's editor or the television station's news director.

The Separated Journalist

A third aspect of this priesthood is this: Journalists find they must *separate* themselves from others in the community more than they would were they in another business. Reporters often worry that an assignment down the line will require them to report on this organization or that, this person or that, or this issue or that. When that time comes, the journalist wants to do all he or she can to remain objective and present a balanced and fair report. Personal friendships can get in the way of that kind of separation, so many journalists choose to make most of their friends among other journalists and to be very selective about what groups they join, if they join any at all.

Peter Bhatia is executive editor of *The Oregonian,* Portland's metro daily and a leading Pulitzer Prize-winning newspaper. Assessing the characteristic of a journalist's detachment, he says,

> Even in an era where closeness to sources is more common due to the burst of excellent, narrative writing in newspapers, I think the cautions and distance remain important. Balancing: that remains a great test for reporters and editors, and it will always be so, I think.

How does he define "distance"?

"Distance does not mean in writing or voice necessarily," he explains. "That's something we have figured out in recent years. That is, our reporting and writing can be intimate, but we can still maintain an appropriate distance from our sources. The simple equation is to remember our obligation to the reader, to be fair, honest, truthful, and complete in our work. Those old values are still good values."

For many journalists, keeping a distance from people they are reporting on, or may have to report on in the future, is a matter of emotional self-preservation. Penny Owen, veteran reporter for *The Oklahoman* who was one of the key reporters on the Oklahoma City bombing story in 1995, is one of these reporters. Here's how she describes her experience:

> The bombing started a whole new reality of dealing with victims and survivors. It meant getting to know them over years, rather than just a couple weeks on the cop beat. It does change the dynamics when covering victims over the long term. For me, some self-preservation kicked in. It was tempting to get close to these people I got to know. But to do that meant risking the story, i.e., clouding my judgment etc., not to mention the emotional toll it could take. It was already emotional, so why make it more so?
>
> I know other journalists said they kept in touch with long-term victims with cards and so forth, but I didn't do that.

Some journalists, while agreeing that journalism is a higher calling, perceive problems with socializing strictly among other journalists. Jim Redmond, a veteran television journalist who anchored newscasts in Denver and Portland for many years, is one of these, and he explains his view this way:

> I definitely felt it was a calling. I always thought I happened to make a good living, but I didn't do it for the money. I did it because I thought it was important, a special privilege, and, despite its flaws, helped people better understand their world and make decisions about things both on the personal and political life level.
>
> But I always tried to associate with non-journalists outside of work. It didn't take long for me to figure out that when you went over to the bar for a beer with your newsroom colleagues after work, you were pulled into a back-biting, bitching, gossipy kind of deal with a lot of office political overtones, and I didn't need that. In Portland, one of the news directors always went to the bar across the street from the station after work. People would hang out around him over there because he drank too much and he talked too much when he did. It was quite harmful. It was a good opportunity for me as a young employee to see how manipulative people were (he had lots of friends from work wanting to socialize with him all the time to play him like a fiddle) and how petty. So I stayed away from that.
>
> I hung out with my ski school buddies (I had become a certified ski instructor in college and always taught part time as we moved around the country) and also with my military reserve friends. They were ordinary working folks, no other journalists, and we talked about their concerns, not money. I always felt that it is important to have widely diverse circles of influence within which you function. That broadens you, makes the world a more interesting place, and

avoids the social myopia that results when you run with other people just like yourself. I only have a handful of really close friends who were journalists. All my best friends were not journalists.

Journalists as Advocates

Later in this book, we will look at the concept of advocacy journalism and how it is being practiced by some in the mainstream media today. But journalists like Redmond worry about a reporter's becoming an advocate or a voice for individual victims. He explains:

> Much of this new stream of logic is just for promotional purposes. It's part of the current wave of theatrics. Sometimes reporters are caught up in the human events they cover, and that's understandable. But being so emotionally involved, and countenancing being strongly attached to people and issues you're covering, virtually guarantees that you will subconsciously, if not consciously, ignore any logical arguments or evidence to the contrary. You become an advocate. When that happens you're no longer a journalist; you are a participant and a member of a side.

Commenting on one high-profile journalist, CNN's Anderson Cooper, and his victims' advocacy orientation in covering Hurricane Katrina, Redmond sees problems with this approach. Cooper said in a June 2006 interview on *Larry King Live* that he had "made a promise" to the people of New Orleans that CNN would not leave the story until the cleanup was complete and evacuees could return to their homes.[4] Redmond comments on this approach:

> Cooper is a nice guy, and he does some nice things. On the other hand, much of his reporting on Katrina was so focused on the victims he ignored much of the difficulty of disaster response and didn't make much attempt, besides just pro forma gloss, at explaining why some of the "victims" were in such a pickle. There's the issue of all of them who ignored evacuation orders and then apparently didn't expect to be held accountable for their actions. There's the issue of how do you get enough busses into a city to evacuate 50,000 people? The logistics of the whole thing were mind boggling.
>
> That's not to say the response shouldn't have been better. But it so emphasized the easy, sappy, crying people and devastation that it did not help people understand why it was so hard to deal with or why members of Congress who caused much of it by failing to provide adequate funds—as requested repeatedly by the Corp of Engineers to maintain the dikes—were not held accountable for causing much of the tragedy by their decades of pork barreling, etc."

A dilemma—and maybe a rather obvious one at that—exists in this notion of journalists separating themselves from stories (mostly events, often issues) and from the people of those stories. The dilemma is this: How can a journalist fully understand what an event, issue, or person is really like if he or she constructs and maintains a distance in between? On the other hand, if the journalist gets too close to the story and the people of it, the danger of losing a more "objective" orientation could threaten.

Feeling the Pulse

I was a young assistant city editor for the *Dallas Morning News,* and I recall sometimes late at night when a few of us remaining staff members were still ensconced in the then-quiet fourth-floor newsroom. As we passed the time between the last pages sent to the composing room and the start of the presses, oblivious to whatever else might be going on outside our building, we would joke, "Isn't it great to have our hands on the pulse beat of this city?" While it was a favorite line said in jest, there was an irony to it: the very people who are assumed by the readers to know exactly what is going on may well know the least because they haven't left the building all evening. Unless the police scanner started squawking or someone phoned in a news tip about a breaking incident, for all we knew, everything was okay. I always thought it's a bit like the rhetorical question, "If a tree falls in the forest and no one is there to hear it, does it make a sound?"

The debate over attachment and detachment from stories will be the focus of a later chapter, so we won't go into more detail here. But it is part and parcel of the concept of the priesthood of journalists, so it's important to begin thinking about from the beginning.

Granting Confidentiality

Yet a fourth aspect to this priesthood of journalists is found in the granting of confidentiality to persons who act as news sources. These people, when guaranteed confidentiality, will tell journalists things in private that they would not want shared in public. Much like a Catholic priest, a journalist often hears a kind of "confession" from a source that may or may not involve his or her own behavior but that at least concerns the behavior of others. This source material is vital for journalists, as it helps them to understand situations they are reporting on and to present an accurate picture to the public of what's going on.

The aspect of journalism's priesthood that requires the granting of confidentiality to a source has been the focus of many newsroom discussions and has kept many reporters awake at night wondering if they have done the right thing. Like a priest, journalists understand they are bound to honor that granted confidentiality. This thinking has given rise to one of the most hotly debated issues in journalism: when—and when not—to grant confidentiality to sources.

Many sources object—some even flatly refuse—to allow reporters to use their names or any form of identity that would cause others to recognize them. The reasons are varied, some more seemingly legitimate than others. Among those reasons are their fears of

- Loss of job
- Personal harm
- Being ostracized
- Damage to reputation

Journalists understand these reasons and often sympathize with them—especially the first two. So a lot of confidentiality is granted by reporters pursuing the goal of getting the story. However, journalists also realize the down side to granting confidentiality to their sources. The two biggest problems are that stories with anonymous sources are often perceived by readers or viewers as less credible than stories in which the source is named and that granting confidentiality means a source can say whatever he or she wants without having to be accountable for that statement or allegation. The next two sections look at the legal ramifications of granting confidentiality and the reluctance of some editors to allow too many anonymous sources to be used by reporters.

Legal Ramifications of Confidentiality

When it comes to the legal arena, a third major problem surfaces over granting confidentiality. The problem here is associated with anonymous sources making allegations of ethical or legal wrongdoing against another person or persons. If these accused persons decide to sue the newspaper, magazine, television, or radio station for libel—and if the reporter refuses to identify the source of these allegations—the judge can find the reporter in contempt of court. Further, the judge could instruct the jury to presume that—absent an identified source—there is no source for these allegations. Either or both of these outcomes would prove harmful to the reporter and the news operation involved. On the one hand, there is probable jail time for the reporter; on the other, there is the loss of a libel suit by the news operation.

Such was the dilemma outlined in a seminar called "Anatomy of a Libel Case: Business vs. the Media," moderated by Harvard University law professor Arthur Miller, which involved journalists, business leaders, attorneys, and judges. It was a roundtable scenario of what the late Fred Friendly, former dean of the Columbia University Graduate School of Journalism, called a hypothetical case but definitely not a fictitious one.[5] The scenario, or one like it, is often played out in the world of journalism and involves allegations of misconduct made by a source, granted confidentiality by the reporter, against another person.

Because of the way libel law is practiced in the United States, reporters usually have to prove only that they had good reason to believe that what they printed or aired was true. If they can do that, they will—in most cases—at least avoid the heavy punitive damages that make up the bulk of most libel case demands. But proving they had good reason to believe the truthfulness of a statement means showing they had good reason to believe their sources. And that proof is hard to argue if a source—and therefore his or her expertise—cannot be identified.

So the analogy between a journalist and a priest and the confidentiality each grants to the source or confessor can only go so far. Courts will not require priests to reveal the identity of their confessors, but courts can and do demand that reporters reveal the identity of their sources. Therefore, the best advice for reporters is to consider the potential consequences of granting confidentiality to a source, in light of the allegations the source might make and the importance of the story, before granting that confidentiality.

Many journalists are hoping to see a federal shield law become a reality for journalists. The Society of Professional Journalists (SPJ) has been soliciting contributions to a campaign to create such a law, believing it would add needed protection to the public's right to know. In 2008, SPJ raised $30,000 for the campaign. The signs appeared mixed for the success of a federal shield law, however, as the proposal labeled S.2035 (the Senate's version of the Free Flow of Information Act, which is also known as the federal media shield law) stalled in voting. On 30 July 2008, the proposal received only 51 of the necessary 60 votes needed for it to proceed to consideration. Said SPJ President Clint Brewer about the situation, "SPJ will continue to encourage its members and public citizens to contact members of Congress and express part of the Society's mission: to encourage a climate where journalism can be practiced freely. A federal shield law would be a major step toward that goal."[6]

Aside from the contempt-of-court potential, the granting of confidentiality has taken on other legal ramifications as well. For example, a Minneapolis jury awarded $700,000 in damages to a Republican Party activist named Dan Cohen when he sued the Minneapolis *Star Tribune* and *St. Paul Pioneer Press & Dispatch* for breaking an agreement to keep his identity as a source confidential. In that case, the two reporters, Bill Salisbury and Lori Sturdevant, wanted to honor Cohen's request but were overridden by their editors who felt naming Cohen would add credibility to the story.[7]

Time reporter Laurence Zuckerman interviewed one of the editors involved and wrote about the incident:

> "My responsibility is to readers," argues David Hall, editor then of the *Pioneer Press & Dispatch* and now of the *Bergen* (N.J.) *Record,* in defense of his decision. But critics point out that Hall could have kept the bargain with Cohen by simply attributing the information to a "Whitney supporter." "This is a very simple case," says Hennepin County Chief Public Defender William Kennedy, a Democrat. "A promise is a promise."[8]

Editors Discourage Confidentiality

A 2005 study of editors belonging to the nationwide group Associated Press Managing Editors found that many of them discourage the use of anonymous sources in their newspapers. Reporting on the study, the Associated Press wrote the following:

> Editors at about one in four newspapers who responded to a survey say they never allow reporters to quote anonymous sources, and most others have policies designed to limit the practice. One editor said his paper's rules are so strict they would have disqualified Deep Throat [see later explanation] as a source. The use of anonymous sources . . . has been much in the news recently, notably in a case that prompted a *Newsweek* magazine retraction [in 2005 over a story about the supposed desecration of the Koran by guards at Guantanamo Bay, Cuba].

> The Associated Press and the Associated Press Managing Editors association decided to jointly survey American newspapers to find out what their practices are. The project, believed to be the most comprehensive of its kind conducted in recent years, drew replies from 419 publications—about 28 percent of the nation's 1,450 daily newspapers. Editors at 103 papers, nearly all of them in small and mid-size markets, said they do not ever permit reporters to cite anonymous sources in their articles.

"Our policy is to get people on the record. Period," said Eileen Lehnert, editor of the *Jackson* (Mich.) *Citizen Patriot*. "Once you operate from that standpoint, you rarely have to reconsider your position."[9]

Examples of this tightening of policies have been seen since the 1970s when editors, burned by reporters who actually fabricated sources, began implementing new safeguards. One of the most notorious cases involving a fabricated source occurred at the famed *Washington Post*, where a reporter named Janet Cooke fabricated the 8-year-old boy that she focused her entire story on. She named the boy only as "Jimmy," and the story, titled "Jimmy's World," was a tragic account of this young Washington boy who had become hooked on heroin by his mother's boyfriend. The story won a Pulitzer Prize before the paper discovered there was no "Jimmy" and then suffered the humiliation of announcing the fact to readers, apologizing, and returning the coveted prize.

More recently, Jayson Blair of *The New York Times* and Stephen Glass of *The New Republic* have committed similar journalistic sins, fabricating sources and plagiarizing articles. Each of these reporters—Cooke, Blair, and Glass—lost their jobs as a result of their fabrications and became ostracized in the journalistic community.

Anonymous Sources in Washington

Anonymous-source reporting is most prevalent in Washington, DC among reporters assigned to cover the various branches of the federal government and their performance. Most Washington reporters say that much of their work would not be possible without granting confidentiality to sources. Indeed, *The Washington Post* series on Watergate, culminating in the resignation of President Richard Nixon, might not have been possible without reporter Bob Woodward's granting confidentiality to his key source, known for decades only as "Deep Throat" and not identified until 2005 as Mark Felt, former assistant director of the FBI. Any presidential administration—for that matter, any executive department from Justice to Defense—has its share of individuals who are troubled by the practices being followed by its leaders. The decision on whether to become a whistleblower may well depend on the degree of confidentiality such a person may expect from the journalist he or she blows the whistle to. It is up to the journalists to determine the import of the information, vis-à-vis the risks of granting confidentiality, and also to try and determine the source's credibility and motives for blowing the whistle.

The intricate dance practiced by journalists and politicians in Washington is often a manipulative game of intentional "leaks" produced by government officials who are either trying out ideas on the public to get a reaction without committing officially to them or attempting to burn political opponents, or simply to take revenge on them. The latter, of course, happened in 2003 when a top White House aide decided to divulge the name of an undercover CIA operative, Valerie Plame, to reporter Robert Novak. Plame is the wife of former U.S. Ambassador Joseph C. Wilson, who, in 2003, became a vocal critic of the Iraq War. The disclosure backfired, however, as a firestorm of media controversy ensued, culminating in the arrest and 2007 conviction for perjury and obstruction of justice of I. Lewis "Scooter" Libby, chief of staff to Vice President Dick Cheney. Several journalists were called as witnesses during the trial as to the identity of the source who leaked Plame's name.

Notes

1. Jay Rosen, "Journalism is Itself a Religion: A Theological Investigation," *The Revealer: A Daily Review of Religion and the Press*, January 8, 2004, http://www.therevealer.org/archives/timeless_000149.php.

2. Thomas Carlyle, *On Heroes, Hero Worship, and the Heroic in History: Six Lectures* (New York: John Wiley, 1849), 147.

3. Ellen Hume, *Tabloids, Talk Radio, and the Future of News: Technology's Impact on Journalism,*" Washington, DC: The Annenberg Washington Program in Communications Policy Studies of Northwestern University, 1995).

4. Anderson Cooper, interview by Larry King, *Larry King Live*, CNN, June 1, 2006.

5. *Anatomy of a Libel Case: Business vs. the Media*, VHS (Alexandria, VA: PBS Video, 1985).

6. Society of Professional Journalists, "Shield Law Stalls in Senate," SPJ press release, July 30, 2008, www.spj.org/shieldlaw-stall.asp.

7. Laurence Zuckerman, "Breaking the Code of Confidentiality," *Time,* August 1, 1988, http://www.time.com/time/magazine/article/0,9171,968006,00.html.

8. Zuckerman, "Breaking the Code."

9. Associated Press, "APME Study: Nationwide, Newspapers Frown on Anonymous Sourcing," *Editor & Publisher*, June 9, 2005.

3

The Journalist's View of the World

Journalists have just as much of an ideological and cultural framework as other people, and this inevitably conditions their reports on "others" and their interaction with sources. Culture guides all of our interaction and communication. That is why communicating with strangers (or even about them) is so difficult . . . because we are guided by other presuppositions about the nature of truth and reality.[1]

With this statement, global media scholar Jaap van Ginneken puts his finger on one of the key differences in the way many journalists view themselves in relation to the world they cover. As can be seen from some of the comments of the thirteen journalists who were interviewed for this book, however, there are those who deviate from this traditional, arms-length perspective. One of the myths of journalism, often used as a cornerstone of criticism by its detractors, is that there is somehow a uniform approach or perspective that all journalists share about the world. But anyone who has worked in a newsroom for a daily newspaper or television station knows this just isn't true. Like other professionals, journalists are socialized into the norms of the profession—what van Ginneken describes as "secondary socialization" (the first is socialization into one's national culture, and the third is into one's company or organization). But these norms exist to aid reporters in presenting an accurate view of the world they cover.

Journalists, for example, are not uniformly liberal in their politics. The last newsroom I worked in while covering the 1995 Oklahoma City bombing featured a computer one cubicle from mine that sported the bumper sticker, "Rush is Right!" And media critics are often surprised to learn that more daily newspapers have endorsed Republican presidential candidates over the years than Democratic ones. Newspapers, after all, are businesses, and the executives who own and run those businesses are often more conservative than many of the journalists they employ. As a result, the leanings found on the editorial page may be quite different from the personal ideologies of many reporters in the newsroom. We will examine all this in more detail in the chapter concerning journalists and ideologies. The concern here is with broader worldviews, with how journalists see themselves in relation to the world—perspectives that transcend political stances.

How do journalists see themselves in relation to the world they cover? Do they have a worldview through which they filter their stories? Do they consciously try to bend events, issues, and people to conform to their views, as critics often contend? Or do they practice what they preach in maintaining distance and objectivity in their reporting? Is there something going on at a more subconscious level that may escape a journalist's awareness? Possibly a kind of interpretation, which is natural when anyone witnesses something and turns around to tell a friend about what she or he just saw? And finally, what perspectives on the act of reporting and storytelling might journalists have? These are the questions this chapter will address.

The Journalist and Worldviews

Like everyone else, journalists either consciously or subconsciously have views about the world outside themselves. One notion that many have had about journalists is that they have grown up angry at the world and are using journalism as a means of standing outside and throwing rocks at a system that has disillusioned them. Like other perceptions about journalists, this one may be true for some but not for others. Consider Michael Walker, formerly of *The New York Times* and the *Los Angeles Times*.

"I wasn't angry, but I was definitely an outsider," Walker explains. "All my friends were. We didn't participate at all in the high-school infrastructure. Nobody was on the football team or worked the school paper or even student council."

Growing up in rural Illinois and during the 1970s contributed to that feeling of being an outsider, Walker recalls:

The town I grew up in was about 50 miles west of Chicago, and, in those days, it was countryside. I viewed the world as a pretty friendly place as I grew up with the same people. My whole life, nobody moved. It was pretty protected. I walked to school until I was 13. We had to take buses to the nearest large city, Elgin, to go to junior high and senior high school.

That changed my worldview, as Elgin was then a decaying industrial town with a lot of racial tensions in the school. There were race-related disturbances at both my schools. Also, as I got older, I was of course absorbing the crisis in the Nixon White House, the Vietnam War. My friends and I had discussions about whether or not we'd go if we got drafted. But overall I looked at the world as exciting and inviting. I couldn't wait to get out of high school and get into it.

It seems fair to say that a worldview can be all encompassing to the one who holds it. It can be an umbrella that is kept open by the individual spokes protruding from its handle. According to that analogy, it could offer a chance to see what is going on, at least at a close distance, in the middle of an otherwise blinding rain. Or it could be like a wide-angle camera lens that can be zoomed in or out. The photographer is not going to see what is not in the lens at its widest point, but she can also zoom in for a close-up of an individual object within that overall frame. The point is that most people would like to have an umbrella in a driving rainstorm, and photographers can't get very far without using a camera. Worldviews are like that too. They provide us a means of protection from confusion, an ability to focus on what we think is important, and a way of defining what we see. Generally, those definitions are the result of assimilating what we see into what we think we know about the world. It was journalist/philosopher Walter Lippmann who said that most of us define before we see. Specifically, he put it this way:

> For the most part, we do not first see, and then define, we define first and then see. In the great blooming, buzzing confusion of the outer world, we pick out what out culture has already defined for us, and we tend to perceive that which we have picked out in the form stereotyped for us by our culture.[2]

Lippmann, himself a working journalist in New York City, started connecting the words "objective," "science," and "scientific" together and emerged as an advocate for journalists adapting the scientific method to journalism as a counterbalance to subjective reporting. He believed, as did psychiatrist Sigmund Freud, that an individual citizen could not intuit truth because he or she is a creature of a specific culture. That culture, through its propagandists, could easily play on the emotional nature of journalists as human beings. Hence, Lippmann saw the scientific method as a way out and a pretty good defense mechanism. It was a message that resonated years later in the 1960s, within a journalistic approach labeled "precision journalism" by researchers Philip Meyer and later Maxwell McCombs.

I picked up on Lippmann's thoughts in a book I wrote called *The Shadow World: Life Between the News Media and Reality* in which I describe the media's representation of reality as a creation that the journalist hopes is an accurate reflection of reality. This representation does, in fact, become a kind of shadow world, paralleling the real world.[3]

It is not surprising that journalists, who often pride themselves on their "objectivity," bristle at the notion that they even have a worldview. They might feel this is like admitting they have a bias or prejudice when they do their reporting. But a worldview is not a bias, and it's not a prejudice. Two people with different worldviews can still come up with the same set of facts and even present them in the same way in a news story. But the worldview may influence what a journalist chooses to call news on a given day, and it may affect how those precious facts are gathered. It can also affect the mood of the story and, agreed, at times it can affect how the story is presented and the effect it has on the reader or viewer. Let's look at an example of how a worldview might affect a journalist's reporting.

The Importance of Time

Journalists' worldviews affect their definition of what is newsworthy. And different cultural orientations to time factor heavily into these worldviews. Timeliness, which may seem in the West to be of obvious news value, may not factor into the thinking of a journalist from the East or Middle East. Nonverbal communication researchers report that one of the defining differences between cultures is found in "chronemics" or the study of time and how a culture uses it and thinks about it. Some cultures are known as having a faster pace than others do; some are known for their people's abilities to juggle several jobs at once or to focus on one thing at a time; some are known for the relative importance they place on punctuality; and some are more resistant to fads because of their respect for history. All of this can apply to how a journalist defines news.

As a culture, the West is driven by the clock. There are degrees of this time pressure depending on where one might live, but, as a cultural value, it seems to hold true. If you doubt this, try opening a branch of your business in Saudi Arabia, thinking you will practice the same daily efficiency there as in the United States. It won't take long before you realize that Saudis are not driven by the clock, in business or their personal lives. Appointment times mean little as a cultural norm, and you may be lucky if you manage to pull off just one or two appointments a day. Saudi Arabia may be a good example of the belief in some cultures that it is more important to "be" rather than to "do."

How is this relevant to a journalist's criteria regarding what has news value? Remember, we used timeliness as an example of one such criterion. In America, a journalist often defines an event as newsworthy by that element. When did it occur? How recent was this? Is it happening now, or did it happen since the last newspaper edition or the last newscast? The extreme case of how important timeliness is can be seen in live, real-time reporting by a television network or station. As an informational medium, television prides itself on its ability to be immediate, to "go to the scene live." Sometimes this is *the* driving definition of news because of the addictive aspect of apprehension: we just don't know how this event will turn out, and we have the chance to witness any drama it produces as it is happening. Timeliness is the reason that producers often jerk viewers away from the recitation of news by a network's anchors to live coverage of a high-speed freeway chase, which can take precedence over most stories simply because it is "happening right now, even as we speak." Why a person is being chased or what that person is suspected of doing is almost immaterial; the action is the chase itself and its immediacy.

The classic example of this was the police pursuit of O. J. Simpson on an L.A. freeway; the networks took viewers away from a deciding game in the NBA finals to watch a long, relatively slow-speed pursuit of Simpson by police. The event ended in nondramatic fashion when Simpson's white Ford Bronco was driven into the driveway of his Brentwood home. Simpson calmly got out and was arrested by police.

Timeliness is largely a Western news value; it is not necessarily shared by journalists from other cultures, from places where being is more important than doing. Another culture may value obtaining a deeper understanding of an event or issue before speaking about it. Or, because of culture, people may not reach final conclusions, just as there are no conclusions in the famed *wayang* or shadow-puppet theatre of Indonesia.

One of the many enigmatic scenes from the 1982 film *The Year of Living Dangerously* features photojournalist Billy Kwan advising Australian correspondent Guy Hamilton on how to interpret Jakarta. Kwan says, "Most of us become children again when we enter the slums of Asia . . . toy town and the city of fear . . . In the West, we want answers for everything . . . But in the *wayang* no such final conclusions exist."[4] If that is your worldview, if that is your wide-angle camera lens, then the image of timeliness does not even appear in your lens. It is not important.

New Orleans journalist Michael Perlstein said it wasn't always space or time restraints that proved challenging in covering Hurricane Katrina.

Often, he said, it was just the slow, laborious process of getting the story right that proved the greatest challenge:

> Amid this intense reporting experience, we quickly became aware of how easy it was to get the story wrong. We saw false information come from the mouths of top officials, from the governor down to the mayor and police chief. We saw some of the bogus information repeated in news reports, from sensational TV accounts to AP updates. We saw veteran journalists of major newspapers and magazines miss the mark because they didn't understand New Orleans, strived too hard to capture the hopelessly complex aftermath into a made-for-deadline epic.
>
> Clarity slowed us down—made sure we got it right, understood the complexity of New Orleans, knew the landscape, [were] informed enough not to fall for easy stereotypes.

News as a Reflection of the World

A basic notion of most American journalists is that news occurs when a person or event goes wrong and produces a negative effect on other people. It's as if there is an expectation—if not a sense of entitlement—among Americans that only good things should happen. When something bad happens, journalists call it news because that expectation is broken—possibly shattered in the case of an event like 9/11, Hurricane Katrina, or the Oklahoma City bombing. This notion protrudes itself nightly in the first segments of a local or national television newscast where wars, natural disasters, and crime vie for more coverage than all other news categories combined, with the exception of politics. Deviant or negative events are so basic to a journalist's innate understanding of news that this emphasis hardly seems deserving of discussion among American reporters, although some critics might say they should. So it may be surprising for those journalists to learn that this criterion of news value is not shared around the world. Think about it. Americans, as a whole, are an optimistic group. It has been that way through history, and it was the driving reason that the pioneers ever crossed the Appalachians to see what lay to the west. And it's what kept pioneers and settlers moving west, through a broad range of tragedies and challenges, until they ran into another ocean. The fuel of optimism, for most people, is the sense that things will work out all right, or at least that the risk will be worth the danger because the potential prize is so great. Of course, it helps a culture to be optimistic if these challenges are conquered and the enemies to progress are vanquished.

But this is not the history of most countries, and the levels of optimism—even among Western countries—may vary significantly. For example, I once had a conversation with a German television executive in Cologne, who said,

> You Americans can afford to be optimistic! You have won the two world wars and most of the others you've been involved in. You have not been invaded and overrun by other countries. You have a sense of safety. Germany has not won its wars, and we have paid heavily for the wars we have been in. Optimism is not nearly as prevalent here as in the U.S.

If a culture is optimistic and expects things to work out well, then progress and safety become the expectation, and events threatening these are seen as news. But if a country has little in its history to suggest these expectations are realizable—if things haven't worked out well in its history—then news is not necessarily the blunting of progress. Indeed, in some countries, news may be defined as occurring when something good happens for a change, when the expectation of pessimism is shattered by something pleasing or an institution that works right, or, in the case of a country like India, when a mountain train doesn't jump the track and when passengers aren't killed. A journalist from New Delhi explained it this way to me when I was covering the anniversary of the Union Carbide chemical plant disaster in Bhopal:

> In America, you have a different concept of news. Some people die in a train or bus accident, and it is a front-page story. Over here in India, that is not always the case. Here busses run off mountain highways a lot, and many people are killed. It is tragic, yes, but it is not necessarily news because it happens so much. In India, we have learned in our history to deal with tragic deaths. Because of our religious beliefs, we believe this world is not the end and that people pass through to a better place. In short, tragedy is not something that is unexpected here, but rather expected. So it is not always news to people. It may be more of a story when good things happen, because people don't always expect that here.[5]

The Concept of Ethnocentrism

A jingle from an old television commercial about hot dogs ran, "My dog's better than your dog"—and that pretty well sums up the concept of ethnocentrism. A value of most cultures—and especially Western ones it seems—ethnocentrism is the judging of other cultures by the standards of one's own, the perception of other cultures through one's own culture's prism, and the resulting judgments about other cultures, which spring from the perspective that one's own culture is at the center of everything. In his study *Deciding What's News,* Columbia sociologist Herbert Gans discovered that ethnocentrism surfaced more in international stories than anywhere else.[6] Interpretation may come into play more in assessing alien cultures than anywhere else because any culture's journalist is prone to measuring the new and relatively unknown culture by the yardstick of the culture he or she knows best—almost always the journalist's own culture. Sometimes that assessment is on target; sometimes it is not; in all cases, the assessment can be seen differently by members of different cultures.

Cultural Immersion

Certainly there are those individuals in every culture who become disillusioned with their cultural norms, try to shed their culture, and take on the cloak of another culture instead. But they often meet with only varying degrees of success, as the process of shedding a culture and assimilating into another is not easy. One such individual who found this to be true was the famed T. E. Lawrence, a British military officer and adventurer who became disenchanted with his life and, when working as an archaeologist in the Middle East, fell in love with Arab culture. He tried mightily to become one of them, even joining the Arabs in their fight against the Turks, but, in the end, he failed. He wrote about that experience and concluded the following:

> . . . the effort for these years to live in the dress of the Arabs and to imitate their mental foundation, quitted me of my English self and let me look at the West and its conventions with new eyes; they destroyed it all for me. At the same time I could not sincerely take on the Arab *skin;* it was an affectation only. Easily was a man made an infidel, but hardly might he be *converted* to another faith . . . Sometimes these selves would converse in the void. And then *madness* was very near, as I believe it would be near the man who could see things through the veils at once of two customs, two educations, two environments.[7]

Even if it were possible to immerse oneself in a culture so deeply that one truly became a member of that culture, would that guarantee a journalist a truer view of the culture? Maybe, maybe not. Some would argue that the process of eliminating the arms-length detachment might produce the same effect it does in other stories: losing sight of the objective reality and allowing emotional attachments to color the truth. This view, of course, assumes that objectivity is possible for a journalist in the first place, and that is a highly debatable point even among journalists. Some journalists would say, however, that cultural immersion may be the best way of getting to understand another culture: live in it, stay in it for months or even years at a time, understand it as the natives do. Journalist Richard Critchfield, formerly of *The Economist* and the *Washington Star,* believed this to be the best approach to gathering truths about another culture. In an article appropriately titled "The Village Voice of Richard Critchfield," he laid out his reporting method and his reasoning for it. He explained that it is necessary to become a kind of "storytelling anthropologist" to get the truest view of a culture and its meaning to the world. He said that, when he lived with the people of Third World villages for days, weeks, or even months, eating the food they did and doing the work they did in the fields, he came to understand them better. Often with the use of interpreters, he would record the dialogue of the people and the comments of those he interviewed, taking copious notes. Critchfield believed the nature of the villagers would arise from their everyday dialogue and observations, together with his own observations made over time of how they thought, what they believed, and how they acted. He felt that much of the tension in the world could be attributed to what he witnessed in the villages of the Third World: traditional people who were comfortable living in a world of the past finding they had to confront changing technology and values imported by the nations of the West.[8]

The Risk of Involvement

Immersion into the culture on which a journalist reports—be that a foreign culture or simply the local culture of an event such as the Oklahoma City bombing—always carries the risk and opportunity of involvement. This involvement might be mental, emotional, or even physical. In the case of the latter, journalists might wonder if they shouldn't put down the camera or note pad and help relieve the suffering of those around them. In the case of emotional involvement, there is the possibility of a journalist's becoming a voice for those he or she is covering rather than a detached observer.

The journalists of the 1960s and 1970s who gave rise to the concept of "new journalism" believed that reporters needed to immerse themselves in the story, the people of those stories, and the psyche of those people in order to get a maximum view of the truth. So George Plimpton took on the guise of a quarterback from an obscure semi-pro team out of Newfoundland, joining training camp with the Detroit Lions in a seeming attempt to make the squad. Management of the team knew what he was about and agreed to the experiment. As Plimpton donned the practice uniform and spent the weeks undergoing the same physical regime as the other candidates for positions, he felt he came to a deeper understanding of what it takes to make an NFL team. He wrote about his experiences and conversations with other players for *Sports Illustrated*, and, eventually, his writings were published as a classic sports book called *Paper Lion*, which later became a film of the same name starring Alan Alda. Other writers of this movement were Hunter S. Thompson, who once disguised himself as a biker and rode with the Hell's Angels for a while, and Tom Wolfe, who allowed himself to get close to the principals of the early NASA space program to get past the superficial hero-worshipping of the Mercury Seven astronauts, discover what really made them tick, and write his classic book *The Right Stuff*. In more recent years, writers John Howard Griffin, Jon Krakauer, and Sebastian Junger have attached themselves to stories of people in crisis to write such books as *Black Like Me*; *Into Thin Air, Into the Wild*; and *The Perfect Storm*.

One journalist who has wrestled with involvement vs. detachment is veteran *New York Times* reporter Barry Bearak, who now heads up this paper's South African Bureau. In a 2007 interview, Bearak said,

> As a young reporter, I often wanted to befriend sources I liked or admired. But that's a dangerous trap. It's pretty obvious you shouldn't be writing about your friends, but it's just as dangerous to be writing about people you'd like to recruit as your friends. Over time, that problem sorted itself out. I simply drew the line: sources over here, friends over there.

Bearak said other attachments are not so easy to sort out.

> As for other emotional attachments, that's an interesting thing. While I try very hard not to allow my personal beliefs—political or otherwise—to color my reporting, I don't curb my emotions . . . To the contrary, I think my visceral responses work to my benefit. I want to ramp them up, not tamp them down. I want to feel things as strongly as I can. My empathy is the road map to readers' empathy. If someone's hunger or pain or loss is bringing me to tears, I can use that emotion to make the reader feel the same thing.

Emotional attachment is not the only kind of connection that Bearak wrestles with, however. He has thought a lot about *professional* detachment, and he has come to a conclusion about it.

> Your use of the word "detachment" makes me think of something else . . . Some reporters seem to put professional detachment on some sort of

pedestal. I've heard the question asked, "If a man is dying at your feet, do you try to save his life or note the color of his lips?" Some journalists would say your job is to let the person die and record the death accurately. Not me. If I had to make that choice, I'd put my notebook away and try to save the life.

Fortunately, I've never had to make that kind of split-second decision. But I've many times come across people who are sick or injured, and I was their best hope for help. At those times, I've always found that I could have it both ways. I was able to report my story *and* get them medical assistance.

Reporters often learn the rights and wrongs of distancing from vs. engaging in stories through their own day-to-day engagement with fellow reporters and editors. Peter Bhatia, editor of *The Oregonian,* sees both positive and negative aspects in the newsroom culture journalists learn.

"It certainly helps young journalists to be shoulder to shoulder with veterans in the newsroom," Bhatia says. "They can learn a lot from reporters and editors who have spent years—in some cases—decades covering and editing stories. The cautious aspect of this culture, however, is that sometimes it may lead to a kind of inbreeding of ideas and actually work toward blunting innovative techniques and ideas. More than once reporters have been frustrated by a veteran who dismisses an idea too quickly with, 'We tried it that way once, and it didn't work.'"

For as long as there are journalists, there will always be debate about how close a reporter should get to the people in his or her story and about the relative benefits of attachment vs. distance. We see it today in the thinking of journalists like CNN's Anderson Cooper and those who would oppose his view of emotional involvement in stories of tragedy.

The Concept of Ambiguity

Another scale that can serve as a departure point for different cultures is the degree of ambiguity that a culture might be satisfied with. This scale is often referred to as a high-context/low-context scale. A culture that is high context is a culture that is uncomfortable with the ambiguities that exist in communication and needs to have the blanks filled in more explicitly. For example, Germany is a country of laws, and it seems to have many more on the books, for even minor occurrences like jaywalking, than do other countries. Or at least that is the perception of many Americans who visit there and, upon crossing a street at an unmarked place, find someone from behind tapping them on the shoulder and telling them they should cross elsewhere. Many traditional Germans are also uncomfortable with those who respond to questions about dinner arrangements with words such as

"Oh, meet me about 6 p.m." In that response, it is the "about" that throws a German. Is that 6:05 or 6:10 or 5:50? A country that is low context is more comfortable with such ambiguities, and America is said to be such a culture.

If a journalist views his audience as high context, he will feel the need to provide more details in a story. If he is wrong in his perception of readers, however, they may see him as "talking down" to them, in which case he might get a reaction such as "Why is this writer treating me like an idiot?" If he is right, then the readers will appreciate what they feel are needed background details. Trying to discern just how much their readers and viewers know about a story is always a tough decision for journalists. It is often also a moot point, however, because of space and time constraints that would not allow them to add more details even if they wanted to.

Of course, the way a journalist writes a story can produce its own level of ambiguity for the reader. Experts in the "science of readability" encourage writers in the mass media to write for readers with a ninth- or tenth-grade education, the equivalent of high school sophomores. That kind of writing is composed mostly of shorter words and shorter sentences. There are writing indices that measure the level of one's writing. A couple of them are the Gunning Fog Index and the Flesch Reading Ease Formula. They are both based largely on similar criteria of word and sentence length. The premise of writing at these levels is that most people want reading to be easy and pleasurable; if a sentence requires rereading to understand accurately, that story will probably not be finished. Editors know this, and one way or the other encourage their reporters to write clearly and concisely. An optimal sentence length in journalism may run only 16–22 words—shorter with some editors. An optimal paragraph length in newspapers may run only 50 words or fewer, and each paragraph will focus on just one main thought. There is a strong feeling in journalism that the shorter thought will be the less ambiguous thought. The old adage, "Less is more," definitely holds true in journalism.

Diversity Among Journalists

Groups to which we belong and with which we identify help shape how we experience and interpret our world. Some of these groups are defined by

- Geographic region
- Race and ethnicity
- Gender
- Religion
- Socioeconomic levels
- Age

Like everyone else, journalists find themselves grouped with others under these categories, and, like everyone else, their perceptions and worldviews are influenced by these groupings—by whether one is a twenty-something male agnostic from Boston or a fiftyish black female from the Bible Belt. A number of studies have been done that profile journalists and show the kinds of groups that many represent. However, journalists resent the idea that their own background would unduly influence their reporting and the accuracy of that reporting. Often, however, the belief in objectivity is a myth wherein a journalist might refuse to recognize what's going on subconsciously. For example, a male reporter on more than one occasion has referred to a woman in his story as a "single mom," even though that descriptor may have no relevance to the story. The phrase has become such a piece of background noise to many, that a man might not recognize the potential problem the woman might have with the title. It is a gap in understanding brought about by the simple fact that the reporter is male and not female.

A recent nationwide study showed the following about journalists and the different groups they come from:

The number of women in journalism hasn't increased since the previous study was done in 1992. They continue to account for about a third of all full-time journalists. The percentage of women with zero to four years of experience was significantly higher in 2002 (54.2 percent) than in 1992 (44.8 percent). "If the attrition rate doesn't change, that will mean more women journalists with more experience in the future," said principal researcher David Weaver.[9]

Meanwhile the percentage of minority journalists has risen slightly over the years, but, at 9.5 percent by 2002, it has remained much below the minority percentage of the U.S. population and also below the percentage of the minority population with college education. The percentage of African Americans in full-time reporting positions has remained static from 1971 to 2002, from 3.9 percent to 3.7 percent.

U.S. census figures say Hispanics account for 13.4 percent of the total U.S. population, but only 3.3 percent of all reporters and editors in 2002 were Hispanic. This is up from 2.2 percent in 1992 and 0.6 percent in 1982 to 1983. Weaver said he suspects there is a high level of attrition, with many minority and female journalists leaving the profession within a few years.

In terms of academic preparation, almost nine out of ten journalists have at least a bachelor's degree. The proportion of college graduates in journalism rose from 82 percent in 1992 to 89 percent in 2002. When Weaver began his research a quarter century ago, slightly fewer than 75 percent of journalists were college graduates.

Chapter 4 will look more closely at the subject of racial, gender, and ethnic diversity in American newsrooms and the relationship of this diversity to the ethical perspectives and standards of journalists.

The Socialization of Journalists

Certainly, much of a journalist's concept of what news is and is not comes from the socialization process that takes place over time as journalists gather and discuss their craft. A lot of information is exchanged after work as reporters gather for a beer at a local bar (a ritual that seems to have seen better days) or mingle at a convention of the Society of Professional Journalists (SPJ), the Radio and Television News Directors Association (RTNDA), or the American Society of Newspaper Editors (ASNE). Additionally, ongoing professional development workshops run by media organizations, such as the Poynter Institute of Media Studies in St. Petersburg, Florida or the American Press Institute in Reston, Virginia, help inculcate criteria of news value into the minds of reporters and editors. Journalists are often eager to exchange story ideas at these gatherings, and they are especially eager to discuss the successes they've experienced in covering events and issues.

This socialization process is enhanced by at least two other phenomena as well: contests and consultants. The profession of journalism likes to reward those who achieve a certain degree of "excellence" with their stories, editing, and news photography. On the print side, the most prestigious of these awards are the Pulitzer Prizes; on the broadcast side, the Peabody Awards, the Alfred I. duPont-Columbia Awards, and even the Emmy Awards are often cited as the most prestigious. But there are many other awards handed out by groups such as the SPJ, RTNDA, and ASNE, for writing, editing, and news photography. Some in the profession feel there may be too much emphasis on these awards, but most seem to appreciate the recognition of a job well done. Along with these awards and award ceremonies, however, comes a growing awareness in the minds of journalists as to what constitutes a good story. Often, winning journalists will talk about "how I got that story" or "how I wrote that story and why." This is a very real form of indoctrination, especially for the younger journalists in the audience. A lot of attention is paid, especially, to the kinds of stories the Pulitzer or Peabody juries notice and reward.

Consultants come into play, too, especially for television news operations. Every television station of any size contracts with a consultant like Frank N. Magid Associates or Audience Research & Development or a host of others.

Among the contributions that these consultants are expected to make is to monitor the kinds of news and feature stories garnering large audiences around the country and to pass that information on to client stations. So some topics become "hot" topics because news stations in other markets are chasing and producing these stories and are getting good ratings with them. On the print side, consultants may not be used that much (although readership research is being used more than ever). In the place of consultants, however, some large newspapers will contract for newsroom "coaches" who will coach reporters on everything from the kinds of stories they identify and develop to the writing of these stories.

In the jargon of mass communication theory, the journalist is the gatekeeper who opens or closes the gate to the event, issue, or person he or she chooses to call news. Knowing something about the gatekeepers in America should help us understand how the process of professional socialization works to produce another aspect of a journalist's worldview. Among academic researchers, gatekeeping has been a popular focus of studies for many years. In 1950, David Manning White considered the process as a complex series of gates that a news story would go through from the actual event being described to the edited, finished story that hits the morning doorstep. He asked the wire editor of a small daily (he called him "Mr. Gates") to retain all copy that came into his office from three wire services over a one-week period in 1949. Mr. Gates also offered explanations about why certain pieces were used and others were rejected. Writing about the experiment, White discovered the editor's decisions were "highly subjective" and that about 30 percent of the stories coming in over the wires were tossed out by Mr. Gates on the basis of his own personal evaluation of their content. One of Mr. Gates's strongest criteria was the story's perceived credibility.[10] White's findings spurred on other researchers, and the studies have expanded to multiple levels of analysis involving nationwide samples of journalists, all in an effort to identify the criteria gatekeepers use in defining news. One scholar, Pamela Shoemaker, has written widely on the topic.[11]

Given how influential (and influenced) journalists are in deciding what is news and how news should be presented, research on gatekeeping and the social background and socialization of journalists seems important. In large measure, news consumers are dependent upon a person they do not know—or often do not know about—to bring them a focused and accurate picture of reality. So who is this individual? During the late twentieth century, some serious attempts were made at defining the American journalist and, as a matter of fact, *The American Journalist* was the title of a book by a group of researchers at Indiana University in 1971. This comprehensive study of American journalists was updated three other times, in 1982, 1992, and

2002 under a grant from the John S. and James L. Knight Foundation. The study is based on extended telephone interviews with 1,149 full-time journalists (both print and broadcast) in the summer and fall of 2002. Following are some of the key findings from the 2002 edition of this survey:[12]

• Journalistic values persist in the face of profit pressures their news organizations are facing from management and owners. This put them at odds with their perception of what the owners value most. For example, most journalists felt that maintaining as large an audience as possible is the owners' primary motive, while earning high profits ranked second, and producing quality journalism was third. To most journalists, producing quality journalism is the highest priority. Almost two-thirds of journalists believed that, despite profit pressure on the newsrooms, the quality of journalism was still rising at their news operation.

• American journalists rank their journalistic training as the strongest influence on their decisions regarding what constitutes news. In fact, training seems to be a value most journalists respect as some two-thirds said they had received additional training since becoming a journalist.

• More than 70 percent of journalists say the "watchdog" role of journalists is the most important role they have, especially when it comes to investigating government.

• More journalists believe it is more important to get the story right than getting it first.

• Undercover reporting continues to be a controversial practice among American journalists, with just over half of the responding journalists supporting this kind of deceptive reporting tactic.

• About the same percentage of journalists—just over 50 percent—support the practice of badgering unwilling informants to get a story.

• Just over three-fourths of all journalists supported using confidential business or government documents without authorization.

• Overall, about one-third of all full-time journalists are women—the same percentage as in 1982—but the number of women in the younger ranks is increasing dramatically. Among journalists with fewer than five years of experience, women outnumber men, 54 to 46 percent.

• The percentage of full-time journalists of color working for mainstream media is increasing, albeit slightly. Among all journalists with less than five years experience, about 17 percent are people of color. Television employs the highest percentage of journalists of color. Still, with about 30 percent of the American population comprised of people of color, the diversity in the newsroom still lags behind the national percentage.

Beliefs, Attitudes, and Values

When you spiral down through the stages of cultural, group, and organizational socialization, you get to the level of individual socialization or—more correctly—individual diversity. It is at the level of the individual that we start finding traits that may or may not be representative of the three layers of socialization just mentioned. Individuals are unique in any culture, and individual journalists are no exception. The three things that make us each unique, at least to some degree, are our personal beliefs, attitudes, and values. To be sure, these three things are all conditioned by the layers of culture and socialization through which we trek, but we as individuals may not buy into all of what surrounds us. Take, for example, the case of Chris McCandless who was the subject of the Jon Krakauer nonfiction book *Into the Wild*. The son of straight-laced, conservative parents who had bought into the materialistic world and a graduate of the prestigious private school Emory University, McCandless rejected his outer layers of culture and hit the road in 1992 in search of what he called truth and freedom. He became a latter-day hippie at a time when such a culture had almost disappeared. Before leaving, he gave away all his worldly possessions except for his car, wrote a check giving his $24,000 in savings to Oxfam, and left without informing his family of his plans. Before long, he was on foot, heading for the wilds of Alaska. Soon after, he was dead of starvation.

So we are defined individually by our beliefs, attitudes, and values.

Beliefs are convictions about whether something is true or false; attitudes are predispositions to respond one way or the other; values are enduring beliefs about good and evil. Certainly, these are conditioned by the larger cultures of which we are a part, but—as in the case of McCandless—there are always individual exceptions to the rule. Journalists pride themselves on being independent, and, as a group, they do tend to live and socialize apart from the non-journalists' culture, much the same as do those professionals in law enforcement and the military. However, as a group, the journalistic fraternity is not as tightly knit as either the police or military.

Most journalists stay in the business because the motivations that brought them in at the start just refuse to turn loose of them. These motivations, as was seen in the previous chapter, usually involve a desire to change things for the better for the world they cover. The crusading spirit, mixed with a certain degree of skepticism, remains alive in the heart of these journalists, as the following comment from *The Oklahoman*'s Joe Hight shows:

> I've always tried to look at the world optimistically, but I never saw the total-ity of it as friendly. In journalism, you quickly learn that people react to you differently, sometimes just because you're a journalist. Or they want to use you for their own personal or political means. I am realistic in that sense, but I do think that journalism can make the world a much better place, especially our country where these freedoms are guaranteed.

Notes

1. Jaap van Ginneken, *Understanding Global News* (London: Sage, 1998), 69.

2. Walter Lippmann, *Public Opinion* (1922; repr. Mineola, NY: Dover Publications, 2004), 44.

3. Jim Willis, *The Shadow World: Life Between the News Media and Reality* (Westport: Praeger, 1990), 7.

4. *The Year of Living Dangerously*, DVD, directed by Peter Weir, written by C. J. Koch and Peter Weir (1983; Burbank, CA: Warner Home Video, 2000).

5. Jim Willis and Diane Willis, "India: A Case Study in International Reporting," *Nieman Reports* 42, no. 4 (1988), 25–30, 51.

6. Herbert J. Gans, *Deciding What's News* (New York: Vintage Books, 1980), 24.

7. T.E. Lawrence, *The Seven Pillars of Wisdom* (Hertfordshire: Wordsworth Editions, 1997), 14.

8. Richard Critchfield, "The Village Voice of Richard Critchfield," *Washington Journalism Review*, October 1985, 27–28.

9. David Weaver, Randal Beam, Bonnie Brownlee, Paul S. Voakes, and G. Cleveland Wilhoit, *The American Journalist in the 21st Century* (New York: Lawrence Earlbaum, 2006). See also http://newsinfo.iu.edu/news/page/normal/4045.html.

10. Pamela J. Shoemaker, "Media Gatekeeping," in *An Integrated Approach to Communication Theory and Research*, ed. Michael B. Salwen and Don W. Stacks, 79–92 (New York: Lawrence Erlbaum, 1996), 81–82.

11. Pamela J. Shoemaker and Stephen D. Reese, *Mediating the Message: Theories of Influence on Mass Media Content*, 2nd ed. (White Plains, NY: Longman, 1996).

12. Weaver, *American Journalist*.

4

Journalists, Theory, and Ethics

The theory and philosophy of journalism do not constitute topics that occupy the daily thinking or conversation of most practicing journalists in America. These subjects are a bit too abstract for most journalists, who are certainly capable of digesting them intellectually (journalism majors traditionally finish college with some of the highest grades on campus), but who are too busy chasing stories and reporting and writing them to theorize much about the profession. And when that job is over, so is the day. Then it all starts again the next morning. Nevertheless, in the journalist's quiet moments of reflection, there is a fair amount of examination concerning whether sources were treated fairly and whether the story was as accurate and as fair or balanced as it could be. Maybe there is even a resolve to do a better job the next time, and possibly to do it in a different way. In these respects, journalism is an ongoing educational experience for the best reporters, who allow it to be.

In 1991, I wrote a book called *Journalism: State of the Art*, which examined a decade's worth of research about the news media and discussed the practical value of much of this growing body of theory. However, the book also looked at how wide the gap is, at times, between the practitioner of journalism and the media researcher. In fact, a key motivation that spurred me into leaving the newsroom and entering university teaching was to try to find ways of bridging this gap between practitioner and researcher. It is not an easy job convincing each camp that the other has something worthwhile to tell.

The Pragmatics of Journalism

Journalists are among the most pragmatic professionals in the world. The world of the working news media is a fast paced, intense, extremely practical one. Most journalists do not have time to sit and ponder what they are doing, how they are doing it, or what its effects might be—they are too busy just doing it. Too busy feeding the beast, as many say. There is always time or space to fill on the next newscast, newspaper, or Web site, and the time pressure to get it filled with meaningful stories is relentless. At the end of the day, a working journalist goes home tired, then turns around and starts the whole process over anew the next day.

So journalists don't spend too much time examining the processes that occupy the thinking of media researchers and that often form profiles of the work journalists produce. Working journalists are more interested in actual techniques that cause their stories to parallel reality more closely and that make it more enticing for readers and viewers to connect with their stories and graphics. The processes of media effects and agenda setting and the issues of objectivity and subjectivity are topics of considerable academic research, but they are not discussed much in most newsrooms.

Media Effects

When it comes to the different effects that the news media have on society, certainly journalists understand from experience that their stories influence readers or viewers—as well as the principals in the story itself—in very real ways. The most desired of those effects is that a wrong may be righted, a wrongdoer fired or prosecuted, a bad situation made better. Indeed the classic idea of journalism is that reporters expose the problems, public opinion is aroused, and government officials correct the problems. Other effects journalists often think about are whether individuals have been treated fairly, whether victims have been treated with respect instead of being victimized again by their very coverage.

Not part of the normal journalist's thinking, however, are academic concepts such as the "magic bullet theory," "limited effects," "two-step flow," "spiral of silence," or "third-person effect." These are all theories of media effects. Since working journalists usually majored in journalism in college, most have come in contact with these theories in an academic setting. Media theory is a staple course in most journalism and communication programs at universities. So journalists have an understanding that there is disagreement about the level of "macro-effects" the media have on a society, ranging from limited to powerful. They understand that some researchers believe the media influence society uniformly whereas others believe media effect is mediated by other influences, for example, family, schools, and church. Still others believe that the media influence "opinion leaders" in society and that the influence of these leaders is the one mostly felt by the rank and file. Some believe that, in putting media stories into the third person voice, many readers or viewers have a sense that the risks and dangers discussed are greater for other people than themselves. Working journalists may have to shake loose the cobwebs of their memories to latch on to these concepts again, but they do understand them. It's just that they understand them more on a story-by-story, case-by-case basis. They think about how this story affected this family, how that story affected that crime victim, or what changes in government this other story wrought.

A Primer in Media Theory

Having mentioned some of the media theories in the previous section, I will discuss them, albeit briefly, here. While this is not a book a media theory per se (although journalists usually develop their own theory about the practice, perhaps borrowing from an established theory), it is important to know how researchers conceptualize journalism and its effects.

- *The Magic Bullet Theory.* This theory, in vogue during and after World War II, is also known as the "hypodermic needle theory." It implies that mass media have a *direct, immediate,* and *powerful* effect on audiences. The mass media in the 1940s and 1950s were perceived as a powerful influence on behavior change. Several factors contributed to this "strong effects" theory of communication, including the quick rise and popularity of radio and TV; the rise of advertising and public relations; the Payne Fund studies of the 1930s, which focused on the impact of movies, especially on children; and Hitler's use of the media as a propaganda tool to unify Germany under the Nazi banner in the 1930s. Subsequent research and the experience of mediating agents beyond the news media have diminished the strong belief in this theory.[1]

- *The Limited Effects Theory.* Because of the realization that the media is not the only persuasive force in America and that audiences are not inanimate sponges soaking up everything the media offer, research moved to a more limited effects rationale of the media. Under this thesis, the public is viewed as independent and intelligent, fully capable of making up its own mind in discerning truth from falsehood (as well as attempts at manipulation) in media portrayals. This change in dominant thinking came about as the result of continuous research by Paul Lazarsfeld of Princeton and Columbia University. Lazarsfeld developed more sophisticated forms of surveys and experiments to measure the influence of media depictions on the ways people thought and acted. Findings suggested that the heretofore believed direct effects of the media were actually much more limited.[2]

- *The Two-Step Flow Theory.* An outgrowth of Lazarsfeld's limited effects theory was the notion that what the media actually do is influence the opinion leaders in a society and that these people—in turn—influence others. Hence, there are two steps to the media's influence, the latter of which is supplied by non-media entities, namely, by opinion leaders. Empirical evidence for this theory was supplied by two major studies Lazarsfeld did on political campaigns in Ohio and Illinois in 1940 and 1943. Among other things, these studies showed that 55 percent of the responding voters had selected candidates early in the campaign and did not change their minds, even after continual exposure to media messages designed to get them to switch candidates. Another finding stated that the influence of the media was only to reinforce a choice that voters had already made.[3]

- *The Spiral of Silence Theory.* Proposed by German political scientist Elisabeth Noelle-Neumann in the 1970s, this theory states that people are less likely to voice an opinion on a topic if they feel they are in the minority. The reason? They fear isolation—or even some kind of reprisal—from the majority members of that group. So this theory would suggest that silence is not so much a matter of oppression as it is a matter of protection. It also seems to cast doubt upon the existence of what President Nixon and other ideological leaders have called the nation's "silent majority"— a phrase used to suggest that people in support of a proposal don't vocalize their opinions as much as dissenters.[4] According to the spiral of silence theory, people do not keep silent if they believe they are members of a majority; rather, the minority is silent. When applied to media effects, this theory suggests that we cannot always tell how a person is really influenced—or not—by a message because that individual's silence or declared verbal opinion may be conditioned by his or her fear of being seen to be in the minority.

- *Agenda-Setting Theory.* An often-heard theory is that the news and even entertainment media set the agenda for the country and its citizens. It draws upon the magic bullet theory of the media in ascribing a powerful agenda-setting effect to the mass media. Agenda-setting theory contends that the choices editors and producers make in deciding which issues and people to cover will, in turn, cause viewers and readers to focus on those issues as well. In theoretical terms, the central idea of agenda-setting theory is called salience transfer, meaning the capability of the media to influence the importance people attach to various issues, people, and even opinions, in other words, to transfer significance to these things and make them part of the public agenda.[5] A vast amount of research has been done on this theory and its various permutations over the decades. Much of the research has upheld the media's agenda-setting capacity to a limited degree, but there are problems. One of the main challenges to an across-the-board rendition of this theory is this: If people are not exposed to the same media, they will not get the same sense of what issues are deemed important by the media. This age of highly fragmented media choices—in which special-interest news outlets choose vastly different issues to cover and specific news consumer groups choose what media to heed—raises a major challenge to some agenda-setting theories.

- *Third-Person Effect Theory.* Under this theory, perceptions of the influence of media on *others* are found to be consistently greater than perceptions of media influence on oneself.[6] This is an outgrowth of other aspects of interpersonal communication theories, which suggest that individuals evaluate their own abilities to withstand manipulation, or to understand complex issues, more highly than they evaluate the abilities of others to do so. This theory brings to the table the self-concepts that individuals have in evaluating their vulnerability to depictions by the media. Some observers have also suggested that journalists might be engaging in third-person beliefs when they consider themselves a better judge of what is news than the reader or viewer.

The Question of Objectivity

As for discussions of objectivity or subjectivity, journalists prefer instead to think about specific things they may do that might unduly connect them to the people or emotions of the stories they cover. The larger, philosophical aspects of objectivity or subjectivity are among the abstract concepts that most reporters avoid. The focus instead boils down to how they handled a story yesterday and how they're handling the one they're working on today. As mentioned previously, journalists are some of the best educated and most highly intelligent people in the world. It's just that their world is focused daily on the here and now and specifically on how to get an accurate, fair, and balanced story into the newspaper or onto the newscast tonight or tomorrow morning.

As a concept, objectivity is discussed elsewhere in this book, so we won't say much about it here. It is worth noting, however, that journalists do very much pursue the ideal of objectivity, although different journalists might define this ideal somewhat differently. To some, the concept of detachment from stories and the people of those stories is paramount. To others, the concepts of fairness and balance form the hallmark of objectivity. To still others, the absence of a reporter's interpretation is key to a story. And others think that applying the scientific method—in much the same way a behavioral scientist would—is important. These people might use the methods of content analysis, random-sample surveys, and even field experiments. At one extreme are those who believe journalists should be little more than stenographers, taking down what is said and relating it back, word for word, without comment. To some degree, the television network C-Span is like that, on the broadcast side. Very little commentary, and a lot of gavel-to-gavel coverage of congressional committees, meetings, and the like. And then there are those journalists who believe that objectivity can be achieved only by thorough investigation of the statements that sources make, lest journalists do become used as means to someone else's ends.

Most—if not all—of these emphases are good ones to use at different times, but some have caused journalists to miss the truth of a story or to be manipulated by self-serving individuals or institutions. For example, the concept of journalism as stenography has proved inadequate and troublesome. In recent years, America has witnessed the news media too compliantly and unquestioningly buying the rationale for the Iraq War put forth by the Bush Administration. That rationale was the president's insistence that Saddam Hussein had weapons of mass destruction and was ready to use them on all enemies, including the United States. Reporting by journalists such as Judith Miller of *The New York Times* seemed to confirm this scenario, although the key source she used was later discredited and her stories suffered in credibility as a result. The veteran journalist Bill Moyers devoted an entire program of his *Bill Moyers Journal* on April 25, 2007 ("Buying the War") to the failure of the news media to demand more proof of Bush's claim that Saddam had WMDs, which were never found after U.S.-led coalition forces invaded Iraq in 2003.

Another example comes from the early 1950s when Wisconsin Senator Joseph McCarthy was staging his political witch hunt and went looking for Communists in American government. Most of the mainstream media were dutifully taking down his allegations word for word and parroting them back to the readers and viewers. There was little investigation going on by the media about whether McCarthy's diatribes about finding Communists in government and the military were true. This was the era of the Red Scare, and McCarthy was spewing out his charges so fast it was all a journalist could do to keep up with them for fear of missing his latest round of accusations. Some historians have described the time as a three-ring circus; McCarthy was the ringmaster and the press was the wide-eyed audience taking it all in at face value. Others have described McCarthy as a deft magician, tricking the press into believing his illusions. It was a time when journalism as stenography did not serve well, either the country or the concept of truth. It was a time when, upon reflection, many journalists saw the difference between accuracy and truth. The press was largely accurate in reporting McCarthy's charges, but the charges simply were not true. It was not until CBS television pioneer Edward R. Murrow decided to step back and probe McCarthy's challenges that the senator was shown for the deceiver that he was, a politician more out for political gain than anything else and not bothered by ruining other lives in the process.

Some twenty years after the McCarthy era, two journalists at *The Washington Post* showed how far the notion of objective journalism had come from the era of journalism as stenography. The journalists, of course, were Robert Woodward and Carl Bernstein, the story was what has become known as Watergate, and the reporting technique was intrepid investigative reporting that required the rhetoric of top government officials to be tested against the reality of what had actually occurred in the break-in at the Democratic National Headquarters and the subsequent cover-up that was traced all the way to the Oval Office. In that case, generally seen as the high-water mark of objective reporting in America, the intense coverage forced the resignation of a president whereas, twenty years earlier, the coverage of Senator McCarthy made him immensely popular until Murrow finally brought him down.

Ethics and Journalists

Although the abstract aspects of subjectivity and objectivity are not discussed frequently in newsrooms, ethics is the focus of much discussion among many journalists because reporters value the concepts of balance and fairness. Reporters spend many sleepless nights worrying over whether they treated sources and the subjects of their stories fairly or whether any innocents were harmed by the published or aired stories.

Industry wide, ethics is a favorite topic among journalists who attend professional development seminars, such as those held by the Poynter Institute of Media Studies in St. Petersburg, Florida. Many of Poynter's seminars focus on ethics, and even a casual glance at the organization's Web site (www.poynter.org) reveals a widespread interest in the subject, as the school offers many resources discussing ethical cases and the issues underlying them.

As a profession, journalism has several ethical codes to help guide the behavior of its reporters, photojournalists, editors, and producers. Among those codes are ones produced by the Society of Professional Journalists and the American Society of Newspaper Editors. Portions of the SPJ Code of Ethics read as follows:[7]

Preamble

Members of the Society of Professional Journalists believe that public enlightenment is the forerunner of justice and the foundation of democracy. The duty of the journalist is to further those ends by seeking truth and providing a fair and comprehensive account of events and issues. Conscientious journalists from all media and specialties strive to serve the public with thoroughness and honesty. Professional integrity is the cornerstone of a journalist's credibility. Members of the Society share a dedication to ethical behavior and adopt this code to declare the Society's principles and standards of practice.

Seek Truth and Report It

Journalists should be honest, fair and courageous in gathering, reporting and interpreting information.

Minimize Harm

Ethical journalists treat sources, subjects and colleagues as human beings deserving of respect.

Act Independently

Journalists should be free of obligation to any interest other than the public's right to know.

Be Accountable

Journalists are accountable to their readers, listeners, viewers and each other.

Although the SPJ Code of Ethics is probably the dominant one in the profession, it does not represent the profession as a whole but is simply the code of ethics adopted by those journalists who choose voluntarily to join the SPJ.

As noted earlier, there are other ethics codes developed by other organized groups of journalists, but none of them is seen as mandatory, unlike within the professions of medicine or law. Journalism issues no profession-wide sanctions against violators of any of these ethical codes. In that sense, adherence is voluntary among practicing journalists, although individual media organizations may well sanction their staff members for egregious ethical violations.

At least two reasons exist for the voluntary nature of the ethics codes in journalism:

1. By their nature, journalists value their independence and are wary of others imposing restrictions or parameters on their work of inquiry as reporters. This has been seen time and again, and most clearly with the lack of support for the former National News Council, an attempt at an industry-wide council that took consumer complaints about journalists, studied them, and issued findings and sometimes reprimands. Because of the lack of support from the industry, the Council disintegrated.

2. Codes of ethics have been used against media organizations by plaintiffs in libel and invasion-of-privacy lawsuits. The thinking by some plaintiff attorneys is that proving a journalist violated his or her own organization's code of ethics demonstrates that journalist's lack of credibility and honesty. If you can't trust a journalist to stick by the ethical code of the profession, how can you trust this individual not to violate a legal statute like libel or invasion of privacy?

Fabricating News

Journalists differ greatly over how they might go about telling a story and even about various points in codes of ethics, but they all agree on one thing: they are dealing in nonfiction rather than fiction. You may present the truth creatively and even borrow from the novelist in your writing format, but you must always remember that you never make anything up. So one cardinal ethical violation, which will almost certainly result in a reporter's dismissal, is fabrication of facts, sources, or entire stories. Sadly, American journalism has seen too many of these cases over the past few decades.

As the new millennium began, one of these most high-profile cases involved Stephen Glass, a rising star reporter with the Washington magazine, *The New Republic*. Glass developed a reputation as an intrepid reporter who always managed to locate the most interesting people to write about and who told stories in the most vivid and captivating ways. His colleagues sat spellbound at editorial meetings while Glass regaled them with the latest stories on which he was working. His undoing came because of a story called "Hack Heaven," in which he described a young computer hacker who extorted money from a company that paid him to stop hacking into their system. The problem came when a competitor, *Forbes*, tried to track down the people and sources Glass used in his story and found that none of them existed. Soon, the editor of *The New Republic* discovered that "Hack Heaven" was just one of many published Glass stories that had been either partially or totally fabricated. Glass was summarily fired from the magazine, and his career as a journalist came to an end. Ultimately, his story was made into a film, *Shattered Glass,* and he became the subject of a *60 Minutes* interview where he admitted to being what reporter Steve Kroft called "a serial liar."

Glass is not alone in discovering how seriously the profession of journalism takes fabrication. A contemporary of Glass who was caught in fabrication was Jayson Blair of *The New York Times*.

The fact that these publications are considered some of the best in the nation shows how vulnerable all media outlets are to journalists intent on boosting their own careers by deception.

Credibility as "Currency of the Realm"

How does ethics factor into journalists' search for the truth, at either the micro or macro levels, and are journalists paying enough attention to ethical issues today? Jim Robertson, managing editor of the *Columbia Daily Tribune,* says yes, especially if the issue is a practical one faced by journalists in their everyday reporting.

"By the time they get to our newsroom, young journalists have a pretty good awareness of ethical issues," Robertson says. "They recognize when a situation arises that we should discuss. They recognize, and I continually emphasize, that our credibility is the currency of the realm and that an ethical slip can do damage that might be out of proportion to the sin."

However, he adds, "It's my impression there's very little discussion about hypothetical situations. Most of the conversations have to do with specific questions that arise during the reporting and writing of stories."

In cataloguing some of the key ethical issues that confront him and his journalists on a regular basis, Robertson says daily reporting is full of ethical dilemmas, and some of them just keep reappearing.

Pretty basic stuff, really. For example, what do you do when you've identified yourself as a reporter and after a long Q&A session the source says, "It's all off the record"? Another example: Should we always identify ourselves, or is an "undercover" role acceptable? What if we're contacted by someone who trusts us who is a suspect in a crime?

We discuss these questions, consult resources such as Poynter, including professionals we know and respect who might have encountered similar issues. We weigh our role and the potential damage to others affected by our decisions. Then we decide.

And often those newsroom discussions focus on what will work best to produce the candor and truth journalists are after. The philosophical ramifications of the ethical issue are left to others who have more time to consider them. A scene from the humorous film *Broadcast News* comes to mind in articulating this reality. In the scene, a small group of reporters is standing around the water cooler when the following dialogue ensues:

Klein: Okay, what about this? Here's a tough ethical one. Would you tell a source that you loved them just to get some information?

Aaron: Yes.

George: Yes.

Ernie: Me too.

Jennifer: Sure.

Aaron: Jennifer didn't know there was an alternative.

[Jennifer laughs that laugh one always hopes beautiful women will laugh when one says something funny. Aaron smiles at her.]

Aaron: Here's one. They allow us to have cameras at an execution in Florida. Do you broadcast tape of the guy in the chair when they turn on the voltage?

Klein: Sure.

Jennifer: Why not?

Ernie: Absolutely.

George: You bet.

Aaron: Nothing like wrestling with a moral dilemma is there?[8]

New York Times reporter Barry Bearak thinks a lot about the issue of credibility but also sees other ethical issues as paramount, including one or two that don't get discussed that much.

"Ethical issues—things like the use of anonymous sources—are great topics for journalism schools, but the hardest thing about journalism is to get the facts right and to tell the story fairly," Bearak (who has been a visiting journalism professor at Columbia) says. "To me, that's the essence of the journalist's ethical challenge, and it's that responsibility that keeps me awake at night virtually every time I'm ready to publish a story. Beyond that, other ethical concerns aren't usually so immediate and compelling, nor hard to sort out."

It's at this point that Bearak's social conscience protrudes most vividly and touches upon an interesting ethical issue that doesn't get much attention in journalism textbooks. It also reveals how this journalist finds a way to be a good journalist and a good human being at the same time.

> Are there some ethical matters that keep recurring? I suppose so. One involves giving money to the desperately poor or ill. A reporter needs to be strict about not paying for information. But what happens when you come in contact with a child who can be bought out of bondage or some sickly old woman who desperately needs medication or some family that is living on the margins of starvation? I think reporters can scrupulously indulge their impulses for charity. When I want to give money to someone who might appear in my story, I wait until the reporting is absolutely finished. If possible, I'll leave and send the money back with someone reliable.

> Another matter that keeps recurring is whether to use the name of a willing source when I suspect that such use might harm them. A lot of people don't understand the power of a big newspaper. They'll tell you it's okay to use their name even after you tell them about possible consequences like the loss of a job or humiliation for their families. Sometimes, even when someone gives me the go-ahead, I'll override their judgment.

Encouraging Ethics in Politics

Otis Sanford, managing editor of *The Commercial Appeal,* is another editor who encourages discussions of ethics in his newsroom. He would like to see more time spent there on ethical discussions, however:

> We don't spend nearly enough time discussing ethical issues. That is one of my passions. I am viewed as the chief of the ethics police in my shop because I preach ethics all the time. We have those discussions, but not nearly enough. We do have them when issues arise, but I would like to see ongoing dialogues on ethics.

Sanford is particularly interested in ethics relevant to stories concerning politics and the political process. He explains:

One issue is political affiliation and the difficulty some reporters have in being totally neutral during political campaigns, particularly at the national level. I am not sure I know how to go about resolving that. We cannot legislate a person's political beliefs, but we do ask them to keep their views to themselves and, whenever possible, we make sure our reporters who cover politics remain as impartial as possible.

Sanford's passion for sound ethical behavior in politics is documented in his newspaper columns. For example, on August 6, 2007, he wrote an impassioned plea for more ethics in government. In part, the column read as follows:

It's not every day in Memphis that you get honesty from a politician, particularly during an election year.

So imagine the elation that Memphis Rotary Club members felt last week as we listened to refreshing political candor delivered by someone who has never received a single vote in Tennessee.

Arkansas Gov. Mike Beebe was the featured Rotary speaker Tuesday. During his brief talk and a question-and-answer session, Beebe deftly touched on everything from ethics in government to Hillary Clinton's popularity in the state she once called home.

But his overall message was this: Public confidence in elected officials is sputtering on empty. And not enough good people are running for office. His stirring comments should have been recorded, turned into Politics 101 and used as a required short course for everyone seeking elected office in Memphis this year . . . his clarion call for cynicism about the political process to end and for office seekers to reconnect with the electorate was on target. And it resonated with those of us who are weary of polarizing politicians who care more about posturing and protecting their own interests than serving the public.

In essence, politics these days has a serious image problem, leaving in its wake two sets of voters—the ones who are moved to act through anger and those who for various reasons have simply tuned out and may not vote at all.[9]

Diversity in the Newsroom

Closely allied to ethics is the subject of racial, gender, and ethnic diversity in American newsrooms. Many, like former *Philadelphia Inquirer* editor Arlene Notoro Morgan, believe diversity among journalists is vital in producing ethical journalism. In 1995, Morgan was honored with the first Knight Ridder Excellence in Diversity Award for her work to diversify the *Inquirer's* staff and for her leadership in fostering a diverse content and workforce throughout Knight Ridder newspapers, then the corporate owner of the *Inquirer*.

In assessing the status of American journalism today, Morgan sees some things being done right in the profession but also room for improvement. Not surprisingly, given her passions, she counts lack of diversity as one deficiency in journalism.

"I think newspapers have to bring more voices into their stories," Morgan says. "So many stories are still framed around the institutions that we are covering, rather than by the people those institutions are serving," she says. "I also think the news media have to figure out how to better reflect a multiple number of communities who live in the coverage areas. I think if they are to grow, they must move beyond the 'us' (most often white) vs. 'them' (immigrants, people of color) treatment, which to a large extent represents a class issue."

Morgan says her own ethnic background has helped her to understand the issues she has covered over her years as a journalist from the perspectives of the different ethnic groups involved.

"I think growing up as an Italian American in South Philadelphia and attending Catholic schools there gave me an understanding about community reporting that an outside person could never bring to the table," she says.

At one point when we were trying to hone neighborhood coverage, Roberts sent me out to do about three months of reporting on how the paper was perceived by Italian American readers.

I interviewed people from a congressman to relatives. Doors opened for me that would have never opened to anyone else. I think the paper learned a great deal from my being "out there," and Roberts was smart enough to use me as a sounding board. He also did that with several other staffers including Acel Moore in the black community, for instance.

The Oklahoman's Joe Hight sees several serious ethical concerns in journalism today, and he feels reporters need to pay attention to just ways of resolving these dilemmas.

One of those dilemmas deals with separation of fact from opinion in news and feature stories. "It's always tough to keep your own personal opinion, politics or faith from your stories," he says. "I think we fight that—and lose—many times."

He also warns against "victimizing" a person who has already been a victim, simply by reporting a story about him or her unfairly or insensitively. He explains:

I'm of the feeling that certain journalists trample on people's lives in the quest to be Number 1 with a story. In every major tragedy there are instances in which this occurs. I think the journalists, especially those who are inexperienced or lack basic ethical values, feel pressure to do anything possible to get an exclusive. Many of these are stories no one remembers a year later, except those victims or family members who were further harmed by it.

Hight is frustrated by journalists who confuse the First Amendment as granting some sort of unlimited hunting license that can be used to hurt innocent people at times.

"Gosh, I wish journalists would realize that the First Amendment provides journalists with many rights, but it does not give us the right to trample on the lives of innocent people. Idealistically, that's what I got into journalism for in the first place: to help the innocent, not harm them."

Peter Bhatia, executive editor of *The Oregonian,* joins the chorus of editors who encourage more ethical discussions in the newsroom.

"We can always have more conversations about ethics," Bhatia believes. "But I think the events of the past few years . . . have reignited the passion around ethics that perhaps had faded into the routine somewhat or no longer was top of mind. In our newsroom, the newsroom-wide conversations have ramped up in recent months, thanks to having a managing editor for whom that is an important part of her job. All this is good. But it has also served to remind us that ethics is a dynamic process."

How does he define that dynamic aspect, and what does it mean for the journalist who works at *The Oregonian?* Bhatia explains it like this:

> We believe, for example, that being a journalist requires us to forfeit some of our rights as citizens. We should not, for example, contribute to campaigns, sign petitions, participate in marches for causes, or have lawn signs for candidates. For many of us, that is and has been a no-brainer. But there are always some who disagree. Donation lists are public, of course. We weren't happy to find one of our reporters recently contributed to a campaign.

> Regardless, the conversations need to be regular and out in the open. More often than not, they are situational and between a reporter and an editor. But more often, the outcomes of these conversations need to be shared with the rest of the staff and our readers. Many in the public are surprised and pleased to find we have ethical standards that we take seriously.

Bhatia points to an example of a tough ethical issue an *Oregonian* reporter faced recently in discerning how much information to divulge in a story about a teacher's aide.

> There are always ones that stand out, such as a recent story we did on a teacher's aide who had a criminal record that likely would have prevented her

from being hired, but the district didn't check. He [the reporter] wrote the story [after a tip] named her; she was very forthcoming, and people rallied around her. Really interesting, difficult story and ethical case.

Most ethical cases revolve around naming people who may not have wanted to be named in the paper and around anonymity of sources. We generally favor the former—naming—and discourage the latter—granting anonymity. But every case needs to be looked at individually. The facts and circumstances may well lead us against our preferred practice in many cases.

Separating Business From Journalism

Another thing most journalists are agreed on is that the business and marketing concerns of their news company should be separated from the journalistic decisions made in the newsroom. Stories should be done for their journalistic merit and not for selling newspapers or gaining a larger audience share, the belief goes. In reality, of course, this kind of separation is only partly possible, as business and marketing concerns often impinge on what stories are covered, how they are covered, and who covers them. Let's look at some examples:

- A big part of the concept of "citizens journalism" or "public journalism" is that the news consumer should have more of a voice in what the news organization covers.

- Readership studies or Nielsen market surveys may indicate the public wants more emphasis on certain kinds of stories—often feature stories—so those are given more play or air time.

- The need to service a newspaper's large debt or to keep public shareholders happy has produced numerous cutbacks in newsrooms. Fewer reporters means fewer stories covered, and some news beats have been decimated. Cutbacks may also dictate that sports reporters don't cover away games or that a newspaper relies on "stringers" or freelancers in those other towns to e-mail or phone in game stories.

- Audience research may dictate that individuals with shallower news backgrounds get the on-air television jobs of anchoring and, in some cases, reporting over more veteran journalists.

Notes

1. Communication Studies Department, University of Twente, "Hypodermic Needle Theory," *Theory Clusters*, University of Twente, The Netherlands, http://www .cw.utwente.nl/theorieenoverzicht/Theory%20clusters/Mass%20Media/Hypodermic_ Needle_Theory.doc/.

2. Stanley J. Baran and Dennis K. Davis, *Mass Communication Theory: Foundations, Ferment, and Future*, 3rd ed. (New York: Wadsworth, 2002).

3. Baran and Davis, *Mass Communication Theory*.

4. Elisabeth Noelle-Neumann, "The Spiral of Silence: A Theory of Public Opinion," *Journal of Communication* 24 (1974), 43–51.

5. Maxwell McCombs and Donald Shaw, "The Agenda-Setting Function of Mass Media," *Public Opinion Quarterly* 36 (1972), 176–187.

6. Diana C. Mutz, "The Influence of Perceptions of Media Influence: Third Person Effects and the Public Expression of Opinions." *International Journal of Public Opinion Research* 1 (1989), 3–24.

7. Society of Professional Journalists, "Code of Ethics, *SPJ: Society of Professional Journalists*, http://www.spj.org/ethicscode.asp (accessed April 20, 2009).

8. *Broadcast News*, DVD, directed by James L. Brooks (1987; Beverly Hills, CA: 20th Century Fox Home Entertainment, 2005).

9. Otis L. Sanford, "Gov Beebe Delivers Straight Talk on Politics," *The Commercial Appeal*, August 6, 2007.

5

The Journalist as an Ideologue

Objectivity. Detachment. Impartiality. Many journalists wear these credentials as a referee in a football game might wear his pinstripes to indicate his neutral role on the playing field. Ideology doesn't fit into most journalists' thinking about themselves, at least not while they're on the job anyway. Most journalists feel they should check their belief system at the door of the story—before entering in, before describing what lies out in front of them. But "shoulds" sometimes fall short of actual practice, and—in reality—journalists can no more disconnect themselves from their worldviews and value systems than can anyone else. So the trick is figuring out what to do with that worldview and what to do with those values when they start reporting.

Revisiting Objectivity

Pulitzer Prize–winning journalist Jack Fuller, who has also served as president and publisher of the *Chicago Tribune*, is very direct in his assessment of whether objectivity is even possible. In his book *News Values*, he writes:

> No one has ever achieved objective journalism, and no one ever could. The bias of the observer always enters the picture . . . One might have an optimistic bias or a bias toward virtue. It is the inevitable consequence of the combination of one's experience and inbred nature . . . The idea of objectivity came naturally to a group of people seeking legitimacy in an era of scientific discovery. In its purest usage, the term suggested that journalism meant to be so utterly disinterested as to be transparent. The report was to be virtually the

thing itself, unrefracted by the mind of the reporter. This, of course, involved a hopelessly naïve notion from the beginning. And surely every reporter who has ever laid his fingers on the typewriter keys has known it.[1]

This problem is one not just for American journalists but for journalists the world over. Each is a product of his or her culture, and individual perspectives and value systems begin with the macro culture each journalist is from. For many years, nations in the West have been arguing with developing and Middle Eastern countries about this very thing: how to get an unbiased and comprehensive view of what is going on in the world.

Any thinking reporter who has covered tragedies in America, such as 9/11, the Oklahoma City bombing, or Hurricane Katrina, or in other nations understands the difficulty of separating personal feelings from the story itself. That is especially true if the tragedies occur in the hometowns and cities of those reporters. I will address this issue in more detail later in this chapter and in the afterword, where I describe my own reflections as a native Oklahoman covering the Murrah Federal Building bombing in the spring of 1995. Anderson Cooper does a fine job of describing why and how his own emotions have gotten wrapped up in the tragedies he has covered for CNN. Those observations are found in his book *Dispatches from the Edge*.[2]

A journalist more senior than Cooper is Michael Perlstein, a 20-year reporter for *The Times-Picayune* in New Orleans. Perlstein was one of the heroic hometown journalists who stayed behind when the levees broke to record what was happening at "sea-zero" in the flooded city of New Orleans. As with other journalists who have covered traumatic events in their own backyards, Reed was confronted head-on with the pragmatism of objectivity and subjectivity in his daily reporting. In the first appendix of this book is a reprint of the complete article he wrote for *Reed Magazine*, the alumni magazine of his alma mater Reed College, about how that experience of "the storm" affected his thinking about journalism. An excerpt of that article reads as follows:

> As Katrina took aim at New Orleans, I assumed I would remain cool and professional whatever the toll. After all, I was hurricane-hardened. I had chased several, including Andrew when it slammed Franklin, Louisiana, in 1992. But as Katrina's epic tragedy unfolded, I was gradually overwhelmed by my city's descent into apocalypse: the freight-train roar of the wind; the insidious and unstoppable rising water; the haze of unchecked fires, widespread looting, and lawlessness; the masses of desperate evacuees; and, finally, death, depopulation, and military takeover.
>
> Instinct and journalistic experience carried me for that harrowing, exhausting, but intensely wired first week, when it actually seemed plausible that my home for the past 20 years would become the next Atlantis . . .

Erratum for *The Mind of a Journalist:*
How Reporters View Themselves, Their World, and Their Craft

by Jim Willis

One of the journalists contributing to this book is Jim Redmond, who is a former longtime reporter and anchor for KMGH-TV in Denver. The text, however, incorrectly states he was with KUSA-TV, a rival of KMGH in that city.

If any story exposed the myth that journalism is supposed to be objective, this was it. In my side gig as an instructor at Tulane University, I always tell students that for all of journalism's lofty aspirations, objectivity is humanly impossible. A noble goal, perhaps, but a goal that can never be attained. Journalists can and should achieve fairness, balance, and accuracy in every story. But a reporter cannot block out his or her biases, experiences, and gut-level emotions.

The devastating one-two punch of Katrina and Rita hammered that lesson home for me, and it posed a new question: what's wrong with subjectivity in journalism anyway? It works in other Western democracies, where most newspapers openly stake out some wavelength along the political spectrum. It's intellectually honest. And it harkens to the best traditions of advocacy journalism.

If any place needed an advocate after August 29, it was New Orleans.[3]

Some make the case that objectivity is influenced more by the economics of the news business than by anything else. It is not that journalists use the claim of objectivity to try to sell more newspapers or get more viewers for the TV newscast; it is more subconscious than that, these proponents say. "Objectivity" is what comes about when a culture's journalists decide what is "accurate and true" in light of the belief and values system of their own culture, which is, of course, also the culture belonging to their readers and viewers. Confusing? Jaap van Ginneken explains it in his book *Understanding Global News*:

> Objectivity is primarily an economic notion, then. It focuses on those aspects of observations that relevant audience groups may easily agree upon. Other aspects they might differ about, by contrast, are set aside for further debate. But the notion of "relevant audience groups" is the key here, because most global media organizations are primarily geared to the interests and views of audiences in the G-7, the largest Western nations. What they consider objective and true may very well seem rather subjective and questionable to audiences in many non-Western nations.[4]

The Subjective Prisms of Cultures

So the concept of culture emerges in discussions about objectivity, and the idea that Western journalists are objective while journalists in countries unfriendly to the United States are not is a subject of debate for many. In Chapter 3, we saw how sociologist Herbert J. Gans described journalists as *ethnocentric*: as viewing the world through the prism of their own culture and—as is human nature—defining and measuring the "other" world by their own. If many American journalists might argue this point, many people from other cultures in the world would not. In fact, it was this belief that the Western view of the world is not the only one (nor even the most accurate) that propelled the United Nations Educational, Social, and Cultural Organization (UNESCO) into a protracted debate about the way information flows around the world and the pictures that are painted in the process. Known familiarly as the debate over the New World Information and Communication Order (NWICO), this was a call by many nonaligned (developing) nations for, first, more news and views from their own regional media to share space in the flow of global news and, second, new journalistic parameters in coverage of their countries. Worrying that these parameters might include censorship and licensing of journalists, the United States and the United Kingdom temporarily withdrew their membership and their financial support from UNESCO until that debate eventually quelled years later without the NWICO ever becoming a reality.

So, for several more years, the Western domination of global news continued until 1996 when Al Jazeera was launched in the country of Qatar with a $150 million grant from the emir of Qatar. Al Jazeera is a combined news agency, television station, and online magazine that bills itself as the only politically independent television station in the Middle East. It claims to have an estimated 50 million viewers worldwide, rivaling the BBC. It had hoped to become financially independent through advertising by 2001, but missed that mark and remained partially funded by annual grants from the emir. It began an English language channel in 2006, and it is now carried around the world, although it has found difficulty in finding a critical mass of American viewers, even though it was aired by seven regional cable and satellite companies in the United States as of 2007.[5]

Reading or watching international stories in the Western media and then encountering those same stories as done by Al Jazeera often reveal differences in ideologies. The United States and the Middle East, and the issues surrounding both, are often framed differently with different assumptions and different ethnocentricities at work, sometimes in subtle fashion, sometimes in obvious ways. Whether the differences are intentional or not is known only to the reporters writing the stories. In most cases, they are probably unintentional and are instead the product of cultural socialization. Assimilating into a culture other than one's own is difficult at best. For one thing, the new culture may not even contain words found in the person's existing culture, or those words have different meanings. Either could indicate a different way of thinking or acting in a culture. Take the following observation from writer David Hazony in the magazine *Commentary*:

The social linguist Philologos writes [in the online edition of *Forward*[6]] about the gradual assimilation of Arabs into Israeli society, as evidenced by their increasing use of Hebrew words when speaking in Arabic. As with any dual-lingual discourse, the majority are terms that have no easy Arabic equivalent—not just "machsom" (roadblock) or "ramzor" (traffic light) but also "glidah" (ice cream) and "sulamit" (the pound sign on your phone). But the most interesting of these is "m'anyen," which means "interesting." After checking around, the columnist confirms that there is no such word in Arabic. "Is this just a linguistic oddity," Philologos asks, "or is it indicative of a deeper feature of Arab culture—the absence, perhaps, of the very concept of 'interesting' that is so basic to the Western mind, since what isn't unusual enough or noteworthy enough to arouse curiosity is not considered worthy of attention?"[7]

Enduring Values

Ethnocentrism is one of eight "enduring values" that Gans discovered in the news following an intensive study of print and broadcast stories in the early 1980s. Most academics who research and write about the news media are familiar with Gans's enduring values, but many journalistic practitioners are not. Indeed, they are focused on providing the text from which the discernment of these and other values comes. Gans's concept of enduring values refers to the values embedded in the text of the news, values that he believes reveal what American journalists hold near and dear. And, by virtue of the fact that American journalists are writing for American audiences, the implication is that these are also values that Americans hold dear. So the values become criteria of newsworthiness. If a story exemplifies one of these values—or if it depicts *threats* to these values—then it becomes news. Gans explains that he discovered these values by examining the text of many news stories from print and broadcast sources and looking for several things: the kinds of events, issues, or people written about; the sources used; the emphasis used; and the way in which actors and activities were described. For example, if neutral verbiage was available but was not used, then he inferred a value statement. An example he provides is a journalist saying a black activist "showed up" at a meeting, while saying a government official "appeared." In any event, along with ethnocentrism, these are the enduring values Gans found in the stories he examined:[8]

- *Altruistic Democracy.* Many stories about government and government officials evidenced a bias for government for the people and by the people. Stories about officials who violate this value become news because of the threat posed to these values.

- *Responsible Capitalism.* Stories about business and businesspeople were framed with an eye toward this value, and, again, perceived threats to the system were seen as news.

- *Order.* Why does crime dominate as a news story in America? This could be a big reason, Gans might say: it is a threat to order, which is a value that Americans seem to hold as enduring.

- *Moderatism.* Stories done about extremist individuals, groups, and movements become news, Gans believes, because Americans value moderatism and fear extremities like fascism or communism.

- *Leadership.* Like the value of altruistic democracy, leadership is also valued in America and is at the basis of many stories, which focus on poor leaders as well as the heroes who lead others out of trouble.

- *Small-Town Pastoralism.* A whimsical longing for the simpler times, mixed with a sense of nostalgia, drives stories that feature this American value. It is somewhat ironic that, even as Americans have flocked to the nation's cities, their hearts often seem to remain in the country.

- *Rugged Individualism.* If there is one value that seems to be the focal point of so many stories, it is this one. Americans love a good story about an individual or group that stands up to greater odds for a good cause, especially if that cause is individual freedom and liberty.

These, then, are the values that Gans believes American journalists hold, and he asks an interesting question about them: are they politically "liberal" values, the kind that many critics say journalists have? His response is that they are not. Instead, he labels them reformist values, the kind that most Americans seem to have. Taken individually or together, however, they do suggest that journalists are ideologues, just like everyone else.

Journalists and Politics

Are journalists political beings, and is there more of a tendency for journalists to embrace liberal causes than conservative ones? This question was posed to the panel of journalists contributing to this book, and the following are a few of their observations:

- Barry Bearak, foreign correspondent for *The New York Times*, believes, "One of the biggest biases among journalists is the bias toward the bigger story."

> If you have 100 reporters who are Democrats, and you gave them a choice of uncovering the corruption of a Democratic governor or a Republican lieutenant governor, 100 out of 100 would go after the Democrat. The bias is always to catch the bigger fish.

Of course, this hypothetical is artificial in the sense that journalists look under rocks for wrongdoing, and a Democratic reporter may be more likely to suspect that something is amiss under the Republican rocks. So that colors things, too. As for pushing for change, I think liberals and conservatives equally push; just in different directions.

• In assessing how a journalist's own political ideology might affect his or her zeal for chasing certain issues and exposing wrongdoing in government and business, *The Oregonian*'s Peter Bhatia finds a complex issue lurking.

• Certainly all surveys of journalists nationwide show there are more who describe themselves as politically independent or liberal than conservative. Is there any correlation between a journalist's political ideology and his or her interest in exposing corruption? "This is a very complicated issue," Bhatia explains. "One that is prone to simplistic answers from journalists and our critics."

> The notion of the liberal media is way overblown. And if you live in a town like Portland you get it from both sides anyway. The liberals are as vicious as the conservatives.
>
> But the nature of people who go into journalism is they want to make things better; they want to do work that will cause positive change. This is not a political orientation; it is a social orientation. And this is exactly where the liberal media notion becomes an imprecise one. I will not argue for a minute against the fact that most journalists favor liberal political causes.

• What are some of those causes, and does that orientation affect how a journalist writes a story? "Most journalists support abortion rights, gay marriage, and they vote for Democrats," Bhatia explains.

• But our critics forget that most journalists are people of tremendous integrity, and we are trained to set aside our personal feelings to cover whatever is in front of us. The vast majority of newspaper stories are straightforward and honest. The critics may not believe that—especially these days when they want journalism to suit their ideology, as compared to being factual. Are newspapers without bias? Of course not. There is no such thing as an unbiased human being. We can do better at confronting some of our biases that flow from the descriptions above as to who we are. But the bottom line is American journalism has never been better, even in the face of the economic crisis we face today.

• Gretchen Dworznik, a former television news reporter, finds the question of journalists' political leanings tough to address. "This is a hard question to answer because I worked only in local news at a station that did very few investigative pieces—political or otherwise," she says.

> However, I will say this. There were several reporters whom I worked with who had very strong political beliefs. But I never saw any evidence of that affecting how they did a story or what stories they pitched. Our government reporter loved all facets of government and routinely did stories critical of both the Republicans and Democrats in office.
>
> I know there is all this talk about the liberal bias in the media, and maybe, at the national level, there is. But, on a local level, I never saw it. We did the stories we were told to do, whether we agreed with them or not. Maybe those stories that were in line with our own political beliefs turned out to be better pieces, but I think something like that happens on a more subconscious level. Purposely changing the way we did a story for whatever reason would have brought to us much more grief than we were interested in enduring.

• Jim Robertson, managing editor of the *Columbia Daily Tribune*, was asked if he believes reporters who lean toward the liberal political view are better suited for uncovering wrongdoing, or is it a bad rap for conservatives to say they're less inclined to go after corruption in government. "A good friend wrote recently about the differences in the two dominant political parties, and his explanation struck me as a pretty good description of why journalists might lean toward the more liberal end," he explains.

> At the risk of oversimplifying . . . Republicans tend to be oriented toward creation and protection of capital—which they believe drives prosperity—and Democrats are more concerned with basic questions about the welfare of the people.
>
> The legislative friction between the two ideologies is essential to the success of American democracy. That concern about people and their conflicts and struggles is what informs and motivates many journalists. It's what makes good stories. That's about as clear a link as I can see between journalists and progressive politics.

• Joe Hight, managing editor of *The Oklahoman*, has a short and simple answer to the question of whether it makes a difference if a reporter is a liberal or a conservative when it comes to exposing wrongs. "No, as a journalist, I hope there is no correlation," he says. "The desire to uncover wrongdoing in government and/or business should cross political boundaries."

• Otis Sanford, managing editor of Memphis's *The Commercial Appeal*, sees an ethical issue intertwined with reporters' political beliefs. "The issue is political affiliation and the difficulty some reporters have in being totally neutral during political campaigns, particularly at the national level,"

Sanford says. "I am not sure I know how to go about resolving that. We cannot legislate a person's political beliefs, but we do ask them to keep their views to themselves and, whenever possible, we make sure our reporters who cover politics remain as impartial as possible."

• David Waters, editor of the On Faith Web site of the *Washington Post*, believes one of the things he gives up willingly to become a journalist is joining organizations, including political ones.

I've never joined a political party. I joined a church, but only before I began covering religion. I'll never join another. I'm a paper member of the PTA, but I never attend meetings or events. That's one of the "sacrifices" you make as a journalist, in order to maintain at least the appearance of neutrality. Not objectivity. Again, no one can remain perfectly objective about important matters and beliefs. But you can practice and achieve neutrality and be fair and impartial in your reporting.

What the Data Reveal

In 2002, an update of a major study done every ten years since the 1970s discovered that American journalists have actually moved a little further toward the conservative side since the previous study of 1992. However, the findings show that—as a group—journalists are still left of the general public in their political beliefs.[9] The study was reported in the book *The American Journalist in the 21st Century: U.S. News People at the Dawn of a New Millennium*. In the study, survey data gathered during four decades were compared with information obtained by surveying about 1,150 American journalists by phone in 2002. In 2002, four out of ten or 40 percent of American journalists defined themselves as being on the liberal side of the political scale. The authors note that the number was down from 47 percent in 1992. In 2002, 9 percent of the journalists defined themselves as being "pretty far to the left." On the other hand, those journalists describing themselves as "middle of the road" rose slightly to 33 percent in 2002, up from 30 percent in 1992. Those journalists defining themselves as tending toward political conservativism rose to 25 percent, 3 percentage points higher than in 1992. Only 5 percent described themselves as being "pretty far to the right." More specifically, the study stated the following about journalists' political affiliation:[10]

• Only about 37 percent of full-time journalists said they were Democrats, and that figure is 7 percent fewer than in the 1992 survey. This moves journalists closer to the overall percentage of Americans who say they are Democrats. Some media critics, who continue to label most journalists as liberals, might be surprised at this finding.

- Almost 19 percent of full-time journalists said they were Republicans, about a 2 percent jump from the 1992 survey. Some 31 percent of all Americans say they are Republicans.

- About one third of all journalists said they were political "Independents," almost identical to the figure for all U.S. adults.

A 2006 commentary on the study done by The Project for Excellence in Journalism remarked on the differences between the survey's findings as to journalists' political leanings and concurrent data for the political affiliation of the general public:

> If newsrooms have moved slightly rightward, the research shows, however, that journalists are still more liberal than their audiences. According to 2002 Gallup data in "The American Journalist," only 17% of the public character-ized themselves as leaning leftward, and 41% identified themselves as tilting to the right. In other words, journalists are still more than twice as likely to lean leftward than the population overall. When it came to the subject of party affil-iation, 36% of the journalists said they were Democrats in 2002 compared with 44% in 1992. (That's the lowest percentage of self-proclaimed Democrats since 1971.) The percentage of Independents dropped slightly from 1992 to 2002, and the ranks of Republicans grew incrementally from 16% to 18%. (There was actually a notable bump in the percentage of journalists who named another political affiliation or declined to answer the question in 2002.) By comparison, the public's party affiliation is evenly divided with 32% char-acterizing themselves as Democrats and Independents and 31% saying they belonged in the Republican ranks.[11]

Serving as the Victims' Voice

One of the most provocative films ever made about journalists is the 1982 film *The Year of Living Dangerously*.[12] This film has so many layers that it is impossible to summarize them all. Overall, however, the film addresses the question of the journalist's stance or orientation when it comes to covering stories of tragedy. The two main protagonists are an Australian reporter, Guy Hamilton, and an enigmatic photojournalist of mixed ethnicities named Billy Kwan. Both Guy and Billy are committed to their professions, but each has very different ideas on how to cover the suffering of the people in 1960s Jakarta, Indonesia, when President Sukarno is in power. On the night of their first meeting, Billy poses the question to Guy: When confronting tragedy and suffering, "What then must we do?" Billy tells Guy that the words are from the Book of Luke and that Tolstoy also asked the same question of himself and others. The dialogue between Billy and Guy runs like this at that point:

Billy: . . . Tolstoy asked the same question. He wrote a book with that title. He got so upset about the poverty in Moscow that he went one night into the poorest section and just gave away all his money. You could do that now. Five American dollars would be a fortune to one of these people.

Guy: Wouldn't do any good. Just be a drop in the ocean.

Billy: Ah! That's the same conclusion Tolstoy came to. I disagree.

Guy: Oh, what's your solution?

Billy: Well, I support the view that you just don't think about the major issues. You do whatever you can about the misery that's in front of you. Add your light to the sum of light. You think that's naïve, don't you?"

Guy: Yep.

Billy: It's all right, most journalists do.

Guy: We can't afford to get involved.

Billy: Typical journo's answer.

Dialogues like this present themselves as either actual conversations or interior mental debates to many journalists. What is the correct attitude for a journalist? Are there two sides to every story, or are there some stories— like human suffering—for which there is no other side? One of the many evenings when I was covering the aftermath of the Oklahoma City bombing in April of 1995, I was approached by a young reporter for the *Fort Worth Star-Telegram* who asked me about the multicolored ribbon I was wearing. It was one of the blue, yellow, and white ribbons (colors from the Oklahoma state flag) that were handed out after the bombing which claimed 168 lives and left some 800 injured.

"You know, I don't think journalists should be wearing those ribbons," the Texas reporter said.

"Really? Why not?" I asked.

"Because we're not supposed to take sides in stories," she responded.

I told her I wholeheartedly agreed with that statement but that I was not taking sides. I was wearing the ribbon simply as a statement that I was sorry all these people lost their lives and many others suffered injuries and losses of family and friends. Did she think there was another side to that? That we shouldn't be sorry for innocents who were killed? My feeling sorry for them was not going to change the way I wrote the story about the bombing.

But the question about the journalist as advocate is one that can go in several other directions. For example, it can involve the following issues:

- Should a journalist advocate a particular point of view such as, for example, that we should all conserve energy or do what we can to avoid greater global warming?

- Should a journalist put down the notebook or camera and help relieve suffering people by giving them food, getting them medical aid, or helping to dig a well?

- Should a journalist become the voice of those victims whose voices are not being heard by the government?

These are not simply abstract questions. Many journalists face them every day, and Americans are seeing how some of them answer these questions by watching their reporting every night on television. Two such examples of journalists who advocate and empathize are CNN reporters Anderson Cooper and Lou Dobbs. In both cases, these individuals have made decisions to go beyond what traditional journalism might say is appropriate for a "neutral" journalist. Before getting to these two examples, however, let's take a look at three types of language available to writers to convey their stories in the first place and see how gradations of language can affect a report.

Reports, Inferences, and Judgments

Semanticist S. I. Hayakawa wrote in his classic book *Language in Thought and Action* that we all have three types of language available to us when we go to put our observations into words. Those are the language of *reports, inferences,* or *judgments.*[13]

Report language is characterized by its neutrality of verbiage and intent. The objective reporter tries to let the object observed describe itself. Technical writing, such as that found in an instruction manual, might be an example of this kind of language. Dry in tone, the message is explicit and without interpretation, comment, or value judgment. The strictest adherents of traditional journalism might suggest that this should be the language of the journalist. However, describing how to put together a bookshelf is somewhat different than describing a tragedy a journalist has just witnessed or interviewed others about. As Jack Fuller noted earlier, almost every reporter who has ever sat down at a keyboard knows how much subjectivity comes into play when writing stories. An example: A few months after the Oklahoma City bombing, *The Oklahoman* and *The Boston Globe* each carried its own staff-written story on the performance of the Red Cross after the bombing in getting relief support to survivors and families of victims. Each story was built on accurate facts and accurate representations of interviews done. But each story came to a different conclusion: One story indicated that the Red Cross had done a good job; the other, that it had done a bad job. The difference was simply the result of the sources that each reporter chose to use and the anecdotes chosen for inclusion in the story. Adding to the difficulty of using *report* language is that most mainstream journalists are engaging in storytelling, borrowing techniques from other writing genres such as fiction—and even poetry—to convey their message. This is borne of a desire to get people to read stories when people would rather watch images of stories than read or even listen to words. Storytelling techniques involve framing a story a particular way, often via a narrative involving personalization and anecdotes. These techniques recast *report* language, transforming it into the language of *inference.*

Inference language is making a statement about the unknown on the basis of the known. It is interpretation, and journalists do this all the time. It is like the process an artist might use in taking small, individual tile pieces and composing a wall-size mosaic from them. An example of using inferences as opposed to reports can be taken from my own experience. I was editor of a suburban Dallas daily. Our reporters had just covered a controversial meeting of the city council the night before, and the story was on this day's front page. It was local election season, and tempers among the candidates were hot as they pored over every word in the local newspaper about them. This story featured a lot of council members. Late in the morning, one of those elected officials walked into my office and made two statements germane to this discussion of inferences. First, he said, "My mother told me if you can't say something nice about someone, then don't say anything at all!" He was referring to an accurate report of his becoming irate at the council meeting and saying things he later wished he hadn't. Second, he asked why we had to make all those observations about the meeting. Why couldn't we just run the city clerk's official transcript of the meeting minutes instead of writing a *story* about it? I responded that a reporter's job is to cover *what* happened at the meeting as well as *how* it happened. I further stated our story was accurate about the events of the meeting and that we covered both the virtuous things said as well as the things people found stupid. I noted that the journalist's role is not to censor out things people do or say that might make them look bad. A journalist tries to offer an accurate representation of what happened. Being a mother to the offending person is not a part of that role. In any event, in deciding what parts of the meeting to focus on, which quotations to use, and how to describe the meeting, we were engaging in inferences and interpretation. We were using our training as professional observers *and* recorders to form *stories*; we were not simply copying the official minutes of the meeting and printing them. It's hard to imagine that anyone would read the latter. For one thing, that "story" would start with the pledge of allegiance and the reading of the previous meeting's minutes. In journalistic parlance, that story would "bury the lead."

Judgment language takes inferences one step further. It involves making value statements about the events, people, or issues reported on. It brings in the "rightness" or the "wrongness" of those elements. If reporters find they must engage in inferences and interpretation, they should avoid making judgments. There are many different orientations and approaches to mainstream reporting, but journalists from every approach would all agree on this, with the possible exception of advocacy journalists, an orientation explained later. A hallmark of journalism is the separation of news from opinion, and that is the reason for the "op-ed" pages of the newspaper. Journalists may emphasize different aspects of stories, select the sources they use, and use storytelling techniques in conveying their stories, and they may let their emotions fuel that reporting and writing, but they shouldn't be making judgments on what people say or whether certain events are right or wrong.

When Passion Enters In

If Anderson Cooper, host of CNN's nightly *AC 360°*, has seen *The Year of Living Dangerously*, it is easy to see how he might have identified with Billy Kwan's approach of getting close to suffering and telling the story of people adversely affected by government policy. Cooper gained fame covering Hurricane Katrina in New Orleans and coastal Mississippi in 2005 and 2006. Night after night, he was at the center of the storm, both literally and figuratively, often showing his emotions about how he felt about the victims of suffering, often showing anger toward government officials whom he believed were moving too slowly in responding to the disaster. In many ways, he seemed to become the voice for the victims of Katrina. Even casual attention to his reporting style reveals that, but so did an hour-long interview he did in June of 2006 with Larry King. And he wrote about his emotional attachment to stories of tragedy in his book *Dispatches from the Edge*.

Larry King asked Cooper about his emotional stance when covering Katrina: "Most reporters stand on the sidelines and report. You got angry. Why?" King pointed to an interview Cooper did with Senator Mary Landrieu in which she was praising Congress for its response to the tragedy.

Cooper interrupted her in mid-sentence and challenged her response, saying dead bodies were still floating in the flooded streets of New Orleans. He chided her for praising her colleagues when that situation still existed. Cooper responded to King's question by saying he hoped he would never be rude to anyone but that he was after "answers to questions" and "not … responses to questions."[14] He said that, if he had to use his anger to get answers, then he would do it. He also told King that he "made a promise" to the people of New Orleans not to leave until they got the relief they needed. That point itself is an interesting one, and one that some might compare to a police officer promising a murder victim's widow that he would catch the killer. Some would ask whether that is a promise either a journalist or a police officer should make in the first place.

Cooper makes some strong arguments for his approach to journalism. Like Jack Fuller earlier in this chapter, he doesn't believe journalists can remain emotionally neutral in the stories they cover, especially if those stories involve tragedy and human suffering. As a victim of tragedy himself (his brother committed suicide in front of his mother in 1988, and his father died when he as a boy), he finds that contemporary stories of suffering summon up those emotions within him, as he identifies with those in the midst of tragedy.

• About Cooper's approach, *Vanity Fair* magazine wrote, "With his reports from the New Orleans disaster zone, Anderson Cooper became the conscience of a nation. But even as he shared the nightmare of a drowning city, another wall was coming down: the emotional one Cooper had built to shield himself from the memory of his brother's 1988 suicide."[15] And Cooper himself wrote in his book, "For years I tried to compartmentalize my life, distance myself from the world I was reporting on. This year [2005], I realized that this is not possible. In the midst of tragedy, the memories of moments, forgotten feelings, began to feed off one another . . . The past never leaves you."[16]

My own experience in covering the Oklahoma City bombing in 1995 and the F5 tornado that devastated a wide central swath of Oklahoma in 1999 resonates with what Cooper has to say about the connectedness of emotional responses to different tragedies. As the bombing occurred on April 19, 1995, I was experiencing the personal loss of a loved one in another state. When I showed up at the bombing scene to begin three months of coverage, the pain I witnessed collided with the pain I felt inside from my own personal tragedy elsewhere. It was easy to understand the suffering of those who lost loved ones when the Alfred P. Murrah Federal Building was reduced to a hollowed-out carcass. I wrote about that experience in a retrospective piece years later for the newspaper that I represented as a reporter in 1995. My observations sounded nearly identical to the ones Cooper made a decade later in his book. From my own experience I concluded the following:

- There are two types of emotions confronting journalists as they do stories about pain and suffering: factual emotions and hyped emotions. The first are those emotions that are a factual part of the story. To ignore them is to avoid the story. My assignment following the bombing was to cover the events and people of ground zero. That was largely a story of emotions, and they were often the main event. Hyped emotions, on the other hand, are like gratuitous adjectives that a writer might pile on, just in case the reader or viewer doesn't notice the real or factual emotions at the scene. They are hyperbole and are meant for the emotional jugular of the reader or viewer. Clearly, they are the essence of that often-misunderstood term "sensationalism," and they should be avoided at all costs.

- Trying to silence a journalist's own felt emotions at the scene of a tragedy is an exercise not only in denial but also in futility: it does not work. Gathering facts, doing interviews, and piecing together accurate stories—journalists do not do these things in an emotional vacuum. Indeed, a reporter's emotions can actual *fuel* the story she or he is writing and produce a level of clarity and appropriateness unachievable when journalists try to wall off these feelings. Of the dozens of stories I wrote about the Oklahoma City bombing, the one I remember the most was about a memorial service held on the rubble pile of the Murrah Building a couple of weeks after the bombing itself. There was a ceremony under way featuring politicians at the base of the building's carcass, but that was not the story on this day. There was so much to see, so much to take in about the thousand or more rescuers and volunteers gathered—this was a memorial largely in their honor—that the story came not from political speeches but from a reporter's own observations. I remember thinking when I left the scene that this was a story that needed to be told in a different way, that the goal here was to transport my readers to see what I was seeing and to feel what people here—myself included—were feeling. As often happens, I couldn't wait to get to the computer to start working on the story. When I did, I discovered the piece was writing itself. This experience is described in more detail in the epilogue.

- The reporter's emotions should not color his or her pursuit of the best obtainable version of the truth through tireless fact gathering and fact checking, interviewing, and observation. Rather, those emotions should provide the reporter with added "fire in the belly," which forces him or her to get as many facts as possible. Devotion to the story can be heightened by the passion a reporter feels about that story.

Op-Ed News

An early-evening tradition for many Americans is to sit down to the television and watch a newscast. Once dominated by the straightforward and no-nonsense styles of Chet Huntley, David Brinkley, Walter Cronkite, and Peter Jennings, the nightly news, which used to be presented only by the networks, is now available on cable news counterparts, where anchors such as Lou Dobbs take more latitude in describing events of the day. Dobbs, for example, moves into territory that Hayakawa describes as *judgment* language, making value statements about the events he and his reporters cover. Dobbs told *The New York Times*,

> There's nothing fair and balanced about me . . . because there's nothing fair and balanced about the truth. "He says, she says" journalism is a monstrous cop-out. I happen to believe strongly and passionately that we are a nation of immigrants. . . But only fools with an agenda can defend illegal immigration.[17]

In its report on Dobbs, *Times* reporter Rachel L. Swarns had the following to say about his approach:

> . . . for most of his program, he looks and feels like a traditional, nothing-but-the-news television host. Then the topic turns to illegal immigration, and the sober newsman starts breathing fire. Mr. Dobbs batters the Bush administration for doing too little to stop millions of migrants from slipping across the border . . . He slams businesses and advocacy groups for helping illegal aliens thrive here . . . his scorching commentaries spill across the nation's television screens.[18]

In that same article, the reporter notes some of the comments Dobbs has made on air about the immigration issue and the response of the Bush administration. Following, taken from "Lou's Commentary" on CNN are a few of these remarks:

- "Only a fool, Mr. President . . . would believe you when you speak of new legislation. You don't enforce the laws now."[19]
- "Never before in our country's history have both the president and Congress been so out of touch with most Americans."[20]
- "The president and Congress are telling working men and women and their families, American citizens all, to go to hell."[21]

In a 2007 article, another *Times* reporter wrote about Dobbs, noting that his audience has risen 72 percent since 2003:

> Mr. Dobbs argues that the middle class has many enemies: corporate lobby-ists, greedy executives, wimpy journalists, corrupt politicians. But none play a bigger role than illegal immigrants. As he sees it, they are stealing our jobs, depressing our wages and even endangering our lives.[22]

Arlene Notoro Morgan, associate dean of the Columbia University Graduate School of Journalism, finds herself at odds with the latest round of "emotional reporting," which has cropped up with Cooper and Dobbs. "I am not comfortable with this approach," Morgan says.

> I think you let your sources show the anger and that this emotionalism, to my mind, is being used instead of bringing various voices on to debate the issue. I don't watch CNN that much. Anderson's personal style clearly appeals to younger audiences, and, while I think he is more emotional than network anchors, I don't think he crosses the line that often. Dobbs, on the other hand, is obviously appealing to a segment of society who fears that immigrants are taking away their jobs, and I rarely hear the other side in any measured way.

> I think there is a big difference between Dobbs and Cooper in that Cooper is still out there reporting while Dobbs is issuing his opinion but with not much that I can see in reporting all the sides to this complicated issue.

Whether the approach to journalism of Dobbs or Cooper will prevail may well rest with the popularity of either or both reporters among viewers. Figures from the 2005 report *State of the American News Media* show that cable news popularity has surpassed the popularity of network evening newscasts, and the approaches of Cooper, Dobbs, and others (such as Bill O'Reilly on FOX) are plentiful on news programs featured by these cable networks.[23]

Notes

1. Jack Fuller, *News Values: Ideas for an Information Age* (Chicago: University of Chicago Press, 1996), 14–15.

2. Anderson Cooper, *Dispatches from the Edge* (New York: HarperCollins, 2006).

3. Michael Perlstein, "Covering Katrina: On Taking It Personally," *Reed Magazine*, Winter 2006, http://www.reed.edu/reed_magazine/winter06/features/covering_katrina/perlstein1.html.

4. Jaap van Ginneken, *Understanding Global News: A Critical Introduction* (London: Sage, 1998), 63.

5. *Aljazeera* [Online], http://english.aljazeera.net.

6. Philologos, "Israeli Arabs and Hebrew: On Language," *Forward: The Jewish Daily*, May 16, 2008, http://www.forward.com/articles/13312/.

7. David Hazony, "Contentions: Arab Assimilation," *Commentary*, May 11, 2008, http://www.commentarymagazine.com/blogs/index.php/hazony/5501 (accessed April 22, 2009).

8. Herbert Gans, *Deciding What's News* (New York: Vantage, 1980).

9. Pew Research Center, "The American Journalist: Politics and Party Affiliation," *Journalism.org*, October 6, 2006, http://www.journalism.org/node/2304.

10. Pew Research Center, "The American Journalist."

11. Pew Research Center, "The American Journalist."

12. *The Year of Living Dangerously,* DVD, directed by Peter Weir, written by C. J. Koch and Peter Weir (1983; Burbank, CA: Warner Home Video, 2000).

13. S. I. Hayakawa, *Language in Thought and Action* (New York: Harcourt, 1990).

14. Anderson Cooper, interview with Larry King, *Larry King Live*, CNN, June 1, 2006, http://transcripts.cnn.com/TRANSCRIPTS/0606/01/lkl.01.html.

15. "Anderson Cooper's Private Storm," *Vanity Fair*, June 2006, 138.

16. Cooper, *Dispatches from the Edge.*

17. Rachel L. Swarns, "Dobbs's Outspokenness Draws Fans and Fire," *The New York Times,* Februrary 15, 2006, http://www.nytimes.com/2006/02/15/arts/television/15dobb.html.

18. Swarns, "Dobbs's."

19. Lou Dobbs, "Dobbs to President: Do you Take us for Fools?" *Lou Dobbs Tonight: Lou's Commentary*, CNN, May 11, 2006, http://www.cnn.com/2006/US/05/10/dobbs.enforcement/index.html.

20. Lou Dobbs, "Bush, Congress Tell Working Folk to go to Hell," *Lou Dobbs Tonight: Lou's Commentary*, CNN, May 24, 2006, http://www.cnn.com/2006/US/05/23/dobbs.may24/index.html.

21. Dobbs, "Bush, Congress."

22. David Leonhardt, "Truth, Fiction, and Lou Dobbs," *The New York Times,* May 30, 2007, http://www.nytimes.com/2007/05/30/business/30leonhardt.html.

23. Pew Research Center, "The American Journalist."

6

The Journalist and Faith

Journalism has been called "the rough draft of history," and it a history of the world in which we spend our earthly lives as we are in the process of living them. By its nature, journalism is the story of the here and now, the ways in which that present is related to (and formed by) the past, and the implications that current events, issues, and people might have on the future. Given journalism's nature, then, the subject of religion has always been an uneasy fit for many journalists because the substance of religion points to another world beyond this one. Religion is also a controversial subject, connoting discussions of a deity in which some people believe, albeit with varying interpretations, and in which some don't believe at all. Nevertheless, there are intersections between journalism and religion. Some of them are the following:

- Both religion and journalism are disciplines that purport to seek the truth, albeit often in different realms. In that sense, journalists and religious scholars are on similar missions.

- Many people about whom journalists write are inspired by their faith and use their faith in dealing with the challenges and tragedies that they face.

- Societal values on which journalists report are often derived from religious precepts.

- Religious news has become popular in many areas of the country, especially in the South. Some southern newspapers, for example, *The Dallas Morning News*, have introduced more in-depth coverage to religion with expanded sections devoted to that news beat.

- Organized religion in America has become a powerful institution, and it is felt by individuals, families, schools, medical research, and government. In the case of the latter, the rise of the so-called religious right in the 1980s began exerting strong influences on politics and even produced a candidate for the Republican presidential nomination in Pat Robertson.

- Individual journalists may hold particular worldviews that are based on their religious beliefs and, as discussed earlier in this book, individual worldviews of journalists can influence what they choose to call news in the first place and how they view those events and issues.

And there is another interesting intersection between religion and journalism: to journalists, their profession itself is a kind of religion. New York University media ethicist Jay Rosen writes the following in his online blog called Pressthink: "The newsroom is a nest of believers if we include believers in journalism itself. There is a religion of the press. There is also a priesthood. And there can be a crisis of faith."[1] Rosen and editor Jeff Sharlet are publishing a new Web journal called *The Revealer* about religion and the press in a contentious and dynamic world. Rosen writes:

> There is a high church in journalism, with high ceremonies, like the awarding of a Pulitzer Prize, joining the panel on "Meet the Press," having a dart thrown at you by the *Columbia Journalism Review*. One could teach a course about it. Bill Moyers once said this while moderating an event at Columbia: "I think of *CJR* and the J-School as sort of the 'high church' of our craft, reminding us of the better angels of our nature and the demons, powers and principalities of power against which journalism is always wrestling."[2]

A Reluctant Story

This chapter began by noting that religion is a hard-sell story to many news media. Sometimes, it is the journalists themselves reluctant to cover stories involving faith and churches; sometimes, it is the media organizations for which they work. But journalists are often among the first to recognize their faults and to discuss those areas for improvement with other journalists, one on one or at conventions such as the annual meeting of the Society of Professional Journalists. Sometimes, a newspaper's editors will issue guidelines for improvement or hold newsroom sessions where reporters and editors can talk over their challenges. Sometimes, committees are struck to consider important issues. A portion of a document written by Bill Keller, executive editor of *The New York Times*, responded to one such committee, the *Times*'s Credibility Committee. Here is what Keller said about reporting religion:

> I also endorse the committee's recommendation that we cover religion more extensively, but I think the key to that is not to add more reporters who will write about religion as a beat. I think the key is to be more alert to the role religion plays in many stories we cover, stories of politics and policy, national and local, stories of social trends and family life, stories of how we live. This is important to us not because we want to appease believers or pander to conservatives, but because good journalism entails understanding more than just the neighborhood you grew up in.[3]

Writer Gal Beckerman also examined the issue of journalists' coverage of religion. She wrote on the topic, not just for one newspaper but for a broader audience of journalists and media academics, in a 2004 edition of the *Columbia Journalism Review*. Her theme was—like Keller's—that journalists on various news beats are often missing important religious connections to stories. She called on reporters and editors to be more discerning in finding intersections between faith and other issues because religion often provides a context for these issues:

> We live in a religious country. Church steeples punctuate the landscape of even our most secular cities. We have a president who claims Jesus as his favorite political philosopher. And the touchiest societal debates we engage in—over abortion, stem-cell research, the pledge of allegiance, gay marriage—point us back to scripture. In a poll conducted earlier this year by the Pew Research Center for the People and the Press, 81 percent of Americans said that prayer was an important part of their lives and that they believed in the eventuality of a judgment day in which they will have to atone for their sins . . . However central belief and faith might be to the American populace, our news media seldom puncture the surface in their reporting on religion . . . it generally takes scandal or spectacle to get even the large denominations on the front page. And even then, the deeper belief systems of these religions are left unexamined. The theology and faith of the believers is kept at arm's length, and the writing is clinical. The journalist glances at religious community as if staring through the glass of an ant farm, remarking on what the strange creatures are doing, but missing the motivations behind the action.[4]

As an example, Beckerman cites the controversial Mel Gibson film *The Passion of the Christ* and notes how it was covered in the press mainly as a "conflict" story. Reporters talked about whether it was anti-Semitic or whether there was too much violence. But few reporters seemed to notice or report on why it was so popular with Christian believers. Beckerman asks, "Can we afford to overlook the deep well of faith and belief that ensured its success? Isn't this journalism's mandate: to offer not just a simple play-by-play of reality, but also to explore what stirs, inspires, pushes people to action?"[5]

Some might say that religion is already covered well in the publications of the religious press and on some cable television stations in shows produced by evangelists such as Pat Robertson and others. But many of the journalists interviewed for this book, and other journalists quoted elsewhere, suggest strongly that religion and faith are forces that should transcend the religious press and are important issues for the secular press to address as well. Studies show that many Americans are guided by their faith and that others are inspired by it at critical times in their lives. Leaving such a strong motive for actions out of a story about people in crisis seems like ignoring an important part of the story simply because a reporter might fear religion is too controversial a topic to handle or because he or she doesn't want to be seen as promoting religion.

Journalist Terry Mattingly agrees with that assessment. He directs the Washington Journalism Center, an institution run by the Council of Christian Colleges and Universities (CCCU). Mattingly is also a syndicated religion writer for the Scripps Howard News Service and is one of the team of a dozen journalists interviewed for this book. He says it was the realization of how badly the media cover religion that helped get him into the news business in the first place.

Religion has always factored into Mattingly's journalism. Although he originally became a journalism major at Baylor University because he wanted to write about music (a music major seemed doubtful without requisite talent on the piano first), his motivation morphed in the spring semester of his sophomore year.

"I became interested in how the media largely ignored religion," Mattingly says. "[A professor] told me that other students on the college newspaper's staff have already picked up that religion is the worst covered subject in the entire American mainstream press. Then he asked me, 'Do you want to do anything about that?' That's when my interest in covering religion really intensified."

Today, more than 18 years later, Mattingly's column "On Religion" appears in some 300 dailies and another 600 smaller newspapers around the country for the Scripps Howard News Service. Much of Mattingly's thinking about the lax coverage of religious news can be found on the GetReligion.org Web site. Here, in part, is his explanation of what he and his colleagues do and why:

Day after day, millions of Americans who frequent pews see ghosts when they pick up their newspapers or turn on television news.

They read stories that are important to their lives, yet they seem to catch fleeting glimpses of other characters or other plots between the lines. There seem to be other ideas or influences hiding there.

One minute they are there. The next they are gone. There are ghosts in there, hiding in the ink and the pixels. Something is missing in the basic facts or perhaps most of the key facts are there, yet some are twisted. Perhaps there are sins of omission, rather than commission.

A lot of these ghosts are, well, holy ghosts. They are facts and stories and faces linked to the power of religious faith. Now you see them. Now you don't. In fact, a whole lot of the time you don't get to see them. But that doesn't mean they aren't there.[6]

Mattingly has also taught in theological seminaries and enjoys mixing writing and religion. That is controversial territory for many journalists, but Mattingly believes it can be negotiated by paying attention to a few guidelines.

"It's false that a reporter can unplug his ideology and somehow become neutral," Mattingly says. "Objectivity should be more of a methodology thing. Balance is a better word than objectivity. Editors need to produce a paper that's fair to the audience they are trying to reach. If you have a large section of your readership that says your abortion coverage is unbalanced and if one side is saying their views are being distorted, then the editor must take that seriously."

Mattingly believes that journalists can solve many of the problems they face when covering religion simply by applying good journalistic principles.

"The answer to journalistic problems is almost always journalistic solutions," he says. "Journalists get into trouble in covering religion news by applying non-journalistic solutions. Just do more religion coverage and use a wide array of sources."

There are always exceptions to the rule, however, and exceptions exist to the idea that covering religion is anathema to mainstream journalism. Take *The Washington Post*, for example. Long known as the newspaper that broke the Watergate story, which resulted in the forced resignation of a U.S. president, the *Post* has made its mark in religion coverage over the years. Most recently, it has launched a separate Web site focusing on religion called On Faith (http://Newsweek.Washingtonpost.com/Onfaith). Produced by David Waters, former award-winning religion editor for *The Commercial-Appeal* in Memphis, On Faith is a joint project of *The Washington Post* and *Newsweek* magazine featuring discussions on the intersection of faith, social, and government issues. Its lead discussants are reporters Sally Quinn and Jon Meacham, and they are joined by an extensive panel of contributors representing the various disciplines of the clergy, journalism, and higher education. The Web site describes itself and its mission as follows:

> Religion is the most pervasive yet least understood topic in global life. From the caves of the Afghan-Pakistan border to the cul-de-sacs of the American Sunbelt, faith shapes and suffuses the way billions of people—Christian, Muslim, Jewish, Hindu, Buddhist, and nonbelievers—think and act, vote and fight, love and, tragically, hate. It is the most ancient of forces ... And so, in a time of extremism . . . how can people engage in a conversation about faith and its implications in a way that sheds light rather than generates heat? At *The Washington Post* and *Newsweek*, we believe the first step is conversation—intelligent, informed, eclectic, respectful conversation—among specialists and generalists who devote a good part of their lives to understanding and delineating religion's influence on the life of the world. The point of our new online religion feature is to provide a forum for such sane and spirited talk, drawing on a remarkable panel of distinguished figures from the academy, the faith traditions, and journalism.[7]

The Washington Post also distinguished itself in religion reporting by winning a 2002 Pulitzer Prize for National Reporting because of its coverage on America's war on terrorism. In one article cited as worthy of this award, Bob Woodward intertwined the religious foundations of 9/11 terrorist Mohamed Atta with his operational instructions to his fellow conspirators before the 2001 attacks in New York and Washington. A portion of Woodward's story shows how even political reporters can find the spiritual connection in stories that, at first glance, are not about religion:

> The haunting writings urge the hijackers to crave death and "be optimistic." At the same time, the document starkly addresses fear on the eve of their suicide mission.

> "Everybody hates death, fears death," according to a translation of highlights of the document obtained by *The Washington Post*. "But only those, the believers who know the life after death and the reward after death, would be the ones who will be seeking death."

> This appears in a section of the document beneath the words, "The last night." That section begins, "Remind yourself that in this night you will face many challenges. But you have to face them and understand it 100 percent. . . . Obey God, his messenger, and don't fight among yourself where you become weak, and stand fast, God will stand with those who stood fast."[8]

It is interesting to hear the observations of the On Faith Web site producer David Waters, as he reflects on the intersections of journalism and religion. One of the panelists contributing to the insights in this book, Waters noted in a 2007 interview that religion should be an important area of coverage.

"This [reporting religion] is a subject near and dear to my heart," says Waters. "I could write for hours about it. Generally, I think religion confounds and maybe even scares most reporters. It's so subjective and emotional and visceral and experiential and theoretical and so on. It's not an easy or comfortable subject to cover. So most reporters either ignore it or treat it as any other subject—by gathering quotes through interviews, reading reports or other documents, attending events and meetings, etc."

In short, there is little of what reporters and editors call "enterprise reporting" or "investigative reporting" when it comes to religion, despite its importance in the lives of just about everyone, he says.

> Religion is the most important topic out there. It matters to nearly everyone, even to atheists and agnostics. It affects nearly everything—from how we raise and educate our kids, to how we make and spend our money, to how we run corporations, communities, and even countries.

Waters first started covering religion as if it were any other beat. He attended meetings and events, talked to leaders, read documents, and looked for trends. He soon realized, however, something was missing in the way he was approaching the subject.

"It wasn't going well. I kept looking for a focal point—like a mayor, a CEO, a team, a building, etc.—but there wasn't one, or so I thought," he explains.

Things were about to change for Waters and his approach, however.

> Then I found the focal point. I decided I shouldn't be covering religion. I should be covering God [or god]. I should cover, in the words of Rabbi Harold Kushner, "the difference God makes in the way we live." The whole beat opened up to me, and I realized that I could and should cover "the difference God makes" in the way we live, work, worship, play, pray, eat, vote, wage war, help others, etc. It's the best beat there is.

On the broadcast side, ABC News decided to boost its level of religion coverage at the behest of the late Peter Jennings, then longtime anchor of its *World News Tonight*. It took this step at a time when no network news operation even had a religion reporter. Jennings described his position in the following way:

> I think what comes as a surprise to people just descending on America for the first time is the degree and intensity of religion in public life, as it has always been in this society . . . There are a lot of people in the country who believe very strongly that the country is in moral danger and that religion is another way to have bearings, moral bearings. I'm not surprised by that. I find it fascinating.[9]

Jon Banner, executive producer for *World News Tonight*, described religion as one of Jennings's "passions" and said he forced the network to hire a religion reporter and to start covering religion as a beat. "He started really to care about faith in all of our lives," Banner said. "He found it remarkable, given how important religion is to the American public, that we weren't covering it more often."[10]

Jeanmarie Condon produced several of Jennings's documentaries on religion, including "Jerusalem Stories," "The Search for Jesus," and "Jesus and Paul: The Word and the Witness." She echoed Banner's point about the importance Jennings placed on religion. "He had lived in the Middle East . . . So he had seen firsthand the ways in which religion moves through history and changes people's lives and changes the course of history . . . He thought journalists didn't take it seriously enough," she said.[11]

Jennings himself said,

> There is a fundamental difference in the way we, as secular journalists, see the truth and the definition of the truth accepted by many people of religious faith. People of faith believe that what they believe is true. We secular journalists are trained to believe that it is our obligation to put what we encounter to a rational test that we can comprehend. Someone pointed out that Saint Thomas, doubting Thomas, could well be journalism's patron saint.[12]

The result of Jennings urging ABC to hire a full-time religion reporter was Peggy Wehmeyer, who reported for ABC from 1994–2002. Commenting on Jennings's own religious faith, Wehmeyer said,

> Religion is a very personal thing. I don't know exactly what Peter believed, although we talked about faith a lot. We talked about different religions and the role of religion. The thing that impressed me most about Peter was that he wasn't closed-minded to religion. He wasn't contemptuous toward people who believed things that he might have found different or odd. I think the most interesting thing about Peter was that he was always pursuing and curious and interested about why people believed what they believed, and how did they believe it, and he wanted to know more about it.[13]

Top Religion Stories for 2007

In his classic study of values and journalism, which was discussed in Chapter 5, Columbia sociologist Herbert J. Gans suggests that, if we want to know what is important to journalists, we should look at the work they produce. Embedded in choices regarding what reporters call "news," what sources they use, and the way they tell stories are the "enduring values" of journalists.[14] If that is the case, then looking at the kinds of stories the media do about religion should say something about the values they feel are important in society. Despite the fact that many journalists are reluctant to cover religion, sometimes it is impossible to ignore religious stories or stories with religious overtones. Consider the year 2007 and the several stories with faith elements that became big news, including the 2008 presidential campaign itself. After all, the field of candidates did include a Baptist preacher and a devout Mormon. A poll of the nation's leading religion writers selected the presidential election and the fight for votes among GOP candidates as the top religion story of 2007, according to a press release issued to the public by the Religion Newswriters Association.[15] Close behind as the number two story was the campaign by Democrats to win over voters by showcasing their faith. The association's press release states the following:

> For the top religion newsmaker of the year, the journalists chose the Buddhist monks in Myanmar. Hundreds of monks protested last September in support of democracy but were squelched by the military-backed government. More than half of those responding to the survey chose the monks over Pope Benedict XVI, President George W. Bush and U.S. Supreme Court Chief Justice John Roberts, among others.

> The 2007 Top Religion Stories as selected by Religion Newswriters are:

> 1. Evangelical voters ponder whether they will be able to support the eventual Republican candidate, as they did in 2004, because of questions about the leaders' faith and/or platform. Many say they would be reluctant to vote for Mormon Mitt Romney.

> 2. Leading Democratic presidential candidates make conscious efforts to woo faith-based voters after admitting failure to do so in 2004.

> 3. The role of gays and lesbians in clergy continues as a deeply dividing issue. An Episcopal Church promise to exercise restraint on gay issues fails to stem the number of congregations seeking to leave the mainline denomination, while in a close vote, Canadian Anglican bishops vote to nullify lay and clerical approval of same-sex blessings. Meanwhile, Conservative Jews become more open to gay leadership.

> 4. Global warming rises in importance among religious groups, with many mainline leaders giving it high priority and evangelical leaders split over its importance compared to other social and moral causes.

> 5. The question of what to do about illegal immigration is debated by religious leaders and groups on both sides of the issue. Some take an active role in supporting undocumented immigrants.

6. Thousands of Buddhist monks lead pro-democracy protest in Myanmar, which is brutally crushed after a week.

7. Some conservative U.S. Episcopalians realign with Anglican bishops in Africa and elsewhere in the global South, initiating legal disputes about church property ownership.

8. The Supreme Court by a 5–4 vote rules on the conservative side in three major cases with religious implications: upholding a ban on partial-birth abortions, allowing schools to establish some limits on students' free speech, and denying a challenge to the Office of Faith-based and Community Initiatives.

9. Death takes evangelical leaders known, among other things, for their television work: Jerry Falwell, Rex Humbard, D. James Kennedy, plus Billy Graham's wife, Ruth, and Jim Bakker's ex-wife, Tammy Faye Messner. Other deaths include Gilbert Patterson, presiding bishop of the Church of God in Christ, and Bible scholar Bruce Metzger.

10. The cost of priestly sex-abuse to the Roman Catholic Church in the United States surpasses $2.1 billion with a record $660 million settlement involving the Archdiocese of Los Angeles, and earlier settlements this year totaling $100 million in Portland, Ore., and Spokane, Wash.[16]

Active members of the Religion Newswriters were polled for this survey, and some 80 responded in an electronic ballot from December 7–13, 2007. The writers selected 10 stories they felt most important from a listing of 20 possible stories. The Religion Newswriters Association is the world's only membership association for people who write about religion in the general circulation media. The association has conducted this survey for more than 35 years.

Resources for Religion Writers

A number of resources exist for journalists who cover the religion beat, now often referred to as "faith and values" by many newspapers and magazines. Industry wide, there is the Religion Newswriters Association (www.rna.org), a membership-based group of journalists whose job is to cover stories of faith. The RNA is a not-for-profit trade association founded in 1949 to encourage excellence in religion reporting among journalists working for secular media and to offer an interactive forum for those religion writers. Its vision is to offer education and other resources and increase the awareness of the importance of religion coverage in the mainstream secular news media. It holds conferences and offers several award contests for its members, handing out prizes totaling $10,000 each year.[17]

Another good resource for religion writers is the Poynter Institute for Media Studies, headquartered in St. Petersburg, Florida. The institute has a wonderful Web site (www.poynter.org), chocked full of free articles, news about relevant conferences and seminars, and easy-to-read tip sheets on covering religion. An excerpt from one of many such articles reads as follows:

> All news is religious news. That's not a statement of faith or an assertion about the importance of religion to society. Rather, it's a lot like saying all news is political news because there's nothing that's not touched by some politician's interests or some piece of legislation. Religion is the same way, with tendrils of connection to everything. Sept. 11 has made that more obvious than ever in modern history.
>
> The difference between political news and religion news is that most papers have a political or city hall reporter, but many don't have someone dedicated to religion. It's not hard to imagine how that happened; it is a secular press, after all, and religion can seem a step removed from the practical world of sewers and subpoenas. But it is not.[18]

Two excellent magazines that sometimes offer in-depth coverage of religion reporting are the *Columbia Journalism Review* and the *American Journalism Review*. Academic research articles on religion coverage can be found in journals of the Association for Education in Journalism and Mass Communication (AEJMC) such as the *Journalism & Mass Communication Quarterly*, the *Newspaper Research Journal*, and *Journalism History*.

An Interesting Study

On April 30, 2003, the findings of a study on the portrayal of religion in American newspapers were released on the Web site of the Department of Religion and Classics at the University of Rochester (www.rochester.edu/College/REL/relnews). The content analysis study assessed how American newspapers cover religion by examining a large group of national and metro dailies across the United States. Newspapers included in the study were *The New York Times, The Washington Post, The Wall Street Journal, The Dallas Morning News,* the *Los Angeles Times,* the *Seattle Post-Intelligencer, USA Today,* the *Rochester Democrat & Chronicle, The Boston Globe,* the *Chicago Tribune,* the *Denver Post,* and *The Atlanta Journal-Constitution.* The researchers studied the papers for the month of

February 3 to March 3 of 2003. The study reported the following findings and recommendations:

Key Findings

1. Religion is mentioned far more often than it is the subject of a story.

2. Religion is widely used as a criterion of identity.

3. Religion stories most frequently describe religion in political and legal terms.

4. Coverage of the religious lives of African-Americans, Hispanics, and women is disproportionately low.

5. Coverage of Islam is disproportionate to the percentage of Muslims in the U.S. Its coverage is predominantly associated with criminality and bad deeds.

6. Roman Catholicism is more often linked with bad deeds and criminality than with Catholic beliefs and values.

7. Coverage of Protestantism, Judaism, and other religions is more balanced than coverage of Catholicism.

8. Coverage of religion in response to tragedy and death was more generic than particular.

9. Coverage of the Iraqi war presented religious anti-war views more prominently than pro-war views.

10. Print popularization of some religious terms is widespread. However, these terms are often used incorrectly.

11. Religion sections appear in a minority of newspapers. These sections treat religions in depth and show how beliefs, values, and practices relate to and influence their readers' lives.

12. Some newspapers reflect better than others their community and religion's beliefs, values, and practices.

Recommendations

1. Remember that context is the key to the complete reporting of a story.

2. Distinguish between the group and the action.

3. Consider a religion section.

4. Accentuate religion close to home.

5. Be balanced in terms of coverage.

6. Reflect a newspaper's region and country.

7. Develop a means of obtaining advice and expertise about religion.[19]

A Journalist's Own Religion

What role, if any, should a journalist's own religious faith play in identifying which stories to cover, in reporting, and in framing those stories? Should a reporter distance himself or herself from personal spiritual values, or is that even possible? Can journalists allow their own faith to fuel their worldviews and—treating religious belief like other individual biases—bring intellectual and moral honesty to bear in understanding their personal values and in keeping them from slanting or distorting their reporting and writing? Here are some responses from the panel of journalists contributing to this book.

"I think this is a fascinating question," responds Arlene Morgan, associate dean of the Columbia Graduate School of Journalism, "especially pertaining to issues of racial and ethnic intolerance and how religious beliefs enter into those discussions. I actually think journalists are much more spiritual, if not religious, than most understand." She continues,

> At *The Philadelphia Inquirer,* one of our managing editors was a lay minister in the Catholic Church; one of our editorial board editors was a very strict Jew. The list goes on and on about how many of our reporters and editors were religious and actually brought that perspective to their reporting in terms of looking for that perspective in their stories.

> As we have seen over the past years, religious convictions permeate almost every aspect of life and policy, from stem cell to Islamic fanaticism. I strongly believe that reporters should learn all they can about how spiritual and religious convictions can impact one's decision making. Perhaps, had we been more in tune to the rise of Islam in the world, we would not have had to struggle so much to understand the context of what happened on 9/11.

When asked what journalists should do with their faith when they go out on a reporting assignment, David Waters of *The Washington Post* answers, "Depends on the assignment." The context of the story should affect how reporters handle their beliefs and values:

> If I'm a Methodist and I'm reporting on the Methodist quadrennial meeting, I need to check my personal experiences and beliefs at the door and just report what happens, regardless of how I feel about it. If I'm a Methodist covering a

Democratic convention, my faith isn't going to be an issue, although my politics might be. So then I need to check my politics at the door and just report.

Our personal faith deeply affects who we are and what we believe, but it doesn't always have to affect what we do. Far as I know, only one person of faith in the history of the world always practiced what he believed. He would have made a lousy reporter and an even worse politician.

Reporters, after all, are not writing philosophy, although they may seek to present daily insights into the truth of our present circumstances. Waters, then, sides with what writer Roger Rosenblatt once wrote in an essay for *Time* magazine: people have come to expect too much from daily journalism if they are looking for "the larger truth." Rosenblatt thinks that the job of the reporter is to report where the ball is at the moment and not where it is not.

"I totally agree," Waters reacts. "We can't handle the truth. There is more truth in fiction than in nonfiction. We can point toward the truth. Give people a glimpse of it, a sense of it." He continues,

I do think that daily journalists either aim too high or too low. We either try to be instant historians or court reporters. Daily journalism is information— useful, relevant, interesting, important information.

But that information should be delivered with as much *context* as possible. That's the value of daily journalism. We tell you what happened, but we also tell you why and why it matters.

This brings journalists into the realm of practicing good ethics, and accurate context setting is one of those ethical practices. But there are many others. Waters believes journalists spend a fair amount of time thinking about the ethical implications of their work.

Jim Robertson, managing editor of the *Columbia Daily Tribune*, was asked if stories involving spiritual faith are beyond the pale of daily journalism and how reporters should handle their own faith when covering stories. He responded, "Our coverage, like that in many newspapers, is event based. We mainstream our coverage—mostly wire service produced—of big events such as debate about gay clergy, papal visits and pronouncements, etc. It's probably not terribly satisfying for those whose faith is a large part of their lives."

However, Robertson does not apologize for this event-based reporting, and he concedes that religion and journalism often approach truth differently: "Journalism and religion is a tough mix. Religion depends on faith, and journalism demands proof."

Republican presidential candidate Mike Huckabee once said that he would "consider it an extraordinarily shallow faith that does not really impact the way we think about other human beings and the way we respond to them." Robertson has a mixed reaction to that thought, especially when it comes to journalists' personal faith.

> That's the tough part for some reporters I've worked with. One young reporter, very involved in his fundamentalist church, refused to write about things his church found repugnant. I let it slide with the first refused assignment and discussed our responsibility to report fairly about things we might find uncomfortable. I asked him to rethink his career decision if he found that impossible.

> After the second refusal, we agreed to end his employment. I have to believe it's possible to practice journalism at the highest standards of balance and fairness and still retain a religious faith. But it takes effort and accommodation. Like voters, newspaper readers come in all sizes, shapes, colors, and ideologies, and our coverage should reflect the richness of that mixture.

The Oklahoman's Joe Hight believes reporters must remain fair and balanced in their reporting, regardless of their own spiritual beliefs.

"In your own personal time, you have to try to make sense of it through your faith," he says. "However, when you're reporting, you must understand that people have different values than you, and you must be as fair and balanced with them as you would with people of your own faith."

Since journalists mostly cover the here and now of the secular world, should they be exclusively secular in their worldviews? Do journalists tend to steer away from matters of faith that cannot be verified? Should they look for spiritual motivations in how people react to crises?

"In the United States, the First Amendment defines rights for all of its citizens, which includes journalists," Hight responds. "Journalists should have every right to practice their religion but should be wary about any causes that might seem political in nature. With the advent of religion sections in newspapers, I think journalists are taking more serious looks at how religion and spirituality affect people's lives. It's something that we, as journalists, should not ignore."

But he issues a warning to those reporters who might be tempted to inject their religious beliefs into their reporting.

"You can't preach to people and report at the same time. I've witnessed reporters who tried, and it never works and tends to turn off people. It also borders on being unethical. I've resisted signing petitions at my church or in my community because I know that people's perceptions of my fairness to them can depend on it. One time, a person in my church attacked me for it. I felt bad, but it didn't cause me to back down and sign his petition."

Gretchen Dworznik, a former television journalist turned college professor, notes that she used to avoid stories with a religious focus, when possible, in order to maintain fairness:

> I believe in God, but I am not an openly religious person. In fact, openly religious people, those who are overzealous about it, tend to make me really uncomfortable. As a result, I've never volunteered for any story that had even the slightest religious tones. Even those silly ones where people see Jesus in an apple pie. I just knew I wouldn't believe that it was Jesus, or see it, so what was the point? The only stories I ever did that involved religion were abortion issues. And even then, I did not use bites that spoke about God's will and whatever. I don't know that it was because those claims couldn't be proven, but I think it was because I knew those religious-based comments would cause a stir, and I didn't want the phone calls. I still got some anyway for not including the religious angle, but I think it would have been worse if I had.

A religion writer for the *Los Angeles Times* was candid in describing the effect that covering the religion beat had on his own personal faith. After making a decision to become a Christian, William Lobdell said he lobbied the newspaper to write about religion and was excited that, in 1998, he was assigned to write "Getting Religion," a weekly column about faith in Orange County. However, as Lobdell covered story after story of faith-based institutions and individuals failing to practice what they preached and as he found person after person victimized by these institutions, his own faith became challenged. In 2008, he went so far as to write a book called *Losing My Religion: How I Lost My Faith Covering Religion in America.* He noted in an e-mail that he went from being "a devout Christian to a reluctant Atheist."[20] One of the institutions he covered was the Catholic Church, which became the target of several judicial probes when so many stories surfaced about its priests molesting children. Eventually, in the Los Angeles Catholic Diocese alone, judgments against the church rose to some $600 million in out-of-court settlements to victims. Lobdell decided he could no longer consider becoming a Catholic, but he found disheartening cases involving other religious sects too. So he came to the point that he describes in a column he wrote for the *Los Angeles Times*:

> For some time, I had tried to push away doubts and reconcile an all-powerful and infinitely loving God with what I saw, but I was losing ground. I wondered if my born-again experience at the mountain retreat was more about fatigue, spiritual longing and emotional vulnerability than being touched by Jesus.
>
> And I considered another possibility: Maybe God didn't exist . . .

Toward the end of my tenure as a religion reporter, I traveled to Nome, Alaska . . . I had come from Southern California to report on a generation of Eskimo boys who had been molested by a Catholic missionary. . . .

It's not God's work what happened to me," he [Peter "Packy" Kobuk, serving three months for assault] said softly, running his fingers along the beads. "They were breaking God's commandments—even the people who didn't help. They weren't loving their neighbors as themselves."

He said he regularly got down on his knees in his jail cell to pray. . . .

Tears spilled from his eyes. Packy's faith, though severely tested, had survived. I looked at him with envy. Where he found comfort, I was finding emptiness.

My problem was that none of that surprised me anymore. As I walked into the long twilight of a Portland summer evening, I felt used up and numb.

My soul, for lack of a better term, had lost faith long ago—probably around the time I stopped going to church. My brain, which had been in denial, had finally caught up.

Clearly, I saw now that belief in God, no matter how grounded, requires at some point a leap of faith. Either you have the gift of faith or you don't. It's not a choice. It can't be willed into existence. And there's no faking it if you're honest about the state of your soul.

Sitting in a park across the street from the courthouse, I called my wife on a cell phone. I told her I was putting in for a new beat at the paper.[21]

Nearly all mainstream journalists warn against a reporter's passing on his or her own religious beliefs. However, some daily newspapers take greater liberty in expressing their religious views, just as they do their political views, on the editorial page. A case in point was the lead editorial for *The Oklahoman* on Christmas Day, 2007. Headlined "Eternal Light," the editorial read in part:

No one ever spoke like him. He came from out of nowhere, or so it seemed. He had no national name recognition, no family connections, no rich uncle. Yet he built a coalition that remains today . . . He pulled unspeakable joy out of the bellies of the downcast yet stuffed self-righteousness down the throats of the sanctimonious . . . He could be all things to all people, if only the people would let him. He offered drunks, dopers and sex addicts two steps—not 12—to recovery. He told people they were responsible for their own actions and to stop wearing their piety on their sleeves. He ran a lost and found service. His door was always open . . . Some say this is his birthday. Scholars have debated that for years. Nobody really knows when he was born, just that he was—and in a most unusual way. He named as his successor an Advocate, who is still on the job. Birthday greetings to you, kind Sir. And, a happy return.[22]

Faith-Based Journalistic Organizations

At least two Washington-based organizations that help train journalists encourage reporters and editors to use their faith as they survey the landscape of possible stories and decide how to cover them. Those organizations are the Christian-based World Journalism Institute and the Washington Journalism Center. Both are founded on evangelical Christian principles, which form the basis of their worldviews.

The World Journalism Institute lists its mission as recruiting, equipping, placing, and encouraging journalists who are Christians in America's mainstream, secular newsrooms. It attempts to identify young people who are Christians and who want to become journalists, and it helps train them in the skills they will need for that profession. The primary pool of WJI students comes from the ranks of colleges and universities who send students to the institute's conferences and training programs. The WJI believes in focusing on mainstream news media outlets, rather than on Christian media, because they are the main providers of information about the world. The group's rationale states, "Christians, joining those of many persuasions in the newsroom, can be beneficial in accurately understanding and reporting the events of the day ... The theological understandings of the Institute inform our approach to journalism. While reforming our understanding of the craft is a continuing and never-ending process, our theology does suggest several practices."[23] The WJI uses the Christian Nicene Creed as its basic doctrine, feeling that this is a doctrine that Protestant, Roman Catholic, and Greek Orthodox journalists embrace. As noted on the WJI Web site, the practices it encourages aspiring journalists to adopt are as follows:

- All people are created in the image of God; therefore all people are to be treated with respect and integrity.

- Journalism is a noble calling for a Christian. The Christian in journalism is in the newsroom to report, write, and explain in accordance with the highest standards of the profession. Factual accuracy in news reporting, undiminished and undistorted by attitudes and outlooks, is the bedrock of the trade. When reporters and editors get that right, they serve the public honorably and well.

- If asked about one's Christian convictions, the Christian in journalism should have the freedom to answer any question in a warm-hearted and gracious manner without fear of professional or personal reprisal.

- The spiritual fall of all humanity has affected our moral and rational judgments. Each individual is influenced by upbringing, education, and environment. Choices are made in any given story development—choices that require value judgments on the part of journalists and editors. The Christian in journalism aims to be fair, accurate, honest, impartial, and humble in chasing the story. This approach, of course, is not a uniquely Christian position.

- [The WJI believes] . . . in a personal God who is truth and who is sovereign over the affairs of this world; therefore the Christian journalist should be fearless in presenting all views of a given issue and should not intend to be the censor of ideas before those ideas reach the marketplace. The Christian in journalism will let the Lord of truth sort things out in the marketplace of ideas.[24]

The World Journalism Institute invites mainstream Christian journalists to deliver talks to its students and then publishes many of those speeches as monographs. A few of the recent titles show the focus on the connection of journalists to their faith:

- "Mightier Than the Sword: The Ministry of Journalism," by John W. Fountain.
- "The Three Callings of a Christian in Journalism," by David Aikman.
- "A Christian Journalism," by Bryan Chappell.
- "Journalism & Humility," by Marvin Olasky.

The Washington Journalism Center is the other organization we'll examine, and it is a project of the Council of Christian Colleges and Universities (CCCU). That council represents more than 110 colleges and universities that identify themselves as intentionally Christian schools upholding mainstream evangelical values.

The Washington Journalism Center (WJC) offers semester-long training programs in the nation's capital to students who are primarily from colleges and universities that belong to the CCCU. The WJC's Web site proclaims its mission: "The Washington Journalism Center is an advanced, experiential semester on Capitol Hill that will cultivate professional news skills and encourage students to think through the implications of being a Christian working in the news media in a city that is home to the powerful and the powerless."[25] Its director is Terry Mattingly, a religion columnist for Scripps Howard who is also a panelist for this book. His comments about journalism and religion are featured earlier in this chapter and elsewhere throughout the book.

Faith-Based Media

Of course the mainstream news media are also joined by faith-based media, largely evangelical Christian in nature, on both the print and broadcast side. These news organizations exist to provide the news in a context consistent with the beliefs of their various faiths. Some of the better known of these media are the Christian Broadcast Network (CBN), *Christianity Today*, and *The Christian Century*. CBN airs its *Newswatch* program nightly, anchored by Lee Webb from its Washington, DC studios. The newscast at first looks like all other network and cable newscasts, but it carries a higher percentage of faith-related stories, and it intersperses segments of standard reporting with segments of commentary by its founder, Pat Robertson, who leads its parent program, *The 700 Club*. Robertson is the televangelist who made a run for the 1988 Republican presidential nomination.

A 2005 article in *Columbia Journalism Review* titled "Stations of the Cross" had this to say about CBN and the Christian faith-based media:

> CBN, or Christian Broadcasting Network, is just one star in a vast and growing Christian media universe, which has sprung up largely under the mainstream's radar. Conservative evangelicals control at least six national television networks, each reaching tens of millions of homes, and virtually all of the nation's more than 2,000 religious radio stations. Thanks to Christian radio's rapid growth, religious stations now outnumber every other format except country music and news-talk. If they want to dwell solely in this alternative universe, believers can now choose to have only Christian programs piped into their homes. Sky Angel, one of the nation's three direct-broadcast satellite networks, carries thirty-six channels of Christian radio and television—and nothing else. As Christian broadcasting has grown, pulpit-based ministries have largely given way to a robust programming mix that includes music, movies, sitcoms, reality shows, and cartoons. But the largest constellation may be news and talk shows. Christian public affairs programming exploded after September 11, and again in the run-up to the 2004 presidential election. And this growth shows no signs of flagging.[26]

Faith-based magazines are not a new phenomenon, however. For example, two periodicals, *Commentary* and *The Christian Century*, have offered news and opinions from particular religious perspectives for decades. *Commentary*, a nationally circulated magazine and a leading periodical of the Jewish faith, focuses on American intellectual life. Its Web site states, "Since its inception in 1945, and increasingly after it emerged as the flagship of neoconservatism in the 1970's, the magazine has been consistently engaged with several large, interrelated questions: the fate of democracy and of democratic ideas in a world threatened by totalitarian ideologies; the state of American and Western security; the future of the Jews, Judaism, and Jewish culture in Israel, the United States, and around the world; and the preservation of high culture in an age of political correctness and the collapse of critical standards."[27]

The Christian Century has an even longer history. It was established in 1884 in Des Moines as the *Christian Oracle*. Currently, it is a monthly

Chicago-based magazine focusing on issues of faith and society and it is one of the leading Christian periodicals. Its editors describe the magazine as follows: "*The Christian Century* magazine believes that the Christian faith calls Christians to a profound engagement with the world—an engagement of both head and heart. We think Christians can and must articulate their faith in a way that is meaningful and intellectually compelling to those around them. That's why the *Century* examines issues of politics and culture as well as theology, and that's why it pays attention to the challenges of faith that arise in our everyday lives as parents, friends, spouses and citizens."[28]

Christianity Today is the leading evangelical, nondenominational Christian magazine in America, and Christianity Today International actually publishes eleven different magazines. The company's flagship magazine was started in 1956 by evangelist Billy Graham, and, today, the weekly *Christianity Today* circulates around the world. Its January 3, 2008 issue featured the following stories: "What Does Iowa Mean?" (an examination of the Iowa caucus held that day), "Violent Christianity" (a report of what Muslims think of Christian concerns about Islamic violence), and "Hindus and Christians Clash in India" (a story on violence that began on Christmas Eve that was then in its fifth day).

Stepping Into Another's Faith

Reporters are always asked to cover things they may know little about; it is one of the reasons that many journalists say they enjoy their craft—they get to learn something new every day, and life becomes an ongoing educational experience. The same is true about covering religion, especially faiths different from one's own. Journalists who may hold to one faith can be asked to cover stories of other faiths, and it is here that reporters have to be extremely careful. A reporter should try to let the adherents of a faith define their belief system rather than filtering that system through the reporter's own beliefs. That is always a hazard in reporting, as the study by sociologist Herbert Gans found when he identified ethnocentrism (the belief in the rightness of one's own culture or subculture) as a value that permeates many news stories. For a fuller discussion of that study, see Chapter 5.

One reporter who told a story about people of a faith other than his was Barry Bearak, foreign correspondent for *The New York Times*. He won a national writing award for his story about Catholics in Texas. Bearak is Jewish. The story was called "Visions of Holiness in Lubbock," and he wrote it while serving the *Los Angeles Times* as a national correspondent in 1989. Bearak was actually based in Miami, but he heard about an incident that became controversial in a West Texas Catholic diocese and went to investigate. It involved three parishioners in St. John Neumann's Catholic Church of Lubbock who believed they had seen the Virgin Mary. Bearak paid particular attention to one of the parishioners, a young woman named Theresa Werner. Her pronouncements and her certainty caused a split to develop in her Catholic community in Lubbock, and the Catholic Church called in a committee to decide if the sightings were valid.[29] Bearak's engaging story began, "From the mists above and a hunger within, Theresa Werner thought she saw God."[30] It continued to describe, in detail, the young woman's faith and the images and voices she experienced, which she believed to be God.

In religion, Bearak feels reporters can find issues that connect with many readers, and they should not be shy about tackling them. He refers to them as "crossroads events" and calls them important.

> I don't know that journalists are tone deaf to religion, but they certainly have trouble playing the tune in newspapers. Daily newspapers aren't so good at the day-to-day things that pack most of the meaning into life. That would include religion, but it also includes love and family and friendship. I've always thought newspapers ought to do more with the crossroads events in everyday lives: the day we had to put Mom in a nursing home, the day Joe quit the factory and opened a bait and tackle shop, the day Jack and Jill dropped their kid off at college, the day Bill decided to become a priest, and the day Bill yielded to his doubts and dropped out of seminary. The joys and pains of everyday life.

Bearak says these are stories that should not be ignored: "These are really great stories but, like most great stories, they're hard to do well. They need time and space. They need reporters and editors with talent and editors with patience."

To some degree, covering religion may be easier or harder depending on where a journalist is reporting from, Bearak believes.

> Religion, I think, is an easier topic for foreign correspondents. Like other beat reporters, foreign correspondents are at the mercy of news events. Wars, disasters, elections all have to be covered, but, during the course of a foreign posting (which usually lasts three or four years), correspondents are also expected to paint a mosaic of how the people in a region live. You could make a checklist of things to include in the mosaic. There are major social issues like schools, courts, police, healthcare, housing, and the like. At the same time, the mosaic ought to show what people are eating, reading, watching on TV, what their weddings and funeral are like. Religion is an obvious part of the mosaic.

An Ongoing Tension

This chapter has examined some of the intersections of journalism and religion: why religion is both an important story to many people in the country and one that is often reluctantly covered by journalists. In a larger setting, a tension exists between the two institutions of journalism and religion. It was hinted at in an earlier statement: journalism is usually about the here and now while religion is often about the spiritual realm and the hereafter. Certainly, there are plenty of stories about how people's faiths, or lack of them, influence their reaction to events in the here and now, and editors like *The New York Times*'s Bill Keller are encouraging their reporters to look for these stories. But many devout Christian believers—especially the Christian dogmatists often found in the conservative camps—still have a problem with journalism: it seems reluctant to validate the beliefs these Christians see as the cornerstone of truth. A born-again believer sees all truth as coming from God, from a deity that, according to this faith, the Bible defines. These believers are often critical of secular journalism because it will not embrace their truth but instead keeps Christianity at arms length, treating their certainty as a doctrine that only some believe is true.   In addition, many Christian conservatives feel that mainstream journalists poke fun at their beliefs and treat them as naïve and anti-intellectual. To the mainstream media, however, Christianity is one of many religions and, in fact, exists on a scale of different principles ranging from narrow-minded exclusion to ecumenicism and tolerance for all faiths. In one sense, mainstream journalists might well put a comma after the beliefs of born-again believers, while those believers would put a period. A phrase often heard in conservative Christian circles is "God said it, I believe it, that's the end of it." But to a journalist, the "end" is not so quickly discovered, and their profession is one of continually searching for the truth. Advocating any particular faith or belief system in their news and feature stories runs counter to most journalistic orientations and to the nature of daily journalism itself. Many reporters are also students of history and recall vividly how leaders of organized religion have lived double lives, preaching one morality while living another. The history of evangelical preachers is strewn with examples of this from Jimmy Swaggart and Jim Bakker to Ted Haggard, former president of the National Association of Evangelicals. All veteran journalists fight an ongoing battle between skepticism and cynicism, trying to stay on the side of the former while resisting being pulled across the line into the latter. But the accumulation of the stories done on people who claim to have a corner on the truth, yet whose own lives evidence another truth, causes some journalists to become cynics and to keep searching for that elusive concept.

A Final Thought

When I began work on this chapter, I wondered if there was enough discussion about religion among journalists to warrant a distinct chapter or whether to include this material in another segment of the book. The journalists I had interviewed talked a lot about it, although they reminded me that stories on religion were not very popular among the mainstream news media. It was not long before I discovered that journalists pay as much or more attention to issues of religion and faith as to any other. The result is that this is, by far, the longest chapter of the book. Not surprising, I suppose, when you look historically at the influence of the media in publicizing issues of faith in America. One case in particular comes to mind—the case of America's best-known evangelist, Billy Graham. In 1949, Graham was 30 and was having some success in local areas as a traveling evangelist, mostly staging crusades for Youth for Christ. He was much better known in Christian circles, however, than by the public at large. As he later told two writers for *Time* magazine, most of the people he preached to in those days were probably already converted.[31] All that began to change quickly in that year, however, when publishing mogul William Randolph Hearst, then publisher of the *New York Journal American* and several other newspapers in the country, attended a Graham rally in Los Angeles. He was impressed by the turnout, by the attendees' reaction to Graham's message, and by Graham's style of presentation. He reasoned that, if so many people were so moved by what this preacher had to say, then he was news. He immediately sent a message to the editors at all Hearst papers saying "Puff Graham!" And the young evangelist soon became a household name around America. Graham later called Hearst one of the two most important reasons for his success in those early years, and the other one was another publisher, Henry Luce, founder of *Time* magazine. Luce was the son of a missionary and a committed Presbyterian Calvinist, and he thought Graham and his message were important. So *Time* also began covering Graham in earnest. Graham says that because of Hearst and Luce and the publicity they provided him, his crusades grew geometrically in size, and more Americans were exposed to the gospel than ever before.[32] And, not insignificantly, he began to gain the attention of every president since Harry S. Truman, becoming the spiritual confidant of nearly every one of them.

Notes

   1. Jay Rosen, "Journalism is Itself a Religion," *PRESSthink*, January 7, 2004, http://journalism.nyu.edu/pubzone/weblogs/pressthink/2004/01/07/press_religion.html.

    2. Rosen, "Journalism."

    3. Bill Keller, "Assuring Our Credibility," June 23, 2005, http://www.nytco
.com/pdf/assuring-our-credibility.pdf.

    4. Gal Beckerman, "Across the Great Divide: Faith," *Columbia Journalism
Review*, May/June 2004.

    5. Beckerman, "Across the Great Divide."

    6. Terry Mattingly, "What We Do, Why We Do It," *GetReligion.org* [online
posting], February 1, 2004.

    7. Sally Quinn and Jon Meacham, "About On Faith: The Question," *On Faith*,
http://newsweek.washingtonpost.com/onfaith/2006/11/about_on_faith/comments.html.

    8. Bob Woodward, "In Hijacker's Bag, a Call to Planning, Prayer, and
Death," *The Washington Post*, September 28, 2001, A01.

    9. Kate Darnton, Kayee Freed Jennings, and Lynn Sherr, eds., *A Reporter's Life:
Peter Jennings* (Philadelphia: Public Affairs/Perseus Book Publishing Group, 2007), 179.

    10. Darnton, Freed Jennings, and Sheer, *A Reporter's Life*, 180.

    11. Darnton, Freed Jennings, and Sheer, *A Reporter's Life*, 180.

    12. Darnton, Freed Jennings, and Sheer, *A Reporter's Life*, 182.

    13. Darnton, Freed Jennings, and Sheer, *A Reporter's Life*, 188.

    14. Herbert J. Gans, *Deciding What's News* (New York: Vintage Books, 1980).

    15. Debra Mason, "Religion's Role in U.S. Presidential Election Tops 2007
Religion News Stories of the Year" (press release, Religion News Writers Association,
December 14, 2007), *Religion/Newswriters* , http://www.rna.org/2007top10.php.

    16. Mason, "Religion's Role in U.S. Presidential Election."

    17. Religion Newswriters Association, "About RNA," *Religion Newswriters*,
http://www.rna.org/whoweare.php (accessed January 3, 2008).

    18. Robin Sloan, "Covering Communities of Faith: Tips for Thinking About
and Covering Religion," *Poynter Online: Reporting, Writing and Editing*,
December 11, 2002, http://www.poynter.org/content/content_view.asp?id=12002.

    19. University of Rochester, Department of Religion and Classics, "Religion in
American Newspapers" (news release, April 30, 2003), *University of Rochester*,
http://www.rochester.edu/College/REL/relnews.html.

    20. William Lobdell, e-mail message titled "Losing My Religion . . . the Book"
about the book *Losing My Religion: How I Lost My Faith Reporting on Religion in
America*, July 10, 2008.

    21. William Lobdell, "Religion Beat Becomes a Test of Faith," *Los Angeles
Times*, July 21, 2007, A1.

    22. "Eternal Light," *The Oklahoman*, December 25, 2007, A20.

    23. World Journalism Institute, "Mission," World Journalism Institute,
http://www.worldji.com/mission.asp.

    24. Excerpted and reordered from the Web site of the World Journalism Institute,
"Mission," World Journalism Institute, http://www.worldji.com/mission.asp.

    25. Washington Journalism Center, "Overview," Washington Journalism Center,
http://wjc.bestsemester.com/overview.

    26. Mariah Blake, "Stations of the Cross," *Columbia Journalism Review* 44,
no. 1 (May/June 2005): 32–40.

27. *Commentary*, "About Us / Who We Are," *CommentaryMagazine.com*, http://www.commentarymagazine.com/abouthistory.cfm (accessed January 3, 2008).

28. "Our Mission," *The Christian Century*, http://www.christiancentury.org/cpage.lasso?cpage=about (accessed January 3, 2008).

29. Barry Bearak, "Visions of Holiness in Lubbock: Divine or Imagined?" *Los Angeles Times*, April 9, 1989, 1, 36–38, 40.

30. Bearak, "Visions of Holiness."

31. Nancy Gibbs and Michael Duffy, *The Preacher and the Presidents: Billy Graham in the White House* (New York: Center Street, 2007).

32. Gibbs and Duffy, *The Preacher.*

7

The Journalist as Celebrity

Journalists struggle with many issues, as the previous chapters have pointed out. One issue that directly affects many journalists—especially those whose stories are broadcast on television—is whether the public perceives them more as reporters or celebrities. The distinction is important because, when a celebrity shows up at a scene, his or her presence can change that scene dramatically. But journalists don't want scenes to change. They want to report on what is happening naturally in the world; they don't want that world contaminated by the presence of a celebrity. So this is a challenge for celebrity journalists. For other journalists, those whose faces are not well known, the issue is still important because it is difficult enough, they say, to separate news from entertainment without having journalists themselves thought of as part of the entertainment scene. So this chapter deals with the views of some journalists who have been celebrities themselves and others who see a problem with combining news and entertainment.

Probably the best operational definition of "celebrity" comes not from a journalist but from a historian. He is Daniel Boorstin, and, in 1962, he wrote a groundbreaking book that has great journalistic relevance: *The Image: A Guide to Pseudo-Events in America*. The book is about what Boorstin calls the "menace of unreality," which he believes defines American culture. Much of the book focuses on "the celebrity," which Boorstin defines as "a person who is well-known for his well-knowness." He argues that public life is comprised more of "pseudo-events" that are staged and scripted than of spontaneous life as it happens. He also states that too much media attention is paid to "pseudo-people," to those known as celebrities whose identities are manufactured—sometimes by themselves and sometimes by the media—to create purposive illusions.[1] Those are observations that many Americans find even more on target today than in 1962.

An Obsession With Celebrity

Echoing Boorstin's observations is Tony Burnham, editor in chief of the Canadian Broadcasting Company's *CBC News* from 2002 to 2007. Burnham quoted Boorstin in a 2007 editorial and then made comments of his own:

> "Celebrity-worship and hero-worship should not be confused. Yet we confuse them every day, and by doing so we come dangerously close to depriving ourselves of all real models. We lose sight of the men and women who do not simply seem great because they are famous but are famous because they are great. We come closer and closer to degrading all fame into notoriety."

> Boorstin died three years ago so we cannot know how he would assess the media culture of 2007. However, since he is the one who wrote these words 45 years ago: "Nothing is really real to us unless it happens on television"— we can guess.

> The growing influence of celebrity culture is not only a business decision to increase profits. For many established news organizations, it's also an effort to connect with new audiences—particularly young people—who may be turning their backs on traditional journalism. But that has its risks. As Boorstin warned, it often means that "stories" that would otherwise be ignored assume gigantic importance.[2]

British journalist Mick Hume has also expressed concern that the media obsession with celebrities "clogs up the news with trivia." He adds, "As serious public and political life has withered, so celebrity culture has expanded to fill the gap, often with the encouragement of political leaders desperate for some celebrity cover."[3]

Burnham notes that Hume cites the controversy over Madonna's adoption of a Malawi toddler as an example of his point:

> What she is doing embodies the new "caring colonialism" underpinning Western attitudes towards Africa. It is based on the assumption that we know what is best for them, and the West must save Africans from themselves.[4]

One of the most-heard critiques of journalism today is that it spends too much time focusing on celebrities. The year 2007 was a classic case in point, as much of the nation's media was fixated on how long Paris Hilton would have to stay in jail for her DUI conviction, whether Lindsay Lohan would ever straighten up her lifestyle, what was up with Britney Spears and her head-shaving incident, and which lover would wind up with custody of Anna Nicole Smith's baby. Even O. J. Simpson was back in the news, as the legal trouble brought on by his Las Vegas gambit made headlines, especially when he was convicted and sent to prison. The public's obsession with celebrity news items such as these and the journalist's role in feeding or encouraging this obsession has been the focus of serious debate for many years, both around the newsroom and at journalism conferences. Let's look more closely at this issue.

USC Targets the Issue

The media's coverage of celebrities was the focus of a 2004 conference at the University of Southern California called "Reporting on Celebrities: The Ethics of News Coverage." It was cosponsored by USC's Annenberg School for Communication and the Poynter Institute for Media Studies. The conference was held just after the California election that moved actor Arnold Schwarzenegger into the governor's mansion. The *Los Angeles Times* reported that some 10,000 of its subscribers cancelled their subscriptions in protest of the newspaper probe into allegations of groping by Schwarzenegger. The story was published just a few days before the election. Managing Editor Dean Baquet argued that the story and its timing were valid. He also rejected claims by critics that Schwarzenegger himself received more coverage than other candidates because of his status as a Hollywood celebrity.[5]

Peter Bhatia, executive editor of *The Oregonian*, disagreed with critics who complained his newspaper has given too much coverage to the sexual assault case against Los Angeles Lakers star Kobe Bryant, causing other important news to be minimized. Bhatia responded that readers should assess how a newspaper reports on community issues "over a passage of time" before criticizing the amount of coverage it gives to celebrities.[6]

One panelist who defended celebrity status as a criterion of news value was Dan Rosenheim, news director of KPIX-TV in San Francisco. Rosenheim said, "A person's celebrity status should be one of the factors in determining news value. One ignores viewers or reader interest at your own peril. We risk trivializing ourselves and marginalizing ourselves."[7]

Celebrity Journalists

One of the big stories of 2006 was the repackaging of lighthearted Katie Couric, longtime host of NBC's *Today* show, into a more serious persona befitting of the *CBS Evening News* anchor desk. When she made that transition in the fall of 2006, Ms. Couric became the first woman to anchor a network evening newscast solo. In a failed experiment from the late 1970s, Barbara Walters, another longtime celebrity journalist, was half of an *ABC News* anchor team (the late Harry Reasoner was the other half). And, of course, America has been witnessing the specter for many years of celebrity journalists interviewing other celebrities. In fact, Barbara Walters has made her celebrity interview shows a fixture at ABC. Her shows are usually aired on the same night as the annual Academy Awards ceremony, and serve as a warm-up for that program.

So journalists are covering celebrities, they are often becoming celebrities themselves, and the result is celebrities covering celebrities. But there is still one more convergence of journalism and celebrity: We live in an age when celebrities who have no training in journalism and no mainstream media experience have become more credible with young people as newscasters than trained and experienced journalists. For example, MTV took all this to new heights with its *Choose or Lose* coverage of the 2004 presidential election. In an experiment to make the campaign more relevant to its young viewers in the 18–24 age range, MTV redefined journalists by pressing celebrities such as Drew Barrymore and Christina Aguilera into service as "correspondents" who interviewed presidential candidates about issues important to young people. Even hip-hop music artist P. Diddy had a key on-air role as part of MTV's coverage of the candidates. P. Diddy reported from the floor of the Democratic National Convention and interviewed several political luminaries including Sen. Hillary Rodham Clinton and the Rev. Jesse Jackson. About MTV's approach, media researcher Geoffrey Baym reported in a 2006 study that MTV effectively used pseudo-journalists more known for their comedy routines than their reporting, such as Jon Stewart. These celebrity journalists moved into the void of political news targeting young people, and many of the nation's youth became interested in politics because of MTV's coverage. Baym explains:

> Comedian Jon Stewart has become an important voice in the landscape of broadcast news. Indeed, at the start of the 2004 presidential campaign, *Newsday* named Stewart as the single most important newscaster in the country, ahead of Tom Brokaw, Dan Rather, Tim Russert, and every other network newscaster. It is not surprising the Brokaw and Rather's age and style rendered them irrelevant in the eyes of many people . . . As young people continue to

turn away from news, the entire issue of credibility—of journalistic authority—is now in play in profound ways. Bill Moyers recognized the point in an (2003 PBS) interview with Jon Stewart: "When I report the news on the broadcast," Moyers said, "people say I'm making it up. When you make it up, they say you're telling the truth. For many, the traditional newscaster has lost credibility, but the comedian speaks the truth."[8]

Critics From Within

A growing number of journalists have joined the ranks of media critics who believe the focus of news—especially television news—has moved too far to the coverage of celebrities and lightweight issues.

"Television news just keeps getting worse," says Jim Redmond, former longtime news anchor for KUSA-TV in Denver. " The audience continues to abandon it in droves. That's being caused by both a combination of new technology being available to the audience and a lot of outright rejection too. The latest Pew studies show continuous decline in audience believability, credence, and trust in TV news. It's mostly a lot of hustle, gloss, and bluster now with increasingly less of any serious content or context. The vacuous superficiality of TV news is quickly killing the golden goose, and the egg that came with it."

Redmond explains that "Edward R. Murrow's famous 1958 RTNDA [Radio and Television News Directors Association] speech echoes in its perceptive truth," and he goes on to quote a portion of that famous speech from the CBS pioneering journalist usually seen as the conscience of television news:

> One of the basic troubles with radio and television news is that both instruments have grown up as an incompatible combination of show business, advertising and news. Each of the three is a rather bizarre and demanding profession. And when you get all three under one roof, the dust never settles.

> The top management of the networks, with a few notable exceptions, has been trained in advertising, research, or show business. But by the nature of the corporate structure, they also make the final and crucial decisions having to do with news and public affairs. Frequently they have neither the time nor the competence to do this. I began by saying that our history will be what we make it. If we go on as we are, then history will take its revenge, and retribution will not limp in catching up with us.[9]

"And so 1958 evolved to 2007," Redmond continues. "What was once somewhat respectable is now more of a current events sideshow of market-driven news where the stories of the day are decided based on audience research studies of what people say they want. And there is a hollow echo left by the footsteps of what they need retreating daily from what is served up as news but has been rendered to mere infotainment."

Where does it go from here? Redmond foresees a death by "syphilis of market-driven news" where there is only a "vacuum" in store for journalists who really care about good reporting, followed by a time when the media will use every kind of content imaginable to try to fill that void.

Another longtime television news anchor, Diane Willis, often found herself unable to do the kind of reporting she wanted to do because of all the personal-appearance duties that her stations heaped upon her. Willis, who anchored the evening news at WRTV in Indianapolis and WNEV (now WHDH) in Boston, often found her days and nights full of speaking and appearance events, which left her little time for anything other than showing up on the set to anchor the 6 and 11 p.m. newscasts. And often the stories she did do were ones designed to enhance her image.

"There were times I longed for the opportunity to get out on rough, breaking news stories and get my hair mussed up a little in covering the stories," she said. "But station management didn't feel that fit my image or persona as a blow-dried anchor who appealed to the demographics they wanted me to reach."

Sometimes, the dual roles of journalist and celebrity can cause apparent conflicts of interest for television newscasters. One case that surfaced in the news recently involved CNBC star business news anchor Maria Bartiromo. It was revealed that she was a friend of Todd Thomson, chief of Citigroup's global wealth management unit, and traveled with him on trips. *The Wall Street Journal* reported that she might have been part of the reason for his being ousted. The *Journal* said Thomson spent more than $5 million to sponsor a Sundance Channel program, which was to be cohosted by Bartiromo and veteran actor Robert Redford.[10]

As *Washington Post* reporter Howard Kurtz reported, Bartiromo made almost fifty personal appearances in 2006 for corporations, trade associations, and other organizations, traveling to places such as Hong Kong and London, and all but three of these involved Citigroup. According to Kurtz, although Bartiromo's employer did endorse and fund her travels, they did cause concern among some journalists:

> CNBC executives say they approved and paid for each trip, and reimbursed Citigroup for the corporate flight. But the time and distance involved raise questions about how close Bartiromo has gotten to some companies she covers and whether she has become more of a celebrity journalist than the Wall Street workhorse of her earlier years.[11]

The cable news network, however, defended its anchor, and Kurtz quoted this defense:

> Maria Bartiromo is one of the most prolific and well-respected financial jour-nalists in the industry, who works tirelessly around the world in the service of business journalism . . . In 2006 alone, she made 46 public appearances on behalf of CNBC. Her travel has been company-related and approved, and involved legitimate business assignments. Her record and reporting speak for themselves.[12]

A Double Standard, an Expected Deference

In Boston, the sports anchor would often rib Diane Willis about her lack of sports knowledge, to which she was supposed to giggle, smile, and get the answer wrong. One of the favorite shticks played during the sports segment in baseball season was for the sports anchor to show a close play at home plate and "surprise" Willis with the question, "Okay Diane! Safe or out?" Usually, the answer was a toss-up for even the most knowledgeable sports fan, but hav-ing her get it wrong and giggle, "Oh no!" when she was told she was wrong was meant to be a self-fulfilling prophecy for male sports fans—something that would probably make them feel smarter than they were. The sports anchor and Willis's male coanchor would guffaw, and that would be that.

Willis managed to fight for—and receive—coverage of some significant stories in spite of what she sometimes found to be a sexist attitude in some of the newsrooms in which she worked. Among her most significant assign-ments were the three weeks she spent in Ethiopia and Eritrea in 1984, covering the famine and civil war there, and her coverage of the New Hampshire pri-mary in 1984. But her experiences with station management left her with mixed feelings about working in television.

Her experiences followed on the heels of those of a Kansas City anchor who gained notoriety in the industry when she sued her television station, alleging that sexual discrimination had forced her into a posture of deference to the male anchors on the set. The anchor was Christine Craft, a former California surfer turned English teacher who was discovered by CBS, which launched her career as a television journalist. Craft rebelled at the physical makeover CBS required of her, which included having her hair bleached to a platinum blonde. After a year at CBS, Craft returned to California to work in local television and then received an invitation from KMBC in Kansas City to audition for an evening news anchor position there. She got the job, but, for a woman news anchor, the demands of television remained the same, she discovered. An excerpt from the Web site of the Museum of Broadcast Communication delivers her story:

> Based on her experience at CBS, Craft states that she told the station management that she "showed signs of her age and experience" and was not willing to be made over. She interviewed and auditioned in the KMBC studios, and was hired as co-anchor with a two-year contract. Eight months later, in July 1981, Craft was informed that she had been demoted to reporter because focus group research had indicated that she was "too old, too unattractive and wouldn't defer to men." Craft decided to challenge the action of management, and when asked for a comment on why she was no longer anchor, told a Kansas City newspaper what had occurred. Craft left the station in Kansas City and returned to television news in Santa Barbara, where for two years she prepared a breach of contract lawsuit against Metromedia. In August 1983 a ten-day trial was held at Federal District Court in Kansas City, at the conclusion of which the jury unanimously returned a verdict in favor of Craft, awarding her $500,000 in damages.[13]

But that was just the beginning. A U.S. District Court judge threw out the verdict and called instead for a second trial. That trail was held in Joplin, Missouri, and—again—the jury found for Craft. That verdict was then appealed, and again it was overturned. When the U.S. Supreme Court refused to hear the case on appeal, the legal issue was over.

Craft decided to tell her story in a book she wrote in 1986 called, *Too Old, Too Ugly, Not Deferential to Men.* The book brought to light a double standard in television that most TV news reporters know about but seldom talk about in public: Male anchors, as a rule, do not encounter the same kind of age discrimination that women anchors do in television news. A 2000 study in the *Journal of Broadcasting and Electronic Media* discovered that the average age for male anchors was 10 years older than the average age for female anchors.[14] As for Craft, she managed to persevere. Although she saw her second appeal overturned, she moved on with her life after writing her book, graduating in 1995 from law school at the University of the Pacific. She continued to appear as a broadcast journalist on radio and television in San Francisco.[15]

Katie Couric's New Persona

A high-profile television celebrity journalist recently in the spotlight would have to be Katie Couric. She underwent a makeover from bubbly early-morning cohost of NBC's popular *Today* show to the anchor of the *CBS Evening News*, with its long tradition of serious male news anchors that began with Douglas Edwards and continued through Walter Cronkite ("the most trusted man in America") and Dan Rather. In a time when television network news was fighting for its life against the upstart cable news channels of CNN, Fox News, and MSNBC, CBS felt the time was right in the summer of 2006 to hire a well-known female celebrity talk show host as television's first solo woman news anchor for its weekday network evening newscast. Katie Couric was the network's choice. Hence, the *CBS Evening News with Katie Couric* was rolled out in September 2006.

It isn't that Couric is without journalistic credentials. Indeed, NBC hired her in 1989 as a deputy Pentagon correspondent, and she became national correspondent in 1990 for a short time before becoming cohost of *Today* in 1991. Also, over those years, she was a substitute coanchor for Tom Brokaw on NBC's evening newscast and had covered most of the major breaking news events for the fifteen years prior to 2006, including the 9/11 attacks. She had interviewed many significant newsmakers around the world in the process.

But Couric was best known by the American public as the sprightly and often giggly cohost of *Today* where, over a fifteen-year period, she seemed to spend more time interviewing celebrities than anyone else. She also engaged in game playing on the show, once donning a red wig and the guise of Lucille Ball's Lucy Ricardo one Halloween, spoofing the actress from the 1950s sitcom *I Love Lucy*. Indeed, the centerpiece of her final appearance on *Today* in June 2006 was wrapped in a bombastic, tearful, and long ceremony that could have been staged by a Hollywood producer. The showstopper was the cast of the hit Broadway musical *Jersey Boys* singing a tribute to Couric. It was a slightly tweaked version of the *Four Seasons* hit "Bye, Bye Baby," refashioned as "Bye, Bye Katie." The four handsome young "Jersey Boys" crooned "Katie couldn't we stay together / Couldn't we keep it *Today* forever" as the throngs of Katie supporters and well-wishers, gathered in the plaza outside the NBC studio in New York City, watched through their tears.

CBS let the summer pass before launching the new persona of Katie Couric, serious-minded news anchor and managing editor of its network evening newscast. The network also attempted to strengthen that persona by adding her to the reporting crew of its venerable Sunday night newsmagazine *60 Minutes,* along with another new face, Anderson Cooper, the new celebrity journalist star of CNN.

Washington journalist Howard Kurtz wrote in 2007 about Couric's first night on the *CBS Evening News* anchor desk:

> She felt like she was under a high-powered microscope. All the hype, all the attention, it was far more than she wanted. Couric knew that a lot was riding on her performance. CBS had made a huge investment in her. She had come to personify the shifting epicenter of network news. No matter what she did,

Couric felt, she would be picked apart. Of course she had jitters. She did not have ice water in her veins . . . She had already decided to dispense with the two words—"good evening"—that seemed grafted onto the front of every nightly newscast . . . "Hi everyone," Couric said. "I'm very happy to be with you tonight." She was the audience's friend.[16]

On September 24, 2008, Couric's journalistic credentials received a welcome boost when she interviewed Sarah Palin, the GOP candidate for vice president. Couric's questions were hard hitting and revealed a Palin who seemed unprepared or at least unable to articulate her meanings clearly.

Cooper's Emotional Journalism

Anderson Cooper is another example of a personable, good-looking, and intelligent television celebrity journalist who, like Couric, has had to work hard to overcome celebrity status and gain credibility as a serious journalist. Of course he works in television, which is a medium of personalities, so his network (CNN) does all it can to play up his personality. Cooper fits well into CNN's pantheon of news and commentary programs, each of which is named for the anchor hosting it. The prime-time centerpiece of those shows is Cooper's two-hour weeknight show *Anderson Cooper 360°,* but there are others, including CNN's 6 p.m. nightly newscast *Lou Dobbs Tonight* and its longstanding interview show *Larry King Live,* which bumps next to Cooper's show. CNN likes to play up what it sees as Cooper's uniqueness: his ability to bring edgy emotions—most notably anger—into his on-air interviews. Here is how the CNN Web site on Cooper's show describes him:

> "ANDERSON COOPER 360°" is a provocative alternative to the typical network evening newscast, going beyond the headlines to tell stories in-depth and from many points of view so you can make up your own mind about the news that affects you. The show's hallmark is its "Keeping Them Honest" franchise—demanding answers and finding the truth. Backed by the global resources of CNN, Anderson's anchor desk is Central Command for a 360-degree look at world events.[17]

And then, as if to underscore the idea that viewers should watch the show to see Cooper as much as the stories he is reporting on, the description continues:

> "ANDERSON COOPER 360°" does not shy away from strong opinions, provocative stories and challenging issues. Regular features include Anderson's take on the world of media and the news, with in-depth coverage of justice, politics, health and pop culture, all from contributors who are as engaged, and engaging, as Anderson.[18]

Cooper's entrance into the world of television journalism is an interesting one in and of itself. A former child model and graduate of Yale, Cooper wanted desperately to become a foreign correspondent but had no luck in getting any of the networks to hire him as a reporter. So the son of Gloria Vanderbilt financed himself as a freelancer who went first to Burma and then to the other hot spots of the world, offering up news footage to anyone who would take it. The educational news agency Channel One began using much of his material, and he was noticed by ABC, which hired him as a correspondent for ABC News. He rose to the position of coanchor of *World News Now*, briefly hosted ABC's short-lived reality show *The Mole*, and eventually became a news reporter for ABC. He was hired by CNN in 2001 where he gained fame for his nightly coverage in 2005 and 2006 of Hurricane Katrina. That coverage catapulted him into his own two-hour nightly news and commentary show.

Cooper's dual status as a celebrity and a journalist, however, causes some degree of angst among television viewers who want to believe he is genuine in his zeal to get to the bottom of stories and correct problems for the victims of tragedy. He seems committed to his cause of investigative journalism and to helping give voice to those who have no voice. And yet he is part of an industry that is, at heart, an entertainment medium. And his own network seems to work overtime to promote its newscasters as personalities as much—or more—than as credible reporters. Especially in New Orleans, Cooper engendered different reactions from victims of Katrina: some believed he was an outsider using their misery to grandstand; some were angry with him for openly challenging a popular U.S. senator (Mary Landrieu), disagreeing with her on air; and others believed he was genuinely concerned and was trying to bring about a quicker and more comprehensive government response.

Cooper has made valiant attempts to convince others that he is genuine in what he does. In 2006, he wrote a book of his reporting experiences called *Dispatches from the Edge* in which he talked about how reporters have to be real in what they do and about how stories wind up affecting journalists personally. Cooper describes his view of the role of the television news anchor in this way:

> I think the notion of a traditional anchor is fading away, the all-knowing, all-seeing person who speaks from on high. I don't think the audience really buys that anymore. As a viewer, I know I don't buy it. I think you have to be yourself, and you have to be real and you have to admit what you don't know, and talk about what you do know, and talk about what you don't know as long as you say you don't know it. I tend to relate more to people on television who are just themselves, for good or for bad, than I do to someone who I believe is putting on some sort of persona. The anchorman on *The Simpsons* is a reasonable facsimile of some anchors who have that problem.[19]

So the mixing of journalist and celebrity, especially in the world of television news, is a problem when it comes to gauging the credibility and sincerity of TV journalists. "Television is a world of smoke and mirrors," Diane Willis used to say of her years in Indianapolis and Boston as a television news anchor. In such a world, how does the viewer really know who is a credible journalist and who is simply good at *acting* like one?

A Possible Distortion

One of the things that print journalists enjoy about their work as opposed to that of television newscasters is their relative anonymity. It takes a long time for a newspaper or magazine byline to become well known among the public. In the first place, only a minority of the American people still read newspapers or news stories in magazines. So a print journalist's byline does not have that much reach. Second, even if a byline does become well known, the face that goes with that byline stays invisible to the general public. The only way people might come to know the journalist on sight is if that reporter winds up as a regular guest on television interviews or talk shows.

On dealing with the celebrity factor that confronts television journalists, former Toledo TV news reporter Gretchen Dworznik said she remembers only two times when it got in the way of a story. One was when she covered a story about pickets. Before she showed up with the cameraman, the picketers were just sitting around. But, upon her arrival, they jumped to their feet, starting marching, and one guy started banging a drum. She got after the picketers later and said she didn't want them changing things just because she was there.

Print journalists find anonymity useful because it allows them to blend into the situations they cover without having their mere presence distort these situations. When celebrity journalists show up to cover events, the focus—at least for a while—can turn to that celebrity and away from the event. And the event itself can change because the television camera is there. This has always been a potential problem. During the antiwar demonstrations on college campuses across America, television's popularity had hit its stride, and the power of the television camera was well understood by the organizers of these demonstrations. On numerous occasions, the mere presence of a television news crew upgraded a minor event into a major one, as a quiet demonstration turned into a loud and boisterous protest with many participants.

Print journalists have understood this distortive possibility for a long time, and it is one reason that many newspapers have had trouble convincing some reporters to allow their mug shots to be used when they write analyses or even columns. As managing editor of a Dallas area daily, I once asked some of my best reporters to write weekly columns and told them we were going to run their mug shots with those columns. I encountered sustained resistance from two reporters who felt this plan would damage their personal anonymity.

The Latest in a Trend?

Is the temptation for journalists to give in to their celebrity status a new phenomenon? Noted Australian journalist Mark Day says no, it's been around ever since there have been writers. He cites, as examples, Mark Twain, Charles Dickens, and even Winston Churchill. He explains:

> Charles Dickens began his journalistic career reproducing the speeches in Parliament for his readership, a feat requiring phenomenal powers of recall. In the meanwhile, he was churning out hugely popular fictional tales which made up an outstanding social commentary of the times. Dickens as performing celebrity became even more the centre of his stories. Then there was young Winston, whose exploits seem to have had some parallels with those of the first of the Murdoch dynasty, Keith. Churchill's reports from the Boer War made him famous and wealthy. His fame outlasted his periodic bursts of affluence. But fame and wealth came from his creative tales in which we wrote himself as the central character. And what about Mark Twain, yet another itinerant journalist whose genius with words excused him from proximity with factual reality as he reported on his journeys? These were early celebrity journalists. They were at times hugely influential. Another example, this time from France, is Emile Zola in exposing the Dreyfus scandal. In this case, the author used his fame to help promote the story, rather than using the story to promote his fame.[20]

If Day is correct, then the modern-day crop of celebrity journalists find themselves in very esteemed company, although that doesn't make their job any easier. They still must present themselves as credible and sincere journalists as opposed to career-hungry personalities who do a good job acting as if they are sincere.

The history of daily journalism in the nineteenth and early twentieth century is also full of celebrities. Many newspapers of that time were known as much for the personality of their editors as for the newspapers themselves. Such was the case with flamboyant editors like James Gordon Bennett (the *New York Herald*), Horace Greeley (the *New York Tribune*), William Randolph Hearst (the *New York Journal*), and Elinor "Cissy" Patterson (the *Washington Herald*).

Bennett's paper featured lively and graphic crime news and financed special expeditions, like reporter Henry Stanley's long-publicized search for Dr. Livingston in Africa. Greeley became known as "Uncle Horace" and was attributed with the encouragement of pioneers to "Go west, young man." Many of those pioneers had the weekly version of his newspaper next to their Bible in their frontier cabins. Hearst's eccentricities were chronicled in the thinly disguised movie *Citizen Kane*. Most historians credit the Spanish-American War to the sometimes-exaggerated coverage that Hearst gave Cuba's struggle for independence from Spain. At one point, Hearst (publisher of the *New York Journal*) himself became a reporter, going to Cuba and covering the battle at El Caney. Hearst had already sent his star reporter, James Creelman, to cover the action, but that wasn't enough for him. He had to get in on the action too. Creelman had already crossed the line between journalist and participant in taking it upon himself to lead a charge of American troops up the hill at El Caney to capture a Spanish blockhouse. He was wounded by a bullet in the process. His actions are described as follows:

Crawling forward to an adjacent hill, Creelman caught up with General Chaffee of the American force. Bullets came uncomfortably close. One clipped a button from the general's breast. It seemed better to be shot at fighting than to die watching. The only man to know the back road up the hill, Creelman suggested a bayonet charge and offered to lead the way . . . Creelman, in the next few moments, ceased to be a journalist and found himself a hero.[21]

In a book containing several of his news reports, Creelman recalls being wounded in the attack, staggering to a hammock in a small room at the fort, "hearing my own blood drip."[22] He was carried down the hill where he lay among the other wounded soldiers. To his surprise, he found a familiar, colorful figure towering above him. He continues the story:

Someone knelt in the grass beside me and put his hand on my fevered head. Opening my eyes, I saw Mr. Hearst, the straw hat with a bright ribbon on his head, a revolver at his belt, and a pencil and notebook in his hand. The man who had provoked the war had come to see the result with his own eyes and, finding one of his correspondents prostrate, was doing the work himself. Slowly he took down my story of the fight as he said, "I'm sorry that you're hurt, but"—and his face was radiant with enthusiasm—"wasn't it a splendid fight? We must beat every paper in the world!"[23]

As eccentric a celebrity editor as Hearst was, however, it was probably a female editor who was even more flamboyant—"Cissy" Patterson. The wealthy member of a publishing dynasty herself, this Washington socialite had many escapades, including a snap marriage to an Austrian count in 1904, a divorce, and the count's kidnapping of their daughter and demand for a million-dollar ransom. All of this drove Patterson to move to Wyoming and becoming a cowgirl. Ironically, it was Hearst who brought her back to Washington, DC to make her editor of the *Washington Herald* in 1930. She made it a success with her unique formula of focusing on stories for women. (Her motto was "Tell it to Mrs. Sweeney!" a twist on her brother Joseph's motto at his *New York Daily News* of "Tell it to Sweeney!") But the focus in Washington was as often as not on Patterson herself, who was a fixture at posh parties and would show up at work in expensive furs with her dog in tow.

In short, celebrity journalists have been around for a very long time, and there is no reason to assume they will fade from the scene now or in the future.

Notes

1. Daniel Boorstin, *The Image: A Guide to Pseudo-Events in America* (New York: Atheneum, 1985).

2. Tom Burnham, "The Rise of Celebrity Journalism," Letters from the Editor in Chief, *CBC News*, January 17, 2007, www.cbc.ca/news/about/burman/letters/2007/01/the_rise_of_celebrity_journali.html.

3. Mick Hume, "When Celebrities Rule the Earth," *Spiked*, http://www.spiked-online.com/index.php?/site/printable/1978/ (accessed April 17, 2009).

4. Burnham, "The Rise of Celebrity Journalism."

5. Victor Merina, "Celebrities in Journalism: The Ethics of News Coverage," *PoynterOnline*, January 22, 2004, http://www.poynter.org/content/content_view.asp?id=59603.

6. Merina, "Celebrities in Journalism."

7. Merina, "Celebrities in Journalism."

8. Geoffrey Baym, "Political News for the Hip-Hop Generation: MTV and the 2004 Presidential Election" (presentation, annual meeting of the Central States Communication Association, Indianapolis, IN, April 5–9, 2006) .

9. Edward R. Murrow, "Lights and Wires in a Box" (speech, Radio-Television News Directors Association Convention, Chicago, IL, October 15, 1958).

10. Howard Kurtz, "CNBC's Bartiromo Flies Into Citigroup Controversy," *Washington Post*, January 26, 2007, C07.

11. Kurtz, "CNBC's Bartiromo Flies."

12. Kurtz, "CNBC's Bartiromo Flies."

13. Thomas A. Birk, "Christine Craft: U.S. Broadcast Journalist," *MBC: Museum of Broadcast Communication*, http://www.museum.tv/archives/etv/C/htmlC/craftchrist/craftchrist.htm (accessed December 21, 2007).

14. Engstrom, Erika, and Anthony J. Ferri, "Looking Through a Gendered Lens: Local U.S. Television News Anchors' Perceived Career Barriers," *Journal of Broadcasting and Electronic Media*, 44 (Fall 2000): 614–635.

15. Birk, "Christine Craft."

16. Howard Kurtz, *Reality Show: Inside the Last Great Television News War* (New York: Free Press, 2007) 270.

17. CNN, "Anderson Cooper 360°," *AC 360°*, http://www.cnn.com/CNN/Programs/anderson.cooper.360/ (accessed December 21, 2007).

18. CNN, "Anderson Cooper 360°."

19. David S. Hirschman, "So what do you do, Anderson Cooper?" *Mediabistro.com*, http://www.mediabistro.com/articles/cache/a1582.asp (accessed June 30, 2007).

20. Mark Day, "Celebrity Journalists as Thought Leaders," *The Leaders We Deserve*, http://leaderswedeserve.wordpress.com/2007/12/07/celebrity-journalists-as-thought-leaders-the-case-of-robert-peston/ (accessed December 21, 2007).

21. Louis L. Snyder and Richard B. Morris, eds. *A Treasury of Great Reporting* (New York: Simon and Schuster, 1962), 241.

22. Snyder and Morris, 245.

23. James Creelman, qtd. in Snyder and Morris, 246–247.

8

Questions Vexing Journalists

M any journalists seem to have a love/hate relationship with their profession. They love the ideals of journalism, and they love the times when they can turn those ideals into reality. Get to the bottom of the story; right the wrongs. But they hate the encroaching business pressures that translate into the bottom-line journalism of severe newsroom cutbacks and more entertainment-driven reporting. The longer a journalist stays in the business, the more he or she grapples with the downside and wonders whether the upside is winning or losing.

The average age of journalists in America is 41, according to a study at Indiana University, and the average journalist is older than was the case in previous decades, as baby boomers are deciding to remain in the profession, although some reluctantly. The study reports that the largest increase in the number of reporters as the twenty-first century began was in the 45–54 age group and that almost two out of every three journalists are now over the age of 35.[1] However, the overall number of journalists—especially working in print—is shrinking because of payroll cutbacks at newspapers. Indeed, the whole newspaper landscape is changing as ink-on-paper newspapers—*The New York Times* included—are finding it hard to stay in business. One major metro daily, the *Rocky Mountain News*, folded in 2009 while the *Seattle Post-Intelligencer* converted to online delivery only. Newspaper analysts expect many other dailies to follow the digital-only delivery model sooner rather than later. And, as was noted in *The Atlantic*, revenues from an online-only *New York Times* would support only 20 percent of the current news staff.[2]

Commenting on the career longevity of many journalists, principal researcher David Weaver notes, "A lot of younger people who are hired into journalism don't stay that long." Also, according to Weaver, "There are enough journalists who work their way up into some of the middle- and upper-management jobs and are hanging on until retirement that it forces the average up."[3]

Following huge growths in news media staffs in the 1970s and early 1980s, the late 1990s and first decade of the twenty-first century saw deep cutbacks in most print media—especially newspapers—around the country, resulting in the loss of 8,400 jobs at daily newspapers and 3,268 jobs at all other print media outlets. The main reasons cited are the loss of advertising revenues to other media and the push to produce higher profits by corporations who paid a lot of money to acquire them. Conversely, the employment picture on the television side was much brighter, with jobs growing by about 2,500 between 1982 and 1992.[4] However, the problems caused by competition from newer types of media, such as the Internet, have also plagued television. As a result, television stations have been experiencing cutbacks as well, although not to the degree that newspapers have in the early twenty-first century.

Nevertheless, a 2007 study of the journalism job market done by the Henry W. Grady School of Journalism at the University of Georgia shows that nearly all of the 2007 bachelor's degree recipients who looked for work had at least one in-person job interview within eight months of graduation. Further, 78 percent of journalism graduates had at least one job offer on graduation. And, as in past years, women had even more success than did men.[5]

It is often said that daily journalism is a "young person's sport," but the economics of the business—especially the cutbacks in print media news organizations—and the changing definition of "journalism" in the minds of young people may be causing that to change, judging from the above findings. Traditionally, there have been reasons for older journalists to leave the profession. First, reporting is a demanding job, which, as we noted in the first chapter, many journalists see more as a mission or a calling. Missions and callings are easier to carry out when one is young and relatively unencumbered by a family and the needs that must be attended to there. Second, reporting doesn't pay that much. The Weaver study quoted above showed the average reporter in America making about $43,000. In today's economy, that is a salary that is more befitting a 20-something professional than one in their 40s or 50s. Third, the idealistic view of journalism that brings many people into this profession often gives way to the grimmer realities of the news business as time goes on. Many young and idealistic reporters find it impossible to make the kinds of compromises that newspapers and television often require.

As a result of these and other reasons, many journalists wind up leaving the daily news business earlier than other professionals might change careers. There may be more older than younger journalists working at the nation's newspapers, but the overall numbers of those journalists have thinned dramatically since the 1990s because of the severe newsroom cutbacks already mentioned. Some journalists who move on to other careers are sanguine about the shift, welcome what journalism has given them, and accept the fact that it is time for them to move on. Some turn bitter over the harsh realities of a profession that lured them in with idealism and the offer of a chance to right societal wrongs and then seemed to turn on them as economic realities left little appreciation of or room for serious news reporting.

A Young Journalist Weighs In

Tim Posada is a 26-year-old journalist in Southern California who went to work for the *Park Labrea News / Beverly Press* in 2007 as a general assignment reporter. (The newspaper had a circulation of 12,000.) Like many young journalists, especially those at community newspapers, Posada was often called upon to perform other tasks as well. In Posada's case, this meant writing film reviews and even doing general page layouts. These were things he enjoyed, although he was surprised by the jack-of-all-trades needs of community newspapers. "I hadn't really learned in college about community journalism," Posada said in an interview for this book. "Most of my courses focused on larger journalism issues and larger media. I was surprised also by the fact that much of my job was in taking press releases and rewriting them, and was amazed how much time I actually spent at a desk, doing interviews over the telephone. But I still like it."

Posada says he found community journalism to be pleasing, especially because he enjoyed the community he was reporting on. "I like getting to know the area of West Hollywood and its people," he explains. "They are very interesting and it's fun getting to hang out with them."

His frustrations have dealt mainly with surprises about the news culture in newspapers and with the traditionalism of older editors and publishers, who haven't seen the need to update obsolete technology to newer software. "We've had to use 15-year-old software because the editor hasn't really seen the need to update it. He feels it's been working okay, so why change it? Editors can get pretty set in their ways."

Posada decided to branch out from reporting to teach part time at two area colleges and help advise a college newspaper. "I love it," he says. "It's fun to introduce college students to writing and reporting." Posada plans to stay in journalism—hopefully both in writing and teaching—for a long time to come.

One Frustrated Anchor

Many journalists leave because their news operations have been forced to become entertainment providers more than information providers. They often believe that marketing consultants are defining news more these days than are editors and reporters. One journalist who left the profession for these reasons is Jim Redmond, former KUSA-TV news anchor in Denver. Redmond left the business to enter university teaching, eventually becoming chair of the Department of Journalism at the University of Memphis. The recently retired Memphis journalism professor says that, in his television news career, he encountered a strong and growing focus on what looked good rather than what was important:

> What is hard for TV journalists is no one cares about the journalism anymore. The consultants have taken over, and now we have a generation of news managers who were not even in the business before about 1985. They don't know what good TV journalism is because they came in after the consultants had already doctored newscasts with an emphasis on good pictures, happy-talk air-head anchors, stripping manipulated series to hype ratings that often have nothing to do with any real news of the day, etc.

> It had become so cosmetically obsessed. On top of that, consultants had already destroyed the way news was gathered and the decisions were made about what to cover, moving into market-research manufacturing of current events that fit whatever the surveys indicated people "wanted" on TV news. No survey I ever saw in the business (and I saw many of them) ever asked what people "needed" on TV news. It became all "want" driven by about 1980, certainly in the major markets.

> So newscasts are manufactured to fit a top 10 or top 20 list of the topics people said they were interested in during the survey taken weeks or months ago. The problem is news happens, and then people find out about it. For example, if I had taken a huge survey with about 10,000 respondents a week before the Tiananmen Square massacre and asked, "would you be interested in knowing more about the intricacies of Chinese politics?" I would have probably ended up with a goose egg. Huh? But if I'd done such a survey after the little guy was on the cover of *Time* magazine stopping the tank, I would have had a significant

response from people wondering what was going on over there. When you decide what goes in a newscast based on market research you are no longer really in the news business. And that's where we are.

Redmond and other news anchors, such as Diane Willis, former anchor of WNEV-TV in Boston and WRTV in Indianapolis, found that they were sometimes asked to do stories simply because those stories had worked in other markets. The consultants for WNEV (now WHDH) encouraged the station's news director to do a five-part series on house cats because it had worked so well in the Phoenix market when it had aired. So Willis drew the assignment and spent weeks researching and reporting on cats. The series didn't fare as well in the ratings in Boston as in Phoenix, probably confounding the consultants who seemed to assume that, whatever Phoenix viewers liked, Boston viewers would like too. Redmond found the same kind of thinking prevailed in Denver as well.

"In about 1985, I think it was, McHugh Hoffman was our consultant in Denver," Redmond recalls. "They did a big survey and came up with a list of subjects people were interested in hearing about in the news. It ended up being 19 subjects. Stuff like weather, crime, state politics, etc. So they printed up the list on big poster-size cards and put them up on the walls of the conference room where we held the meetings for each show's news budget of the day. The items were ranked in descending order with the most important up at the top. It was "weather" followed by "crime." Then the news director put out a memo to all the producers saying that the top five had to be in every show, and the first producer who did not do that would be replaced."

This directive severely restricted the news content, as Redmond explains: "Well, by the time you blocked a half-hour newscast—which actually has about 12 minutes of content in it by the time you subtract for weather, sports, commercials, and anchor chit-chat—you only had stories about the five topics and barely had room for any thing else. That is called now 'market-driven news,' and it's everywhere. It's in the newspapers too, which have increasingly used market research to determine content."

Redmond's conclusion: "The news is no longer developed with an overpowering sense of providing the people what they need to know. It is developed with an overpowering sense of creating content that the market study says we should have. So news is manufactured, in effect just made up, to fit that mold. Witness the stupid series that always appear in rating periods. Most of the time those have nothing to do with the news of the day but are manufactured content driven by the consultants. In fact, Magid [an Iowa-based national television consultant agency] faxes suggested news series to every client news director every week during major rating periods. You'll be in Toledo and see a series, and fly to Salinas and see the same series, and then up to Portland and see it again (if you jump on a plane that week and flit around)."

Redmond saw the handwriting on the wall and made plans for another career, pursing a PhD at the nearby University of Colorado, graduating, and moving into university teaching at the University of Memphis. In the process, he says he was more than willing to take a drastic pay cut and turn his back on a new anchoring opportunity in Dallas, which would have paid him more than he could ever have earned in teaching.

"I didn't go into television for the money, and money wasn't enough to keep me in it when I saw things going irretrievably bad,' Redmond says.

Rays of Hope

Although the dissatisfaction Redmond and other journalists experienced in the news business convinced them to move on to other careers, some journalists see rays of hope in what the mainstream media is doing today. One of those is Arlene Notoro Morgan, a veteran reporter and editor at *The Philadelphia Inquirer* who is now associate dean of the Columbia University Graduate School of Journalism. She seems proud of the way most of the major media conduct themselves today, in terms of providing news and information of value to the public.

"I think mainstream is still doing public service watchdog journalism better than any other media in a consistent way," she says.

Yes, magazines and TV news—the *New Yorker* or *Frontline*, for instance—do occasional "wow 'em" pieces, but nothing in comparison to the work *The Wall Street Journal* did last year in China, the *Los Angeles Times*'s "Altered Oceans" on the environment, or *The Washington Post's* examination of what was going on at Walter Reed Hospital.

I think newspapers still can be depended on to give us information and stories that we don't know we need or want. They continue to surprise us, dig beneath the surface, and help a community change. Over the past decade, newspapers have also become easier to use, and they now produce Web sites that can link you to almost every piece of information you need to live your life, not only in the community but the world. That is an enormous public service.

Morgan says she has not altered her views over the years about journalists remaining detached from their sources ("not being in bed with your sources or carrying out your own agenda," as she states it). She believes reporters must be better prepared to understand their sources, however, especially before beginning interviews.

"Parachute journalism does not do anyone much good," she quips. "Beat reporters, in particular, should constantly be improving their knowledge through self-education, workshops, and just getting out on the streets to meet the real people their stories affect."

And again, the topic of diversity enters into her thinking: "I believe that multiple perspectives are now more required to make a story fair and complete than the traditional, 'he said, she said' formula."

If journalists are so committed to the profession of making objective observations to the world and exposing corruption and sham, why do so many leave the profession and move into business, politics, public relations, and advertising—the very professions most journalists would say fuel manipulation and obfuscation?

"Actually," Morgan responds, "I do not agree that every journalist comes into the business to be objective or to expose corruption and sham. That might be 20–30 percent of the profession. And I have not seen many of the journalists who are committed to those ideals leave the business." Morgan thinks other motives are responsible for journalists joining and then leaving the profession:

You have to acknowledge that some people come into it for their own glory and ego. And I have known a lot of journalists—they are human after all—who are not always objective. Just look at TV journalist Lou Dobbs right now. He's certainly not objective about immigration, but he is getting good numbers out there. So, obviously, people may not care as much about so-called objectivity as they do [about] finding someone who will confirm their views.

I think objectivity is an ideal that, sadly, is not always reached. The best we can ask for these days is that every journalist does work that is fair.

As for leaving the business to pursue financial, political, or other goals, I think again that it is human nature to seek what you think is best for you. I would not want to stereotype anyone who leaves the business for financial gain because so many news jobs just don't pay enough to meet the living standards required to raise a family and have a decent life. So I am not going to condemn anyone for taking a job outside of journalism as long as they do that job with integrity and are not corrupted.

New York Times reporter Barry Bearak also finds enough positives to remain optimistic about the news business, so much so that he remains in it as a committed reporter, trying to do what he does best: report the news accurately and fairly and, hopefully, help change the world. But, as he explains, altruism did not motivate him to join the profession:

I didn't get into journalism in order to change the world, but as I experienced more and more of the world and observed the people who ran it, I increasingly thought change was fairly urgent. And reporters are better positioned than most to grab people by the lapels, shake them up, and say, "Hey you! Things are a mess. Fix it!" For nearly fifteen years as a roving national correspondent for the *Los Angeles Times,* I had one of the best newspaper jobs imaginable. I was given huge chunks of time and huge amounts of space to write whatever stories caught my eye.

I used the opportunity to dig into social issues—most every topic on the poverty hit parade: housing, drugs, AIDS, racism, corporate greed. I suppose I had hopes that my stories would force people to think in a more compassionate way. And, on rare occasions, I probably hoped to force lawmakers to rewrite laws. Did those expectations go unfulfilled? I think the stories were good enough to make people think, and there's some evidence that some appropriate brainwaves were provoked.

As time went on, Bearak came to the conclusion that, if he really wanted to make a more significant difference, he might have to have a bigger megaphone.

As for changing policy, I'd come away disappointed. Actually, that was one of the things that led me to *The New York Times.* It had a more powerful audience and that meant more influence, and I think that has proven to be true to some degree. But I still usually come away disappointed. I haven't stopped trying to change the world, but I have decidedly diminished expectations.

Some Stay, Some Move On

Gretchen Dworznik left the television news business after less than a decade, although, like many other former journalists, she moved into teaching journalism at the college level. The former Toledo reporter has given some thought to why dedicated journalists often leave the profession to pursue careers in business, public relations, or advertising—the very institutions they were skeptical of as journalists.

"I think this happens for two reasons," she says.

First, compared to television, all of those professions are so much easier. It's kind of the "If you can't beat them, join them" idea. You get so tired of fighting the power that you just give up and join it. Being skeptical and challenging all the time can be exhausting. It's much easier to be the person trying to fool the media than it is to be the media person trying to figure out whose fooling them.

Second, I think that television experience tends to make people very marketable to those in the non-TV world. TV journalists tend to stand out from the pack when that pack is full of just the average Joe. So I think they move into those professions because it's so easy to get jobs in them. You make contacts while you're still reporting, and, as soon as you say you want out, chances are some of those contacts will get you a job.

In her own case, Dworznik decided it was time to leave and to turn instead to teaching the news business in a college setting. She picked up her MA at Ashland and received her PhD at Kent State University, taking a full-time teaching position at Ashland University in Ashland, Ohio.

"I talk about the emotional aspect of journalism with my students now," she said. "But for me, it just wasn't fun any more as a reporter. I was doing that battle [between attachment and detachment] every day."

Were there any realities that didn't match her expectations?

For the most part, the realities matched my expectations. There were two things that I didn't expect, however. One was that there was more of "Let's just get a story because we need to fill the time." Sometimes, a producer wouldn't even care if it was a good story idea or not; we just need to fill the time. Second, there was a lot more stress on my emotional well-being than I thought there would be. I wasn't prepared for that. I so desperately wanted everyone to like me, and I wasn't prepared for the reactions I would get sometimes. Some people didn't like me because I was the media, and I just wanted to say, "But I'm still Gretchen!"

Another frustration for her was to see how many of her family and friends didn't really understand what she did or really know much about the importance of journalism:

Some of them would try to bash the media, and it became very frustrating. Most journalists are into the passion of journalism. There is a certain love for news and for all things media, and for "Look at what I did!"

In that sense, journalism is more of a mission or calling than a job, Dworznik believes. So it made the bashing of her business frustrating, and she found herself hanging out more with journalists than non-journalists.

"I don't think a lot of students today get it," she said, referring to the passion of journalism and its mission. "A few of them do, and you can see it in them and in their work. But most of them are into it because they think TV is cool, and you get to wear make-up and wear nice clothes and be on camera."

There is also some confusion as to what journalism and journalists actually are because of all the pseudo news shows and pseudo journalists.

"And some students just don't like the news itself because they think it's all slanted or boring," she continues. "Those are the ones who won't make it in this business."

Dworznik says her favorite compliment would be a thank-you note from a victim's family because she covered a lot of crime and cared deeply about being accurate but also about being sensitive to the innocents, the victims, and their families. "A note just might say 'Thank you for caring and for doing such a nice story for us,'" she explains.

Author Michael Walker found that some of his expectations about journalism failed to materialize in a sustained way. But other expectations were exceeded. From a shaky journalistic start writing music reviews for his high school paper in Elgin, Illinois, to international publication of his rock and roll history book *Laurel Canyon,* Michael Walker is definitely living his dream despite the frustrations he encountered in the business of daily newspaper reporting.

> The *L.A. Times* was . . . a sloppily edited newspaper outside of its A section. There were some very talented writers and reporters, but the editing overall was inconsistent and sometimes nonexistent, especially in the cultural coverage. Also this was . . . when walls between business and editorial were supposed to come down, which ran counter to everything I'd been taught and believed in, at least when it came to newspapers.
>
> Finally, the paper was cutting back in lots of counterproductive ways. The Sunday magazine, for example, was left out of the national edition of the paper. My colleagues and I were doing a lot of really good work that was only being seen in Southern California. It scared me that my future as a journalist and writer was being presented through the prism of this newspaper that wasn't taken very seriously even in its hometown, so I got out.

Since then, life has taken Walker back into the world of freelancing and now into the book-publishing world as an author of a popular bestseller. But he has always considered himself a journalist. He realizes that covering his passion—rock and roll and its legendary leaders from the 1960s and 70s—moves him emotionally closer to the subject than some journalists think appropriate. But he sees value in feeling that passion.

"Interesting. That's what also made the Katrina coverage so compelling," he says. "The only danger I see in getting too close is this: Someone without experience, I would find less trustworthy in telling the story. There's a danger in pandering."

In *Laurel Canyon*, however, Walker provides an incisive study of a singularly important era in American musical and cultural history. Walker tells the inside story of the unprecedented gathering in this Los Angeles neighborhood of some of the baby boom's leading musical lights—including Joni Mitchell; Jim Morrison; Crosby, Stills & Nash; the Mamas and the Papas; Carole King; the Eagles; and Frank Zappa, to name just a few. These artists turned Los Angeles into the music capital of the world and forever changed the way popular music is recorded, marketed, and consumed.

Penny Owen, feature reporter for *The Oklahoman*, has weathered the temptations to leave the news business and remains a full-time working journalist. She understands why some leave the business, but seeing the job as a kind of mission in search for truth is one reason she stays in it.

"I do think what we do is somewhat of a mission," she says. "I don't think it's wise to adopt a cause or anything, however. I'd call it a truth mission. But then we have the Sabbath gasbags spewing opinions every week while reporting the news, so I can see how things get blurred."

What keeps her from becoming burned out with the business of reporting?

> Taking a short break helped some. I'm not sure I'm over my burnout I experienced. I miss my early enthusiasm. But I also miss journalism terribly when I'm not doing it. Creativity helps. Camaraderie helps. Journalists are an interesting breed. I feel entirely comfortable with them, which isn't true of everyone. They're a bit rebellious, always curious, intolerant of small talk. I like that.

How did she finally get off the long series of assignments on the Oklahoma City bombing? "I was on it until McVeigh was executed in 2001," Owen responds. "I didn't ask to get off of it. I guess it did just naturally fade away. I'm glad it did, frankly."

Why was she glad to see the end of the story? "I don't know," she says. "Maybe I have a short attention span. Maybe I think other things have come along that are bigger than what happened there and for us to still write about it is too much. I interviewed McVeigh's father when I went to Terre Haute for the execution. That was a great story. But Bill McVeigh is not a talker, so, yes, it was a hard interview. Plus it was quite sensitive because I was asking him about the last time he'd see his son. So it was emotional."

Another journalist still plying his skill is *The Washington Post*'s David Waters. How has his own idealism about the journalism profession held up over the years? For the most part, fairly well, he says.

> Nearly all of my expectations have been met and exceeded. I wanted my work to be useful and meaningful, and it is and has been. I wanted to be engaged, challenged, pushed to be creative, and given the room to try. I have been and

continue to be. I also wanted to be able to earn a living and support a family. So far, so good.

Lately, however, my hopes and expectations for daily journalism are being challenged and even put in jeopardy, mostly by greed. Wall Street is killing daily journalism, and no one seems too upset about it.

One journalist who left the news business recently was Philip Delves Broughton, a young 32-year-old Paris bureau chief for the *Daily Telegraph* of London. Unlike many other journalists, Broughton felt the business did not offer as much independence as he valued, and he worried about the future of the industry. Frustrated over the problems that newspapers are facing because of media convergence and the declining interest in reading newspapers, he quit the business and entered Harvard Business School to pursue an MBA. A self-described idealist, Broughton found the ideals of journalism too far separated from its daily practice. He also wanted to change his worldview. "I went there [to Harvard] to recover from writing, to stop looking at the world around me as a source of potential stories," he says. "I wanted to learn about business in order to gain control of my own financial fate and, more important, my time. I was tired of living at the end of a cell phone, prey to an employer's demands."[6]

The Oklahoman managing editor Joe Hight is making a life-long career out of a profession he loves and still believes in. How does he interpret the decisions of those journalists who decide to leave journalism and enter into careers such as public relations or advertising, professions that—as journalists—they were cynical of?

Money, recognition, power, working conditions, and the nature of what we cover [violence, tragedy, corruption, etc.] are among the reasons that I think journalists migrate to other professions. We shouldn't be surprised that this is happening either because we cover those areas like public relations, politics, and business consistently and have constant exposure to people in those professions.

Changes in career paths also are becoming more commonplace and, thus, are affecting journalism even more. I would think that most journalists have thought about making changes at some point in their lives. Sometimes the temptations are too much and too hard to resist.

For Otis Sanford, the first African American managing editor of *The Commercial Appeal* in Memphis, newspapers have made good strides in covering the different voices in the South. Much of this has happened by cultivating, hiring, and promoting more journalists of color. In the process, several of his personal goals have been brought to fulfillment by the news business.

"My number one professional expectation early on was to be a good writer and to eventually write columns and opinion pieces, and that has been met," he says. "I also wanted, after several years as a reporter, to see how high I could possibly go in newspaper management, and that expectation has—for the most part—been met. What has gone unfulfilled so far has been the opportunity to be the top editor of a newspaper. I also would love to win a major journalism prize, but basically all of my goals as a journalist have been met."

In his 2007 book *Reality Show,* Washington journalist Howard Kurtz laments the decline of American journalism and discusses the effect of the new realities of the business on the ways television newscasts are being packaged at the network level. His cautionary words make a fitting conclusion:

> The larger reality was that all of organized journalism was in deep trouble, as I was painfully aware after a professional lifetime in the trenches. I had worked for one afternoon paper, the *Washington Star,* that abruptly shut down; then *The Washington Post,* which had been growing by leaps and bounds when I joined, eventually started losing readers and trimming its staff like most big-city dailies. Newspapers, in fact, had been declining for a generation . . . Network magazine shows, which once filled every night of the schedule, had dwindled to a precious few. Cable news channels were drawing a relatively tiny audience . . . Newsmagazines were struggling as well . . . Deep down, media executives wondered whether the younger generation cared about news at all, or whether its members were content to play Xbox games, instant-message each other, download songs from iTunes, and find apartments and dates on Craigslist . . . In the midst of this free-fire zone, high atop a hill . . . the network anchors were trying to hold together a tattered coalition of the middle . . . the networks had to deliver news that was neither too sophisticated nor too dumbed down, too left or to right, too elite or too obvious. They still sought a mass audience when the very concept sounded like a twentieth-century relic.[7]

The news profession is indeed at a crossroads, and journalists must determine individually what they expect to get from a career as a reporter or editor. The favored term in describing the media landscape today is "media convergence," and it is an apt one. It appears that the day of individually separate media platforms is history. In the new reality, every journalist entering the profession must be skillful as an information provider who can present the message across print, broadcast, and online media platforms. That means a number of things beyond simply writing stories differently for print or broadcast. It means understanding the strengths and weaknesses of each media platform and being willing to use those strengths and to live with the weaknesses. It means coping with the rising business pressures and the requisite mixing of news and entertainment. Some journalists will be able and willing to do these things; some won't. The hope is that enough journalists stay with the profession and find ways of continuing to right the wrongs in society and to move people to needed action, even in the midst of a dramatically altered media industry.

Ed Kelley, editor of *The Oklahoman,* disagrees with those who predict an end to newspapers, however. He notes that the two major dailies (*The Rocky Mountain News and The Seattle Post-Intelligencier*) that ceased publication in print form in 2009, were trying to survive in two-newspaper markets. That is extremely difficult to do, he said. However, as an industry, Kelley believes newspapers will survive and added they should continue to produce ink-on-paper publications. He explains:

> To date, newspapers still generate much of their top-line revenue from the print product and have not been able to switch much of it to online ventures. Newspaper-centered organizations that switched to digital only would be pared drastically because the revenue simply wouldn't be there to support large news staffs. So coverage of the basics of democracy—city hall, the county courthouse, the state Capitol—would be spare and perhaps disappear altogether in some markets. This can't be good for a society that has relied on newspapers to be watchdogs in their communities for many years.[8]

Notes

1. David H. Weaver, Randal A. Beam, Bonnie J. Brownlee, Paul S. Voaker, and G. Cleveland Wilhoit, *The American Journalist in the 21st Century* (Mahwah, NJ: Lawrence Erlbaum, 2009).

2. Michael Hirschorn, "End Times," *The Atlantic*, January/February 2009, http://www.theatlantic.com/doc/200901/new-york-times (accessed April 24, 2009).

3. Indiana University, "Big News Covered by Fewer Full-Time Journalists, According to New Book by IU Faculty," IU news release about *The American Journalist in the 21st Century*, http://newsinfo.iu.edu/news/page/normal/4045.html (accessed January 3, 2008).

4. Weaver, *The American Journalist.*

5. Lee B. Becker, Tudor Vlad, Megan Vogel, Stephanie Hanisak, and Donna Wilcox, *2007 Annual Survey of Journalism & Mass Communication Graduates* (Athens, GA: Grady College of Journalism & Mass Communication, University of Georgia, 2007).

6. Philip Delves Broughton, *Ahead of the Curve: Two Years at Harvard Business School* (Boston: Penguin Press, 2008).

7. Howard Kurtz, *Reality Show: Inside the Last Great Television News War* (New York: Free Press, 2007).

8. Interview with Ed Kelley on June 5, 2009, from Oklahoma City, Oklahoma.

Epilogue

Reporting From Iraq
Journalists Talk About Covering War

As Told to Marilyn Thomsen, PhD
La Sierra University

The stories that follow were told by participants in this 2007 study at Claremont Graduate University. The only requirement was that the story focus on the journalist's experiences in Iraq. The stories are included here to provide background and insight into the experiences of the journalists who participated in this study and to add another dimension to the observations of journalists about other subjects presented in this book.

* * *

Ron Harris, *Reporter**

St. Louis Post-Dispatch

I'll tell you one story I've been telling lately about covering a war. The thing about war, and a lot of people think it's some special deal, and it is in that you're under a lot of duress. But the journalism standards don't change.

---

*Ron Harris is a veteran reporter who has worked for several large metropolitan daily newspapers. His first experience covering war came in 2003 when he went to Iraq. He returned to Iraq a second time in 2004.

I'll give you one quick example. We were outside of a military base. I was embedded with 3rd Battalion, 7th Marines. We were preparing to attack that military facility. They were expecting up to 5,000 Iraqis inside the base. It was going to be a night assault. They were going to have air assault before the ground assault. Sounded like it was going to be big stuff.

Right before the attack, we're out on the side of the road, and all these vehicles are in a column on the side of the road. I decided to hand out our company sat phone and let the Marines call their homes. I said, "You've got five minutes," and I just give them the phone and say, "Ok, you call."

While they're doing that, one guy comes up to me and he says, "Hey, I've got a great story for you. There's a marine in this unit over here whose fiancée was killed in 9/11. She was in the World Trade Center when the plane crashed into it. And [he was] so heartbroken and hurt—they were going to get married. He knew we were going to go to war, so he signed up with the Marines because he wanted some payback. He was in the family's landscape business, and he was so integral to the business that, when he left, the business fell apart. Mom and dad couldn't keep it up. So this fellow sacrificed. But now he's on the eve of this really big battle, and he's going to get some payback."

So I go over to interview him, and I say to him, "Get me four or five phone numbers—get me your mom's phone number, your dad's phone number," because they were divorced. I said, "Let me have your fiancée's parents' phone number, so I can call them and talk to them about what you've been through." What you want to do is corroborate your story, make sure it's true.

So I go back and I make phone calls back to the States. Nobody answers the phone. They either don't answer the phone or it's the wrong phone number. And these are the times when people would be home. So I go back to him and I say, "Unfortunately, I must have written these phone numbers down wrong, because none of them work." And he goes, "Well, maybe my mom's number—the numbers are transposed." I'm like, "This guy doesn't know his own mom's phone number?"

So it hit me that he might not be telling the truth. So I said, "OK, I can't write this story. I cannot corroborate his story. I can't prove his story." I only tell you that as a journalism story because you have to understand that when we do our job, we have to report what's true, and you can't drop those standards. I could easily have just said, "This marine said this and he said that and he said this and he said that." And some people would have fallen in love with it and put it on the wire, and put my name all over the place. But I couldn't prove that story to be true, and I wasn't going to send back information that wasn't true. I just make the point that, even in the middle of war, when people think you're playing fast and loose, you're not playing fast and loose. You can't play fast and loose because the same standards that you have over here, you've got to use over there.

* * *

Gidget Fuentes, *West Coast Bureau Chief**

Marine Corps Times

We had flown in, and we got stuck in Baghdad for the weekend because we missed our ride, and we ended up hiring an Iraqi to drive us out to Camp Fallujah. This was in the middle of March 2004, just as things were getting hot. It was two weeks before the contractors were killed. They had just had a couple of anniversaries in late February that stirred up a lot of violence, and things started to heat up in March. We missed our ride at the airport because the flight we took made a stop in Mosul first. It was mostly just me and the photographer and KBR [Kellogg Brown & Root] contractors on that flight. So we missed our convoy to camp where we were linking up with the Marines.

We ended up getting stuck at the airport for hours. There were some military people and contractors who had worked there for months and never left the airport. One guy said, "I've got one more month here and then I'm going home, and if I never see this place again, I'll be better for it." I just remember thinking, "You didn't see anything." I had just gotten there and I'm like, "You didn't get out of this walled-in compound. What have you really seen in Iraq?" That always stuck with me.

We ended up getting a bus ride down that airport road, which was dangerous at the time, and went to the coalition authority to get our badges and military IDs just so they could vouch for us. We found we really didn't need them outside of Baghdad. After spending a few hours there trying to get our military ok, we had to figure out what we were going to do because we had no place to go. We hadn't planned on being in Baghdad at all. We planned on staying with the Marines, getting a tent. We had all our stuff with us. A British army guy, retired, overheard our conversation. He ended up taking us out to this hotel in Baghdad—it was probably about 10 o'clock at night. It was an eye-opening experience—you're not in the United States any more. It wasn't my first time overseas, but, when you're a woman, nobody really cares what you have to say. People look at you funny.

So we're stuck in this hotel, and the photographer was pretty much like, "Let me handle this." So I thought, "Ok, I'll defer to him," which goes against my grain as a woman. But I let him try to haggle for the hotel and all. That was an interesting couple of hours because you didn't know who to trust. Everybody's looking at you funny. They're looking at me funny because I'm a woman. Here I am sort of wearing men's clothes. I had cargo pants on. We had our company hats on, bulletproof vests and helmets; plus we had military packs with us, so we looked really out of place.

---

*Gidget Fuentes was the military reporter for a daily newspaper and very much wanted to cover the war in Iraq. When her paper sent a male reporter instead, she quit. She became West Coast bureau chief for the *Marine Corps Times* and went to Iraq in March 2004.

We ended up spending that whole weekend at the hotel. That first night we heard shooting. I barely slept that night because we were placed in rooms opposite from the elevator on the same floor. CBS had the whole second floor of that hotel. They were pretty much paying for security. There were some American contractors, but it wasn't heavily populated. The hotel had been hit in the bombing in 2003, and had a lot of damage. It was the Mansour Hotel, which is right on the Tigris. In the morning, we could hear military helicopters flying up and down the river. There were car bombs. We saw burning tires. We were trying to make arrangements to get out of there. We didn't feel safe there at all.

It was a long two days. We ended up hiring this guy to drive us out to Camp Fallujah, and he shows up and you realize you're not in New York any more because you can't just hail a cab and say, "Hey, drive me there." He shows up with a buddy in another car. He wanted to split us up, one in each car, and drive out there because he didn't want to drive alone. And we're like, "We're not splitting up." We were two westerners in the Mansour area of Baghdad, which is a nice area, but it's still dangerous. That was a hellish ride out of there, in traffic, two westerners in the back of a car.

We got wrong directions to the camp, and we ended up on the road going right into Fallujah. I was working the phone—we had a satellite phone—trying to call the public affairs office, and [they'd ask] "Now where exactly are you? Go down this road and you'll pass Abu Ghraib prison," which we did, but it was on my right and it should have been on my left. There are two parallel roads that leave Baghdad. The prison's kind of between the two. Well, the one on the south goes into Fallujah, and that was the road we ended up being on. The driver, who was married and had eight children, he wanted to be home that night. He was kind of worried. We saw bombed-out cars on that highway. We didn't think about what it was until afterwards and then we realized, "Oh, that's what that was." It was a checkpoint—they were looking for whoever it was, and they weren't military, Iraqi military. They were just gunmen. I'm trying to get this guy to turn the vehicle around—"Turn around! Turn around! Turn around!"—which luckily we were able to do, but I tell you, that was the longest two minutes or five minutes of my life.

We're driving up to the [Marine] camp in a little Iraqi car, four-door white car, looks like every other car out there, and we were like, "Wait, don't go too far, because they might think we're hostile and shoot at you." So the photographer got out—he goes up the dirt road with the car kind of following behind him, and the guy was really nervous driving. I really felt bad for him. We get up to this one gate and Scott, the photographer, went ahead and was holding his ID in his hand and we were just dressed in khaki. We didn't want to look military; we looked like reporters, I guess. He rounded a corner, and he heard the cocking of a shotgun. The Marines were there. He threw his hands up: "U.S. Press! U.S. Press! Don't shoot!" And I guess they were like, "Who are you with?"

"Marine Corps Times!"

"Oh, *Marine Corps Times*. Oh yeah, we know you guys!"

He said his heart was in his chest when he heard that cocking. He had never been in a war zone—it was his first time. He's been back three times since. So he comes back to tell us, "OK, just go really slow. We have to go all the way around so they will see us." The poor Iraqi guy was just terrified. The Marines were nice enough to give the guy a couple bottles of water because he has to drive back to Baghdad. And they treated him pretty fairly, but, at some point, something exploded in back of our car. We had known that the insurgent fighters would bury stuff outside the fence at night so vehicles would get hit. That was our own little introduction to Fallujah.

That night we went to the dining hall, and there was air conditioning; bright florescent light; clean, fake trees; red, white, and blue tablecloths; and white plastic tables with white plastic chairs. Huge. They could get 500 people in there. They had all kinds of refrigerated sodas, and the food—there was chicken and meat, tons of fruit, salad bar, cakes. I just remember, "Great! This is great!" While we were having dinner, they had big-screen TV; usually they had on CNN or Fox News. We were sitting there chatting with one of the sergeants. We finished up dinner and were starting to eat dessert, and, suddenly, we hear this "Boom boom boom! Boom boom boom!" Everything just stopped, and the sergeant grabbed me and threw me down on the floor. Everybody's coming out of their chairs to get underneath the table. So all of a sudden the sergeant is trying to pull me under a table, and I'm trying to get my helmet on because, after sunset, you had to have your helmet and flak jacket with you all the time. And I looked over at Scott, the photographer, and we were looking at each other, and there's this image of these white tablecloths and like 500 Marines in tan camouflage crouched under plastic tables in an aluminum-covered building as mortars or rockets were exploding outside. I look at Scott, and he realizes, "Shit, I don't have my camera!" He'd left it in the public affairs office. We're like, "What an image! Where's that wide angle!" Five hundred U.S. Marines crouched under plastic tables, taking cover, as if that would have mattered.

And then we started to hear this other counter "boom boom," and it was artillery. We'd heard them during the day. They were practicing. They were shooting up blanks, trying to get their guns in line. They had just gotten there that week, artillery from Camp Pendleton. We heard them, and a lot of people started to stand up, and a lot of people ran out, and we're like, "Where is everyone going? Should we leave?" And someone was like, "No, no, they're just running out to see the fireworks."

I'll never forget this one Marine major. He puts his chair back up and sits down and finishes eating his cake. Like nothing happened. At that point my heart is like thump, thump, thump, thump, thump. I'm like, "Holy shit! We just got attacked!" We found out that, when that happened a few days earlier, it actually killed a few people. A rocket hit right outside the aid station, killed an officer who had gone outside to warn everyone to get inside. He had just spoken to his wife on a cell phone, said, "Honey, I've got to go," and he died. He was an army doctor. And I think a navy corpsman died, and a couple of people got wounded. That was the first time they had a mass casualty at that camp.

That was "Welcome to Fallujah." It was an ongoing joke the whole time. Every time we went in or left Fallujah, something happened. It was either a firefight, mortar attack, or rockets. The last time we left Fallujah, we were in a convoy at midnight, sitting in the back of a truck, and "boom, boom"; 25 yards away a couple of mortars hit. That time we barely blinked, eight weeks later. But that image underneath those plastic tables in an aluminum building—there's a lot of images from meeting up with all the Iraqis—but that was one of the more fascinating ones.

* * *

Emily Harris, *Foreign Correspondent—Berlin**

National Public Radio

This is the story of election day, January 31, 2005. It was an interesting day. First of all, there were huge concerns about security, so the U.S. military and Iraqi officials basically shut down movement around the country as best they could. They certainly shut down movement in Baghdad, which is where I was. We journalists had been led to believe, through a number of extended conversations with the U.S. embassy and the Iraqi Ministry of Defense, that journalists would be allowed to drive around the city and go anywhere they wanted to, talk to anyone at polling places that they wanted to, although we understood that only certain polling places allowed cameras and recording equipment in them.

It turned out, on election day, we weren't going to go out first thing in the morning. We were going to wait and see if bombs went off. But a news crew at the place we were staying went out early in the morning to get to a polling station, and they ran into a U.S. military truck that basically told them to get

---

*Emily Harris majored in Russian studies at Yale and made her way into professional journalism through her work at public radio stations and as a Moscow-based freelancer for U.S. print and broadcast media. She reported from Iraq during six separate tours of duty for National Public Radio and was pregnant with her first child during her sixth time there in early 2005. She was interviewed in Palo Alto, California, while she was a Knight Journalism Fellow at Stanford University.

off the streets or they, the American soldiers, would shoot the American journalists because they didn't have the proper sticker or whatever. We went out later and ran into a similar situation. Driving down the street, we were stopped by an Iraqi military guy who told us to get off the street. When we went to the polling station, we didn't have that problem. Coming back from the polling station, which was probably eight blocks from where we were staying, there was this Iraqi military guy in a truck who blocked us and told us to get off the road. We told him, "We're just trying to drive back to our house. It's like two blocks away." And he finally let us go.

But the story is really later. It was *so* restricted on where you could go on election day. It was so frustrating because you had no idea what was going on around the city. Some areas were so blocked off that, even if we had sent our Iraqi translators places, they wouldn't necessarily get to those places. And there were places that they didn't want to go because they were afraid of violence that day. So I was quite frustrated because we were in a neighborhood that was of mixed ethnicity and religion. There have been bombs there, certainly, but it's not like a Shia neighborhood or Sadr City, or a Sunni neighborhood. I was really frustrated because the people we were able to interview in that situation, they all seemed to want the same thing, and I couldn't go to the places where I knew there were other opinions.

One of the translators I worked with had interviewed a man a couple days before who lived nearby and was very sympathetic to the general Sunni view that these elections were illegitimate—they shouldn't be going forward. I wanted to talk to him. She had his phone number, and so we called him up and asked if we could come over and chat, and that was fine. So we got in the car to drive over there, and we had to drive past a polling station. We got up close to the polling station, and 11 Iraqi police or soldiers—I don't know who they were exactly—pulled their guns on us and made us get out of the car and put down our cell phones and go stand by the wall. They wouldn't let us go until the Americans came and picked us up and took us back to their field base where they were running things for the neighborhood and decided we weren't terrorists.

I didn't get to that guy. I eventually did the interview over the phone. But the most interesting thing that happened after that was with our driver—the NPR [National Public Radio] driver that had worked with us from the very, very beginning. One of our NPR reporters hooked up with him early, early on after the war. He got so furious after this incident. He walked into the room where the translators worked and threw down his keys and said, "I'm never listening to a woman again!"

I'm not exactly sure what kind of feelings it left in me. I knew what I was doing was risky, but I didn't think it was *that* risky, and I really wanted this interview. I really felt like this would make a better story. Not a better story in that you had to have conflict in the story, but it would be a better representation of what was actually going on in the country than if I just had interviewed people when we went to the polling booth, which was also a very important part of that day, but it wasn't the whole thing. And at this point I never was going anywhere without specifically saying to my translators, "Are you comfortable going there? Are you comfortable with me going with you?" Because it's one thing to put your own life at risk, but it's something completely different to put somebody else's life at risk. So this was a risk that I had taken calculatedly, and then the driver later claimed he was never consulted, he was just told, and there were lots of things I didn't know whether had happened or not, because they were all in Arabic.

It was one of the more revealing days of the various layers of Iraqi interaction that was a large part of what I reported in different stories anyway. But it was different when it's two people you know well. You're part of the problem, and it was kind of scary to have these 11 Iraqi guys with guns pointing at you. And then getting out of the car and having to stand over on the street—I was wearing a headscarf and a covering, but I was clearly a foreigner, and then you're just exposed? Who's passing by, who's taking notes of the scene, who knows the car license plate? The tension added up and added up.

* * *

Rick Loomis, *Staff Photographer**

Los Angeles Times

I would preface Iraq by saying how I ended up there, which was basically that, the year before, I had spent about seven months in Afghanistan. During that time, I had embedded with . . . before the "embed" term got really popular . . . I had spent time with the Marines, with the Special Forces, with the army, doing a bunch of different stories. I got back from my last trip to Afghanistan in December of 2002. It was right when things were heating up for Iraq, and the newspaper was assembling a team of people to head in there. Originally, they had me in the second wave of people waiting on the edges to go in right after the war was fought. After I got back from Afghanistan I talked with my boss. He told me about the embed positions that were coming up, and I said, "You know, I'm probably the right person to go do that because I've just had all these experiences." He agreed, so I was going to be one of the embeds. We were supposed to have two slots.

*Rick Loomis won the Photographer of the Year award from the Newspaper Press Photographers Association in 2003. A graduate of the photojournalist program at Western Kentucky University, he has spent his entire career at the *Los Angeles Times*.

So I got back in December, and I left in February of '03 and went to Kuwait with a mass of other journalists. It was a little daunting trying to get everything together and get over there, and, basically, at that point it was vying for position: Who's going to be at the front? I had no idea what to expect from the whole "embed" thing. It just seemed like a joke to me. I really thought, in the beginning, that they wouldn't quite put you in the action. It just didn't seem like the government was going to allow that. In the end, they basically assigned people to units, and whatever those units ran into, that's what you saw. So my experience during the war was sometimes boring, sometimes sad, sometimes exhilarating.

I got assigned to a Marine unit camped out in the middle of the Kuwaiti desert for about three or four days. I had all the gear that I thought I needed—sat phone, flak jacket, helmet, and all sorts of things—just basically waiting. Then, one night, they were listening to Bush, standing around a little radio, and he said, "We're going to war." These guys were pretty geared up to go do it. In the few days of waiting, I'd finagled my way into what I thought was going to be the best position, which was riding with the weapons company of that particular unit I was with. It ended up being in this Humvee that had no armor on it. It was supposed to be an armored Humvee with a TOW missile on it, and these guys rolled it a week or two before the war kicked off. So they got a back-up Humvee, and the biggest weapon on it was a hand-held machine gun, so they got all the crap. They got the journalists. They got the pigeon that was supposed to alarm us if there was a chemical threat. They got the castoffs from all the other units: "Could you carry this for us? Can you carry that?" And they got two medics. So they weren't the toughest truck in the bunch. But we headed off, and the first day or so was sort of frustrating because we knew there was a war going on, and we felt far from it.

Probably the original scary moment for me was when they called "Scud missiles!" And they were supposedly inbound, and we were just sitting out in a vast expanse of desert. I had dug my own sort of grave or fighting hole. It basically looked like a grave. Felt like a grave. "Get in the hole! Get in the hole!"— and you pop in and lay down, face up, and there are guys on either side of you, and you're just laying there, waiting for a missile to hit and see if you live through it. So I'm lying in there, and all this stuff is running through my head: "Well, if I just lay here, I don't do anything to tell anybody about what's going on here. I'm just one of these guys." So I was debating with myself for about 30 seconds: "What am I going to do? What am I going to do?" Then I thought, "Well, I don't hear anything. I've been here for a little while. So I'm going to jump out and shoot a picture." So I jumped out of the hole, and I ran to the hole that was right beside me, and there was a guy lying in there with his gas mask ready to put on, and I stood over the hole, and I was like "Huhhhh." And I shot a bunch of pictures of him, a couple different angles, and then I jumped back into my hole. And the scud missiles came, but they didn't come near us at all. So then the next day we moved ahead in the desert a little bit.

Finally, we went through a little broken fence that was the Iraqi-Kuwait border. We were in Iraq, and we were in this long line of vehicles. It was amazing how many vehicles there were. I remember when I was in Kuwait, staying in a nice hotel, waiting for the whole thing to kick off, I said, "I still think there's a chance this war's not going to happen. It's probably just a really big bluff." When they finally did bring us out to the middle of the desert where all these units were waiting, there was so much military gear there that there was no way that war wasn't going to happen. It was going to go off.

The frustration came from not being able to provide every day for the newspaper. There were bombs heading into Baghdad, but I was 100 miles from there, and there wasn't anything to really photograph at that time that was pertinent news. There were bridges and boats that they would truck on 18-wheelers for crossing canals. Those guys would sometimes pass us up, and I was thinking, "How far back can we possibly be when they have boats on trailers passing us?"

So it was frustrating, in a way. I'm thinking, "Here I am, and I'm not doing any good." And then came Nassariya, which was another scary moment. The U.S. side had already had people injured, and they really got the crap beat out of them going through Nassariya. So, when we went through Nassariya, it was supposedly like a picket line. Other units had one side of the road, and on the other side of the road they had guns aiming out against any enemy, and we were just supposed to push right through the city in the middle of the night. There were fires going off everywhere and mortar rounds exploding, incoming and outgoing, and it definitely started to feel like a war. I knew Afghanistan wasn't much training. It wasn't an out and out war. This started to feel like a real war, and I hadn't been to one before, except for Afghanistan.

So, when we went through Nassariya, it was the middle of the night. I hadn't really had much sleep, and, at night, it was almost impossible to take pictures. They were trying to punch through to the other side of Nassariya. Our guys were on edge trying to go through there, and what happened was we heard over our radio "We've got contact." About 20 seconds later this marine or army guy comes from the side of the road, and he starts yelling right into our truck. And he says, "You got a radio in there?" And the guy driving our rig goes, "Yeah." And he goes, "Well, tell those people to stop fucking shooting! There's friendlies up there!" They had friendly people in the building that our unit just went and shot up. I think it injured two guys. I have no idea whatever happened to them.

So we made it through Nassariya. At some point, dawn broke, and that was a really eerie feeling with nobody on the street, and things were shot up, and we're passing these buses that looked like they had been attacked by helicopter gunships or something like that, and there were bodies spilling out onto the road and injured people lying there. There was a moment when I was trying to photograph some of that and I saw this car that had been shot, sort of sideways in the road. I saw a body in the road, and I thought it was an Iraqi soldier or something. We got closer, and I'm looking through the lens to photograph it, and I take a couple of pictures, and I realized that that body was not a soldier; it was a little kid, and he was still alive. That was really hard. I yelled. You're in a convoy of vehicles, and I yelled to the guys in my truck— "Hey, there's a kid laying in the road, and he's injured!" And I didn't have the power to make anybody stop in this huge convoy. So I shot a couple pictures, and there was nothing I could do. I couldn't stop; I couldn't get out. That was my ride, and I had them radio somebody. I don't know what happened to that kid.

So we kept moving forward, little by little. Some days it would seem like we didn't make any progress at all; other days we were making a lot of progress. One day I think we went through Al Kut, and there was gunfire raining on the side of the road for what seemed like hours. Finally, at some point, these Iraqis started coming out of the woodwork. There were maybe 30 or 40 of them that came out and surrendered. Part of me thought, "We're just throwing a lot of ammunition out, and I don't know what's coming back." You can't tell what's incoming. So to actually see that there were people out there, I was thinking, "Oh, OK, there's people out there, and they must be shooting at us." But at times it was really hard to tell. Other times—there were several times when it was easier to tell. There was a time when there was a whole battery of these Russian rockets that were launched, and they came zinging over our heads. There were times when mortars went off right near us.

It's a little bit tedious at times, and you're thinking, "What am I doing here? What good am I doing?"—especially on the days when you didn't have yield from it as a journalist. You lived through that day, and for what? I did stupid things, like, one day, I had my sat phone, and I was trying to transmit pictures, and I ran the computer over the top of it, and the whole screen blanked out, and I was thinking, "Oh, man, you might as well sign off." If you lose one piece of equipment, you're like what they would call "battle ineffective." When the big dust storm went on for days, the paper wanted pictures to represent that. The day it finally cleared, the U.S. pushed forward.

Then there was a whole battle pause. I still don't know the root of it. You're embedded so deep, you don't know why. Everybody stopped for two days. I suppose it was supply lines or whatever. We finally got back on track, and I was lucky enough on the day it cleared to be pulled over next to a unit that was firing artillery shells that go 12 miles or something like that. I made a good picture that showed clear skies and these guys recoiling from artillery. They put that on the front page the next day.

* * *

David Baumann, *Staff Photographer**

The Press-Enterprise, Riverside, California

When we were in Kuwait, waiting for the military to decide who was going to be embedded with whom and when we were going to get shipped out to our base camps to get the whole thing started, we were told that the military would supply us adequate training in order to deal with the potential weapons of mass destruction attack—that is, scud missiles with chemicals. We were in Kuwait at the official media hotel for over a week, when we were all prepared for just one or two nights, but the military was dragging in their efforts to get everything together and make it happen. It was sort of "hurry up and wait." So, in addition to our news organizations spending literally thousands of more dollars in a stand-off before we even got embedded with these guys, things that the military said that they would take care of hadn't been taken care of yet. This is all about the WMD.

They kept suggesting to us, "Yes, we will train you how to properly prepare for the weapons of mass destruction." They called the chemical suits they gave us "NBC suits"—not National Broadcasting Company—"nuclear, biological, chemical." Well, when they finally got around to saying, "OK, we're going to train you now," it involved 30 minutes out on the tennis courts of this Kuwait Hilton where they said, "This is a gas mask. This is how you put it on. This is a chemical suit. You've each been issued one. And they come vacuum-sealed. But don't open it, because you'll spoil it. You want to keep it in the sealed container. You only open it when you absolutely need it. We're going to have Joe Mo here show you how to put it on. Zip zip zip. You're ready to go. Go to war."

The next day we were on buses being taken to our respective base camps. I went to a camp called Camp Betio with the gas mask that we wore on our sides 24 hours a day. Literally slept with it. Never took it off. And our NBC suits, which we carried on our persons at all times, because you only have x amount of seconds to get into these things. Not even a minute. When the alarm went off, you had to be ready. The military was all about being prepared and telling you they're going to tell you how to do stuff if you need to do it. I got 30 minutes on a tennis court on how to save my life in the event of a WMD attack. I can guarantee you I spent all that night in our hotel room practicing putting on and off this gas mask.

* * *

*David Baumann is a second-generation newspaper photographer who knew from the time he was a child that he wanted to follow his father's footsteps into photojournalism. Iraq was his first experience in covering war.

John Quiñones, *Coanchor**

ABC News PrimeTime Live

I wind up doing a lot of the more emotional and touchy-feely stories for *PrimeTime*—stories involving human rights. The one story that I remember vividly was just a day or two after the war started. We crossed the border from Kuwait into southern Iraq, and it was very tense because I wasn't embedded. I was on my own with my camera crew and a van that had tape on it that said "Television—TV." But the problem with that was, of course, that anybody could get a van and, if you were terrorists, could claim to be TV journalists and attack the American forces. So everybody was suspicious of us—the allied forces (the British and American forces), as well as the Iraqis who might well presume that we were not who we said we were. So it was very touch and go.

We snuck in and out of Iraq from Kuwait. We had spent a lot of time in Kuwait waiting for the war to start. When it started, we then were able to talk our way into southern Iraq, in a place called Um Qasr, which is a port city at the very southern end of Iraq. One of the first stories we did was about the children in that region. I gathered about a dozen kids in that little town and asked them what they thought about the United States, who they thought we were, and whether they had any idea what freedom really means, and democracy. They were all eight and nine and ten years old. It was a real insight as to what they thought of Americans. The misconception was that everyone was rich in America. Freedom—they really didn't know what freedom meant because they had never really been totally free. Freedom of speech, freedom to write what you want, freedom to do what you want and criticize the government in power—they were totally unfamiliar with that.

Then we went to their homes. You get some real insight looking into somebody's refrigerator. It was Diane Sawyer who suggested that I do that, to try to get a sense of what people live on day to day. Now this was at a time the U.S. had just gone in. Things seemed to be under control, and, compared to today, it was relatively safe. Reporters could actually wander in neighborhoods. I remember walking all over Um Qasr with my cameraman and producer, and, obviously we didn't go there at night, but we did that during the day, and now I think it would be highly risky to do that.

Anyway, we went into people's living rooms, kitchens, and saw that they really had very little to live on. Maybe a piece of meat—it was in short supply. They had a lot of rice and potatoes and that was basically it. So that story sticks out.

*John Quiñones, a Texas native and graduate of the Columbia Graduate School of Journalism, was one of the most experienced war journalists in this study, having reported extensively from Central America during the 1980s. He reported from southern Iraq for ABC News shortly after the war began in 2003.

I think the kids, the children and what they had to say about the American invasion and the American presence there, what they wanted, was touching.

* * *

Jules Crittenden, *Reporter (Now City Editor)* *

Boston Herald

A very pivotal moment for me was April 6, 2003. The unit that I was in had been in pretty regular combat for the prior week. I had had a number of close calls, not all of which I fully realized at the time. Sometimes you don't realize for quite some time afterwards exactly how bad a situation could have been. But, in any case, I had found out the night before that Michael Kelly was dead. Then I found out that day that David Bloom was dead. Kelly was in a Humvee that came under fire and went into a canal, and he drowned. Bloom had an embolism, although, at the time, I was told by a staff officer that they thought that he might have had a concussion from being too close to a main gun going off, which would be the big cannon on a tank, because he had been on the thunder run, the first thunder run through southern Baghdad. David Zucchino's book *Thunder Run*—it's definitive about Second Brigade, which I was attached to, and the taking of Baghdad, April 5 through 8. I was on the second thunder run, the second part of his book. I wasn't on the first one.

So I just found out that these two guys were dead. On March 11, the day that we were embedded with the units, we all formed up at the Hilton hotel south of Kuwait City, and they processed us, and they put us on buses. The bus I was placed on was going with the Second Brigade of the Third Infantry Division. I was with A Company, 4/64 Armor Regiment, which is also called Task Force 4/64 because they reconfigure them—they put all kinds of other units with them when they actually go to war. That was part of the Second Brigade of the Third Infantry Division. It was a tank company.

On the bus going to Second Brigade, Bloom was sitting in the front seat, I was sitting in the second seat, and Michael Kelly was sitting in the seat behind me. And first I'm talking to Dave, and we're chatting and showing pictures of wife and kids and this kind of stuff. A little later on, Kelly taps me on the shoulder. Kelly actually lived just north of Boston. And he said, "Oh, you're from the *Boston Herald*. I live outside the city." We talked about baseball, the

---

*Jules Crittenden is a mid-career journalist who, though not a veteran, grew up in Southeast Asia around U.S. military personnel during the Vietnam War. He got a taste of war reporting when he covered the tensions between India and Pakistan in Kashmir. He was present as an embedded reporter early in the Iraq war when an American tank fired on the Palestine Hotel in Baghdad, accidentally killing two journalists.

Globe/Herald rivalry, and various other things. I saw him again just briefly a couple of days before he was killed, at a scene of a battle in a place called Al Hindiya, a very pleasant kind of meeting, kind of in a lull in the fighting. He came along in a vehicle, and we said hello and chatted a bit.

I found out in the space of about 12 hours that both of these guys were dead. And I knew that, the next morning, we were attacking Baghdad. We were going to go in and take the palaces, and the unit I was with was leading that assault. It was a two-pronged assault. Task Force 1/64, which was First Battalion of the 64th, would lead first, and then they would split off and go to the place where the big crossed swords monument is. This is western Baghdad, and that is like a big parade ground. It's all part of the Green Zone now. And we, Task Force 4/64, would go straight ahead into the palaces, which is the heart of the Green Zone. And this was the palace complex. This was the heart of the regime. This is where all the government buildings were, all the biggest palaces. There was one that had these enormous heads of Saddam Hussein on top of it, and that was where we went.

Now our expectation was that the Iraqis had been falling back and falling back and that Baghdad was where they were going to do it to us, the great "mother of all battles," and they were going to trap us in the streets. So we fully expected a very intense fight there. Prior to this, I had been enjoying the action. It wasn't the first time for me. It was much heavier intensity, but I was past all of my initial jitters. I'd found that I can function here. I actually enjoy this. This is like the most intense work that I've ever done. And you kind of get past a lot of your issues. But when I learned that these guys were dead, I thought, "OK, things happen in threes, you know." Literally, I started going through all the threes that I knew in my head because I thought, "I'm sitting between two dead men right now. And we're going into Baghdad tomorrow. I'm going to get killed tomorrow." I felt bad about it, because I knew that they [Kelly and Bloom] had kids, and that was the part that was most upsetting, the idea that their kids were just finding out about this, and I thought, "Well, now I'm going to do this to *my* kids."

I was depressed about that. But there was no question about what I was going to do. This was what I was here for. I was riding with these guys who are all 20-year-old kids who I had been living in very close proximity to, sharing everything, and we had been through a number of fights together. I had already picked up a rifle in one case, although I did not have to use it. We were being ambushed, and I picked up a rifle because, if the vehicle was hit and we had to get out, I didn't intend to get out of it without a rifle. I mean, we were in the middle of a bad situation.

So I was very strongly bonded with these guys, with the idea that, if they went and got killed, I did not want to have to face myself if I had stayed back and lived. That's sort of how far into all this I was at that time. This is a different thing. I had committed myself to seeing it through with them and did not want to break that commitment. I had been in other conflict situations that weren't my conflict situations, but this one was. This is a war that I supported. This was my army, and now these were guys that I had lived with. So I had a strong sense of identification. And I also had a sense that what was going to happen tomorrow was the biggest thing that I would probably ever cover in my life, the taking of Baghdad. In retrospect, it looks a little bit different because it was really just the start of much more. At the time, we thought this was going to be a bloodbath.

I'd been looking at the tanks when I got the news about Bloom. I'd been looking at the tanks that made the run into Baghdad the day before, the first thunder run, and they were just full of holes. They were shot up very badly. They had taken a lot of heavy fire. They had lost a tank. One or two guys were killed. I was looking at these vehicles, and I realized the vehicle that I'm in is a lot softer than these tanks. If we get hit like this or like this or like this, we're all dead. They had big gouges in them, and they have very thick armor. It's like, "That hit goes right through us." So that was my expectation. What I mentally decided in my head was, "I'm going to get killed tomorrow."

Having decided that, it was a very liberating kind of thing because, at that point in time, you could focus on the matter at hand. You set everything aside, all the depression or feelings of guilt and that sort of thing associated with my family. I didn't call my wife that night, or my editors. At that point it was like, "OK, I'm just going." Everything sort of lifts off of you at that point, and you can just do what you want to do, what you need to do, and you don't care any more. It's a very interesting dynamic that I think has got to be a very fundamental, primeval mechanism. I don't know.

Something was kind of interesting after we left. This is something Zucchino writes about in detail, and I didn't find out about it for another four days. The assembly area where this assault took off from was about five miles south of Baghdad. The whole brigade was there. After our column left in the morning, it was attacked. Now there were two reporters—there was a German and a Spaniard—and they had chosen to stay behind. They had called their bosses—this is all documented in the stories at the time as well as Zucchino's book—and said, "It's too dangerous. We're not going to make this run. We're not going into Baghdad. We're going to stay back here in what's called the TOC—the tactical operations center—and listen to the radios, but we're not going in."

I guess around 10:00 in the morning, they're hearing on the radios that we have taken the palaces and accomplished everything that we set out to do, and they are eager to file now because they don't want to get beaten by those of us who are actually there. And they finally get permission—"OK, you can go and report now"—because there are security issues related to when you can report certain things. So they were now told by the operations officer, "OK, now you can go report." They go outside and they set up their sat phones on a Humvee, and, at that moment, an Iraqi antitank missile comes, hits the vehicle, and kills both of them as well as two soldiers.

The point is—and I guess the lesson of the whole thing was—that, in a place like that, you really can't second-guess your options. You've got to use your brains and common sense, but, at a certain point you have to accept what's coming to you, whatever it may be. That is the deal.

* * *

Laura Rauch, *Western Regional Photographer**

Associated Press

I was with the First Marine Division. The unit I was with was India Company, 3rd Battalion, 7th Marine Regiment. I remember sitting on the border of Kuwait waiting to deploy, and everyone was so young, and none of them had combat experience. And, of course, you don't know what's going to happen when you cross the border. There were all sorts of religious services going on. One guy wasn't a Catholic priest, but somehow he was able to give Catholic communion, so the Catholics were all lined up with him, and he was trying to give communion. The chaplain for the battalion was trying to give a service. It wasn't storming, but it was really clouding up like it was going to storm, and I wish I had written all this down because it was such an emotional time for these guys.

In the middle of all these services, they got the call to go. They never got to finish, and it scared the hell out of them! You could see everyone running. It was difficult for them because there wasn't even time for religion. There wasn't even time for God. The U.S. military had sent down the orders, and they were going into Iraq. These were really young men—18-, 19-year-olds—and everyone bugged out. We were already set in position to move. They had been staged in Kuwait, and then the call came in the middle of the night to move up to the border at any moment, so we were sitting up at the border for two or three days, waiting for the orders to move across the line of demarcation. We're sitting there, and the order comes, and I remember just the sheer terror in their eyes. And again, no time for religion.

* * *

*As a mountain climber, Laura Rauch had spent considerable time in the Himalayas. Her knowledge of that region of the world led her to believe she had something to offer professionally after the attacks of September 11, 2001. She covered the war in Afghanistan, then Iraq, but found covering the presidential election of 2004 even more exhausting. She was interviewed while at Stanford University as a Knight Journalism Fellow.

Dean Staley, *Reporter**

KSTP-TV, Minneapolis, Minnesota
(Now Anchor, Northwest Cable News)

One of the big things that people want to talk about when you get back is, "Were you scared?" One of the scariest moments—and I bring it up only because it was a compelling moment for us—was when we were still camped in the desert in Kuwait, before the actual fighting had started. The U.S. was massing troops there, getting ready for the invasion. We were in our tent about 10 o'clock in the evening. There's a meeting going on, what they call a battle update briefing. They were talking about the condition of the equipment, the condition of supplies, oil, all of those things that they were going to need for the invasion. All of a sudden, machine-gun fire sounded like it was right outside the tent.

We had a big earthen berm that they had built up with bulldozers around the encampment. We were always ready and always training with these people for a terrorist attack. You knew that there were people that wanted to hurt American soldiers. Those people generally knew where American soldiers were. They knew where the encampments were. We had patrols and people out in the middle of the night with their night vision goggles watching the perimeter of the camp. The way into the camp was a very secure built-up berm, so no one could get into the camp with a car bomb.

All of a sudden, we hear this machine-gun fire, and it's just "tat tat tat tat tat," and it's loud. And everyone's screaming, "Hit the floor! Hit the floor! Get down!" So everyone is on the floor of the tent, and no one quite knows what to do except for a couple of people who are experienced Army Rangers. We had some experienced soldiers with us. A lot of the soldiers were young, 18, 19 years old. Very quickly, everyone got out of the tent, one at a time, and went into the survival trenches, which were dug around the perimeter of the tents. That was the place we spent a lot of time later when there were scud attacks. When there were scud missiles incoming, everyone would get down there with their chemical suits with their gas masks on anticipating some sort of an explosion nearby and a chemical cloud coming over the camp. This was still in Kuwait.

So you find yourself [there] in the middle of the night with all the lights out, pitch black. You see the stars. One of the soldiers in the trench had a radio,

---

*Dean Staley did his first work as a journalist when he wrote for his elementary school newspaper. In college, he discovered an affinity for television news and, after graduation, worked his way to progressively larger media markets. Iraq was his first war, though not his first experience in covering tragedy. Among other notable stories, he reported on the massacre at Columbine High School.

and he was communicating with the command post: "They're inside the berm. There's a dozen of them, and we don't know where they are." We're just sitting there, and we didn't have weapons. Everyone around us had weapons, but me and my photographer were just sitting there, waiting. And really, you're just waiting to get shot. You're just waiting for someone to run up to the trench and start spraying people with machine-gun fire.

We followed the story throughout the night. A Kuwaiti citizen had rammed the berm in his car, and the soldiers opened fire on him because it was clear that there was something wrong. He had been speeding 70 miles an hour toward the thing. He was the only person in the car. In the initial confusion, there had been reports that there had been a dozen of them, and, because he rammed the berm in a place that wasn't lighted, it wasn't clear whether he had rammed the berm and then a bunch of people in that car jumped out and went over the berm and were inside the camp, so . . . Later it turned out there was only one of them. They tracked him down, got him in custody. He had been wounded, but not killed. They never really determined, as far as we could tell, whether he was intentionally trying to hurt people in the camp. He didn't have any explosives in the car. It was one of the most terrifying moments I've had.

* * *

Moises Saman, *Staff Photographer**

Newsday, Long Island, New York

The most dramatic story that comes to my mind is being arrested during the war and being in a very stressful situation. But there's amazing stories that we encounter every day. That's the nature, a lot of times, of working in war zones. It's such a stressful situation almost on a daily basis. But I guess the most dramatic would be being arrested and put in prison for several days without really knowing what the outcome would be, knowing that there were many people worried and being in a lot of danger and not being able to tell anybody that you're ok or not.

We were arrested a week into the war. The reporter that I was working with and I had been in Baghdad since late February, leading up to the war. About a week before the actual war started, our visa was denied and we were asked to leave the country. After really thinking hard about it and having several discussions with our editors, we decided that, if we were to leave, there was no way of coming back because the borders would be closed. It was impossible to get a

---

*Moises Saman drained his savings to finance his own way as a photographer to cover his first war. At *Newsday*, where he has spent his career to date, his niche is to cover conflict. Just after the start of the Iraq war, he and a colleague were held as prisoners of the Iraqi government in the infamous Abu Ghraib prison. Born in Peru, he is partly of Palestinian heritage.

renewed visa at that point. We could just try to stay under the radar a little bit. We decided to stay in Baghdad because that was our mission, to cover the war from Baghdad from the Iraqi perspective.

A week into the war, we were tracked down, and I guess arrested on suspicion of being spies or working for the government or working for any kind of intelligence service. We were taken to Abu Ghraib prison, which I'm sure you've heard about by now. It took about eight days until things got figured out after very strong international pressure. Everyone from the Red Cross to the Vatican to even the Palestinian Authority got involved—because of my Palestinian background, I suppose. We were released eight days later and deported to Jordan.

We had a unique perspective that a lot of people, I guess, didn't have to see. It was actually quite ironic that, even during the worst of the time we were there, nothing even close to what went on there under the Americans happened to us. It was tense, and there were some moments when there was some screaming and yelling, but there was never any physical harm or humiliation or to the degree to what some Iraqi inmates have to go through under Americans.

* * *

Dennis Anderson, *Editor**

Antelope Valley Press, Palmdale, California

When I went back to Kuwait and Iraq last year in 2004, it was to catch up with the unit that I had covered for more than a year through their stages of preparation and their arrival in country. I stayed with them for about a month after we arrived in the Iraqi Freedom theater and then in Iraq. My interest was how were they doing. I had more or less maintained continuous email contact. I think I was as interested as anything in these fellows from the National Guard that I covered. They reminded me of what the old army might have been like in WW II. I raise that because, for one thing, they trained at a place called Camp Roberts on the central California coast, which had been built in 1941, and it remains a kind of museum piece that kind of looks like the army looked like in 1941. It was deeded over to the National Guard sometime after the Korean War, and it looks like the kind of place that you'd see in very old war movies from the 1940s and 1950s. It looks like that now. And that had a shaping effect on these particular soldiers. They ranged in age from 19 years old to 59. That made them different than the regulars, the Marines, and infantry, whose average age would be about 21. . . .

---

*Dennis Anderson, the only editor in chief among the participants in this study, is a military veteran. His newspaper is located in a community closely affiliated with the military. He went to Iraq on two reporting missions. His son served as a marine in the Iraq war.

April '04 was a terrible month, as it turned out. I had said to [my newspaper's] publisher and the general manager, "I want to go back [to Iraq] for a few weeks to see how things have gone with our guys." The publisher, in a cheerful way, said, "Is it safer now?" And the appropriate reporter's answer is, "Oh, sir, it's much safer. You know, we've only got 25 attacks a day, down from 77. They captured Saddam. I think it should be all right." And he says, "Well, I want you to stay in Kuwait," or words to that effect. No reporter wants to be told to go to the goal line and then don't go past. But, arriving there, it turned out that things were not good at all because, on March 29, the contractors got ambushed, shot, burned, strung up, desecrated, and a new war was on. . . .

I got back in around April 2 . . . I'm returning to the unit, and this unit is ready to go home. They have sweated out their year in the sandbox, and they've been in and out of the box, and they've been in and out of harm's way. People have been sent home loopy, depressed, distressed, divorced, strange, and also wounded for evacuation, and everybody's ready to count their blessings and get out, and then this thing happened in Fallujah.

I'd managed with the guy who was the executive officer of the company to angle a ride into Baghdad. We went down to Kuwait International to get on a C-130 and fly to Baghdad. There's a lot of bureaucracy and sleeping in tents and waiting for people to yell out the manifest. . . . We're trooping onto the C-130 some while around 1:30 at night, and, as we're getting ready to board, the air force manifest guy says, "We have human remains on board. Any objections?" Everybody kind of swallows. "No, I don't think so." A C-130 has its own cavernous interior, and there's an eight-foot steel casket lashed to the center spar of the aircraft, and the instructions from the load master were "Don't put your feet on that." And you're damned right, don't put your feet on that. . . .

Baghdad International was under attack with mortars and rockets. We were coming in to land, and we hurried out of the airplane. April 6 had been the Marine reentry into Fallujah, about a week after this thing happened with the contractors. It was a fight, and it was at peak at that moment.

Baghdad airport is just a bunch of bunkers and netting and contractors milling around and people waiting for flights into there and flights out of there, and it looks chaotic, like a chaotic war movie. It was bizarre because we're in a transit area, which is kind of a hardened hangar, and there was an enormous big-screen TV of Condi Rice giving a 9/11 Commission talk. It had an Orwellian feel to it. It was weird.

And then we heard this enormous "boom!" You develop your ear: "That's not a 105. No, it's not. It's bigger than that." I ran outside the hangar. We saw this enormous column of smoke going up. That was the Kellogg Brown [&] Root convoy. Remember the guy Hamill, the truck driver? He was the civilian trucker who got kidnapped for a couple weeks? That was that one. So we were standing there on the rampart, looking at this thing that looked like 75,000 gallons of fuel going up. It kind of looks like the *U.S.S. Arizona* at Pearl Harbor. We're going, "OK, I guess we're in the shit now. OK, fine, good." We didn't know that that was Hamill, that that was KBR. It was a lot of smoke and "boom." But 10 or 12 Americans who were killed in that attack—that was a big ambush—their bodies were thrown in the ditches. And Hamill—they wanted to kidnap an American. These were inept kidnappers because a couple of weeks later he escaped in Tikrit. But you had the sense at that moment that things were kind of coming unglued. They "black lined" the roads, which meant they were having so many IEDs [improvised explosive device attacks] and ambushes going on at that point they just said, "Stop the travel."

. . . I wanted to get up the road to a place called Al Assad, because we had some Marine Corps air wing guys from Edwards Air Force Base out here that I wanted to talk to. I also wanted to go to a place called Anaconda, where some more guys from Palmdale were just getting in, to begin their tour. But I couldn't go anywhere because they'd stopped all the transit, so we were marooned a little bit. We had no rations or approvals or billeting or anything, and it's about 125 degrees. We all murmured about it like Indian chiefs and said, "Well, whatever the next flight is out of here, we're gonna take that and go wherever that might go." Happened it was back to Kuwait, and I thought, "That might not be the worst thing to get back to Kuwait, file stories, and try to get another flight in when this crazy battle is over."

Got back to Kuwait, filed the stories, and now it's Easter Sunday, and that's when the insurgents started beheading people. I had about six days left to be in country. I'm on a short leash from the publisher because he said, "I want you to go there, and I want you to come back. I want you to spend exactly the time that we say, because I'm not letting go of you for four months like we did last year. We have management considerations here." So [I had to go home and] I didn't get my second bite of the apple.

I got home on a Friday. On April 6, Staff Sergeant Allan Walker of our hometown, Palmdale, had been KIA in the Ramadi ambush. He was the oldest marine in the ambush, 28 years old. He was the senior sergeant in charge. Nobody particularly suffered because there was such a crossfire of RPGs [rocket-propelled grenades] that blew up all the Humvees; everybody was dead in a minute or two. So, whoever was in the casket on my trip into Baghdad, it was a one in 12 chance that it was my townsman Allan Walker. It could have been him just as easily as anybody else. I had left on my trip a couple of weeks before to find out how the Palmdale and Lancaster combat truckers were doing, and I came home to find one of my townsmen had been killed. I was there for his funeral on Sunday. I don't know that I wasn't riding in or out of Baghdad with him a week earlier, and that was the steel casket. It was one of the 12 from this particular day. I was startled to my foundations that the remains in that particular aircraft could have been [those of] Allan Walker, whose parents were, like myself, Marine Corps parents. We have since become extended family to one another.

* * *

Cheryl Diaz Meyer, *Staff Photographer**

The Dallas Morning News

I photographed the Marines of the 2nd Tank Battalion after an incident where they had accidentally killed a minibus full of people—civilians and children. We had had a very difficult day the previous day. We had four men killed and 17 injured, and we sustained three rocket attacks in the midst of the camp where the leadership of the battalion was staying. So everybody was on edge. A couple of vehicles had tried to run the checkpoint immediately next to the camp, and they turned out to be full of ammunition. Between these two vehicles was a minibus, and they had fired warning shots to the minibus to indicate that it should stop, and the driver, probably anxious and nervous and not really knowing what to think, kept driving through the checkpoint. And they shot up the bus. By the next morning, the bus was full of blood and bodies and children with bullet holes in their heads. The only things that were left standing in the bus were the chickens.

So I photographed the aftermath of this, and, sadly for me, it caused a lot of pain to the families of the marines who I was with. I had contextualized what had happened, tried to tell that situation as honestly as possible because, in reality, I had felt everything that they had felt. I was as anxious as they were. The previous night, I had had sort of a meltdown during the rocket attacks. So I knew what they were feeling, and I knew why that accident had happened, but, in the end, the families, the wives of the marines who I was with, they felt, really, that I had done them wrong. So people whom I had grown very fond of and whom I owed my life to, whom I would like to still be in contact with, I'm not in contact with. That saddens me.

I had committed to them to tell the good, the bad, and the ugly, and they knew that from the beginning—that I was a journalist. I wasn't pretending to be their pal. I was there to tell the story. Most of the time the story was a story of hero-ism. I saw a lot of good. They were very kind to me and hospitable, and they were great hosts in the midst of a very stressful situation. I felt really stuck between a rock and a hard place. I did my job, and, in the end, it caused a lot of heartache. That comes with my work, but, in this instance, it leaves me with a lot of sadness, I guess.

---

*Cheryl Diaz Meyer says that no one who studied photojournalism with her at Western Kentucky University would have predicted that she would one day cover war. But she went to Afghanistan and later shared the Pulitzer Prize for her coverage of the war in Iraq.

Afterword

A Personal Odyssey

My own fascination with journalism began in ways similar to those experienced by Barry Bearak, Otis Sanford, Peter Bhatia, and other journalists represented in this book. I can't remember whether the love of reading or the love of writing came first. For as long as I can remember, I was stopping off at the public library that was midway on my walk to and from elementary school in Midwest City, Oklahoma. I remember loving biographies and stories about animals the most. I would sit fascinated for a couple of hours at a time reading about the adventures of Wyatt Earp and Wild Bill Hickock or poring over the old Jack London stories, *The Call of the Wild* or *White Fang*. One of my favorite books was Walter Farley's *The Black Stallion*. And, under the Christmas tree each year, were two or three new Hardy Boys mysteries like *The Tower Treasure* or *The House on the Cliff*. These stories would transport me to magical worlds and light a fire in me to travel and experience as many new places and new adventures as I could.

But also, for as long as I can remember, I loved writing my own stories. I would squirrel myself away in my bedroom—which at various times in my boyhood also served as a cavalry fort, medieval castle, and even a photographic studio and darkroom—put pen to paper and start crafting my own stories of brave dogs, horses, and boys who loved them. It didn't matter that the stories were never read by anyone but me, and sometimes Mom and Dad. It was enough that I had imagined them, written about them, and let them take me on new adventures.

Without knowing it, I had begun a lifelong passion for the printed word, probably fostered by my mother, who was my first teacher at Jack and Jill Pre-School, and my father, who was my first editor. As a pioneering television executive in Oklahoma City, he knew a thing or two about words. The inspiration of those early years translated into three university degrees in journalism and more than a decade as a full-time working journalist with newspapers such as *The Oklahoman* and the *Dallas Morning News*. It was a career that began on a fine community daily in Oklahoma, *The Edmond Evening Sun*. I left full-time newspaper reporting to enter college teaching of journalism and mentor young writers and conduct research that I hoped would benefit future journalists. I have tried to do that at several fine universities including the University of Missouri, the University of Memphis, the University of Oklahoma, and a fine liberal arts school in Southern California, Azusa Pacific University.

As with other journalists, my love of reading and writing came from a deep curiosity about the world, especially the mysterious places of the world. I cannot say for sure why my passions took me in the direction of nonfiction rather than fiction, but I suspect it had something to do with an adolescent passion for photography that stays with me today. My dad had a home engraving workshop in the garage, and he let me turn it into a darkroom after my mother had enough of trying to get developing solutions out of my bedroom carpet. I came at photography via the magic of the darkroom and watching prints come to life in the developing tray. But I retained a love for it through the magic of the camera lens and of the permanent and often enigmatic visual record photography makes of life as we observe its all-too-fleeting moments. It may be that, as I was making those observations through the viewfinder of my Kodak Brownie and later my Nikon 35mm, I discovered that real life, in all its nonfictional nature, could be just as fascinating as the fictional stories I wrote as a kid.

Many years later, as an adult journalist at the 1995 scene of the Oklahoma City bombing, I would have occasion to weave visual and verbal storytelling together to chronicle that horrible chapter of American history. The event I remember the most vividly took place sixteen days after the April 19 bombing of the Murrah Federal Building. I was standing on the rubble of the building, next to what was left of the nine-story carcass. It was a few days before the building's remains were scheduled for demolition, so the Oklahoma winds didn't do the trick more dangerously. The event was a memorial honoring those who died and the many rescuers and volunteers who had spent long days and nights searching for bodies of the 168 who perished at the hands of at least two domestic terrorists. The midday sun was clear and illuminated a vast scene, producing near visual overload.

My story that day came almost totally from my own observations, and those were aided by the Minolta 35mm with telephoto lens that swung from my neck. I used it to record the up-close vignettes of the day that spoke volumes and became important pieces of my story: the rose dangling from the tripod of a tough Reuters photojournalist; the orange highway cone wrapped in gray duct tape and scarred with the black marks that might have been made by a frustrated fireman or two; the trio of stern construction hard hats looking on sadly from a blown-out five-foot window, four floors up in the Journal Record Building across the street. Their gaze was fixed on Murrah's carcass in front of them and the tomb it had become for so many of their fellow Oklahomans.

The wedding of words and pictures. That's how it should be, and that's how it has become in our world of media convergence. It is a marriage that, in the spring of 1995, brought me back to a fascination with both and rekindled in me a passion to be the kind of storyteller that would cause readers to say, "Your story made me feel like I was there." I believe that is one of the highest compliments any journalist can be paid.

I had been away from full-time reporting for several years, after having transitioned into teaching college journalism, but my visit to see my parents in Oklahoma City in April of 1995 brought me back to it. In the days following April 19, all of a stark sudden, the sometimes theoretical and abstract notions of the role of the journalist in American society became abundantly clear to me in a very real way. I was having breakfast on April 19 at a diner in Norman, about twenty minutes south of Oklahoma City, when I heard a distant sound—the blast that came at 9:02 a.m. on that Wednesday morning. I spent the day doing what thousands of other Oklahomans did: responding to calls for various kinds of help. I bought batteries, bottled water, and other items useful to the search and rescue operations at the Murrah Building site, and I drove them to designated drop-off points in Oklahoma City. I gave blood at the local Red Cross. But, at the end of the day, I was still wanting to do more, and then it hit me: although I had moved into college teaching, I was still a journalist, and everyone was hungry for information about what had happened and what it might mean for tomorrow and the day after that. So I called the editor at an area daily that I used to edit myself years before and asked if she needed help. "Yes!" was the response. "Can you come be here tomorrow at 8 a.m.?" I was there at 7:30, and I began on-site coverage of the search and rescue operations at ground zero, coverage that lasted for the next three weeks until the building was imploded. Beyond that, I covered the many memorials held around the city for the victims and their families, as well as the appreciation ceremonies for the thousands of rescuers and volunteers that came from across the country.

Apart from the misery that the tragedy inflicted on so many and the sadness it engendered in me personally as a native Oklahoman, the Murrah Building bombing represented a turning point in my professional life. Before

April 19, 1995, I had been toying with burnout, becoming more cynical about how the profession seemed to be giving into pressures from the business side, which were forcing out serious reporting and forcing in entertainment. Oklahoma City gave me the chance to commit to what I called "pure journalism" once again. By that I mean seeking honest answers to the honest, desperate, and legitimate questions people had. Journalists became a key part of the glue that held Oklahomans together after the bombing, by the daily information they provided about what was—and was not—happening and what it seemed to mean. What a privilege it was to be able to provide some of those answers to all those grieving readers, who seemed to cling to every word. if our stories helped transport readers to the scene and made them feel even more connected to each other, so much the better.

Events like this can also change the way you do business as a journalist, and that's exactly what happened for me. There were stories I covered that literally begged to be told in different and unique ways. When trying to find the human heart of the stories I wrote, I discovered what writer Walt Harrington later described as "intimate journalism." In the spring of 1995 in Oklahoma City, that sort of intimacy was not hard. But it caused my writing to take on new dimensions. Earlier I mentioned the memorial held on the building's rubble. That was an emotional day for me and for the many present at the scene. It was one of many times when I came face to face with the issue of journalists and the emotions they feel in covering tragedies. As I was leaving the site, I was overcome with the belief that this story needed to be told in a different way, that the inverted pyramid would not do it justice and would rob it of its meaning. Underneath, I felt that, most of all, I wanted to bring readers to this scene, so they could see what I saw and feel what the many were feeling on that day. As often happens to journalists who have just witnessed a momentous event, this story began writing itself as I sat down at my computer.

Jon Franklin, a former writer for *The Baltimore Sun*, has said on numerous occasions that, as he was writing his Pulitzer Prize-winning story "Mrs. Kelly's Monster," he realized the story was having a physiological effect on him. "It was like holding fire in my hands," he has said. When I read that passage years later from his book *Intimate Journalism*, I was stunned because that is exactly what happened to me as I wrote the story of this memorial in May of 1995. Before I knew, it was finished. When I began reading it over, I was surprised to find that I had written most of it not in the third person, which tradition dictates, but in the second person.

"You stand here . . . you see this . . . you remember this . . . you feel this . . ."

That is the natural language of a reporter who very much wants to bring others to the scene he or she has just witnessed. When you can do that with words, you get the feeling you have accomplished something important.

In this day of converged communication technology and corporate-owned media trying to please public shareholders with impressive quarterly profits, it is easy to lose site of what lures people into journalism and what can keep them there and keep them on fire for a long time. Despite what some critics say, journalists don't get turned on by developing biased and sensational stories that vent their personal views and sell as many newspapers as possible. In fact, those are all turn-offs for real journalists, as can be seen from several of the comments from working reporters quoted in the chapters of this book. What keeps journalists inspired is the chance—indeed the privilege—of being able to *commit pure journalism:* to seek answers to legitimate questions that caring people in a democracy need and have a right to know, to help us once again understand and feel for our fellow travelers on earth, and to enjoy the creative art of accurate reporting in the process.

It's a lot of fun.

Appendix 1

Covering Katrina
On Taking It Personally

By Michael Perlstein

New Orleans Times-Picayune

As the body count rose with Katrina's flood waters, each of us reached our own point of psychic overload, that inevitable moment when the ruination of our city became too much to bear.

Brian, the *Times-Picayune*'s hard-charging investigative reporter fresh from Iraq, broke down when a building collapsed in front of him as he took a cigarette break. Terri, our editorial page editor, cried quietly as we returned from the field with experiences that seemed too intimately tragic to reduce to standard news stories.

For me, the emotional needle jumped into the red when I bumped into New Orleans police chief Eddie Compass, a man I knew well, a friendly adversary for several years on my beat as the paper's criminal justice reporter.

We were in front of the Convention Center, where more than 15,000 people plucked from rooftops and foul water endured a second round of hell waiting for water, food, and rescue buses. When I caught up to him, Compass was charging toward the valet parking apron in front of Harrah's Casino, the makeshift command post established after police headquarters flooded.

Note: Reprinted with permission by *Reed Magazine*, Winter, 2006.

I grabbed him by the shoulders: "Hey chief," I said. The red-eyed, adrenalin-stoked police chief embraced me in a back-thumping hug. "It's going to be all right, man," he said. "We'll get through this." I'm not sure precisely which accumulated fears and sorrows triggered my reaction, but I began sobbing. He started crying too, and there we were, alpha dog of a gritty urban police department and veteran hard-news reporter, weeping openly in front of thousands.

Then I pulled out my notepad. My questions may not have been articulate, but I walked away with an exclusive interview of a key figure in the nation's worst-ever natural disaster. (I would ride another twist in the roller coaster with Compass two weeks later, when the mayor unexpectedly forced him to resign.)

As Katrina took aim at New Orleans, I assumed I would remain cool and professional whatever the toll. After all, I was hurricane-hardened. I had chased several, including Andrew when it slammed Franklin, Louisiana, in 1992. But as Katrina's epic tragedy unfolded, I was gradually overwhelmed by my city's descent into apocalypse: the freight-train roar of the wind; the insidious and unstoppable rising water; the haze of unchecked fires, widespread looting, and lawlessness; the masses of desperate evacuees; and, finally, death, depopulation, and military takeover.

Instinct and journalistic experience carried me for that harrowing, exhausting, but intensely wired first week, when it actually seemed plausible that my home for the past 20 years would become the next Atlantis.

Months later, my role in chronicling the city's uphill struggle to recover was a bit more deliberate, but one thing hadn't changed: There was no way to separate personal feelings from professional responsibilities. Our house had a blue tarp instead of a roof. I still drove past massive debris piles on my way to work. There were rank refrigerators littering our block. Entire neighborhoods were dark and empty. Most schools were closed, many of our favorite stores and restaurants were shuttered, tens of thousands of families—including some of our friends and most of our neighbors—were still scattered around the country.

Those of us who remain are forced to witness a once-great but always fragile city slowly strangled by government foot-dragging.

If any story exposed the myth that journalism is supposed to be objective, this was it. In my side gig as an instructor at Tulane University, I always tell students that, for all of journalism's lofty aspirations, objectivity is humanly impossible. A noble goal, perhaps, but a goal that can never be attained. Journalists can and should achieve fairness, balance, and accuracy in every story. But a reporter cannot block out his or her biases, experiences, and gut-level emotions.

The devastating one-two punch of Katrina and Rita hammered that lesson home for me, and it posed a new question: what's wrong with subjectivity in journalism anyway? It works in other Western democracies, where most newspapers openly stake out some wavelength along the political spectrum. It's intellectually honest. And it harkens to the best traditions of advocacy journalism.

If any place needed an advocate after August 29, it was New Orleans.

Our newspaper seemed to set the tone in our September 2 edition. It was the first after Katrina forced us to evacuate our flooded office, a handful of reporters and editors piled in the back of several delivery trucks. We were reduced to publishing only an online edition for three days. The banner headline read, "Help Us, Please." It was a quote from a desperate evacuee shown in a front-page photograph on her knees, wailing in prayer. I believe it spoke for all of us.

I know it spoke for me. While most of our staff evacuated to Houma and Baton Rouge to figure out the logistics of putting out a newspaper, I was part of a 10-person team that, weirdly, became the "New Orleans Bureau" of the New Orleans home-town newspaper. Without access to working telephones or computers, I was out of contact with my family for nearly three days. My wife and three young children—four-year-old Max, and one-year-old twins, Eli and Jackie—ended up nearly 1,000 miles away with family in Milwaukee, after evacuating in bumper-to-bumper traffic and riding out the storm's outer fringes in a flea-bag motel near Mobile.

Our rental property in Broadmoor, which housed four Loyola University students, was inundated with several feet of water. It now stands gutted. Even more nerve-wracking, I saw the water rise steadily in front of our own home in what is now known as "the wet part of Uptown," even though the house is five feet off the ground and five miles from the nearest levee breach. As I waded in through chest-deep water on day three, I knew the only way I could return was by boat. When I canoed home a week later, I was humbled to find only a trace of water on our floors from boat wakes and helicopter spray.

We were among the lucky ones. About one-third of my colleagues lost their homes and most everything in them. Many more saw their cars under several feet of water. My Nissan ended up high and dry, but looted. Like everyone along the Central Gulf Coast, we suffered cruelly random degrees of loss.

Working in the storm zone also presented physical and mental challenges. For the first few days, we endured fitful nights in relentless humidity, with little food and water and a maddening inability to communicate with the outside world. When our hygiene reached crisis levels, we bathed by sneaking into a stranger's backyard swimming pool. Things got better after we scrounged some military MREs, a generator to operate box fans and laptops. But somehow our jobs only seemed to get tougher. And more vital.

As our editorial team worked through those first three days after the storm without a printed edition—the first gap in the paper's 168-year history—our website logged an unheard-of 30 million hits. For evacuees scattered around the country, we were a critical thread to the home they left behind. For the rest of the world, we felt an obligation to show that New Orleans was in dire crisis, that the slow government response cost lives, and that our longstanding neglect of the poor had created Third World conditions in a First World country.

Even the broadcast big-foots dropped all pretense of detachment. When Ted Koppel grilled now-disgraced former FEMA Director Michael "Heckuva Job" Brown on *Nightline*, he asked incredulously, "Don't you guys watch television? Don't you guys listen to the radio?"

It seemed that virtually every journalist who descended on the story was overcome by the same impulse. As the crowds began swelling at the Convention Center, reporters were besieged by hungry and exhausted people asking questions like, "Why aren't they sending help? Can you please tell people what's going on down here?" We vowed to do just that.

The first story I co-wrote after we evacuated our offices was about the frenzied mass-looting of a Wal-Mart—by criminal cops as well as opportunistic citizens. The scene was unnerving, at times truly scary, and, in the middle of it all, we managed to become fringe participants in our own story.

Alongside people wheeling out flat-screen TVs and grabbing fistfuls of jewelry, there were others who were careful only to take what they needed to survive: water, food, diapers, medicine. We quickly drew a distinction. Looting for profit was stealing. Looting for survival was foraging. Like the foragers, we didn't know how we were going to eat and drink in the coming days, so we debated whether to grab a cart of supplies. We finally decided to take some necessities, but only after cataloguing the items so we could pay for them later. We actually had the cart out the door when Doug MacCash, the *Times-Picayune* art critic, reopened the debate: Sure, we could justify our actions, he said. But why put ourselves in a position of having to justify anything? We voted unanimously to leave the merchandise behind and worry about feeding ourselves later.

And the story kept skirting the line. I joined tense boat rescues, putting down my notepad to hold crying babies as they were handed to me. I pieced together the chaotic evacuation of the city's 6,400-inmate prison, and the 14 escapees the sheriff tried to cover up. And I accompanied state troopers following up on days-old 911 calls to search for bodies in muck-encrusted houses.

Of course, there were moments when our energy flagged, especially in that first week. But with each trip to the Superdome or Convention Center, we were re-energized by the desperation of mostly poor, mostly African American citizens begging us to tell the outside world of their plight. Police officers begged us to tell the same story. So did firefighters and doctors and elected officials. Many of them still are.

The woeful response to the catastrophe reminded me of a running debate I had during my freshman year at Reed with Ali Raza ('84) in the game room of the since-bulldozed Coleman dormitory: Does "government" exist during Armageddon? I argued that it did, that survivors would look to the remnants of officialdom for direction. Ali maintained that the notion of a governing body would not survive such a societal deconstruction.

I still don't know the answer, but I met untold Katrina victims who openly questioned the existence of authorities as they languished for days without food or water. For those who perished, their bodies unclaimed on rubbish-strewn streets, we can only assume that, at some point in their final hours, all concept of man-made authority ceased to exist.

In many ways, the fact that hurricane victims were needlessly suffering helped me and my colleagues to forget our own hardships. At the end of each day, when we regrouped in the borrowed house we turned into a makeshift newsroom, we shared details of death. One body, that of an elderly woman, was covered with a sheet on a porch a few blocks away, where it remained untouched for a week. The day that two local cops committed suicide, including a public information officer many of us knew well, was especially ominous.

In between tragedies and stories about tragedies, we attended to personal matters. We checked on colleagues' houses, embarked on pet rescues in kayaks and canoes, tracked down family members and friends. We realized there were some people we would never see again: a favorite waiter, perhaps, or a grade-school reading buddy. The contours of our lives were stripped away, and now, months later, it is obvious that some of those touchstones will never return, not even to say goodbye.

That's not to say that covering the story of a lifetime hasn't been exhilarating at times. Contributing to the first draft on such a historic tragedy is a powerful thing. To be personally invested in the story only made it more so.

In journalism, the big stories often bring out strains of competitive tension that cut into the profession's unspoken code of courtesy, but all of that seemed to evaporate with this one. The journalistic mission of Katrina's aftermath was way too important to worry about scoops and bylines.

The camaraderie that was forged among the Katrina reporters, especially in our makeshift "New Orleans Bureau," hasn't gone away. I don't think it ever will. We still greet each other with back thumps instead of polite hand-shakes. Over a long lunch or after-hours cocktails, we fill in the blanks of those first war-like weeks.

If I had a chance to give it all back—the plaudits from peers, the national media appearances (I did CNN, MSNBC, NPR, and others), the gratitude from citizens—I would forgo every byline, every life-altering moment, in exchange for the pre-Katrina New Orleans. But it happened, and now I'm faced with the agonizing dilemma that so many New Orleanians are grappling with. Do I stay and help in the rebuilding process? Do I stick with the amazing story of a city's struggle to regain a semblance of its former glory? Or do I stake out a fresh clean start for my family, in a place where there are no flooded playgrounds and the strength of levees isn't on your mind every time a storm starts brewing in the Gulf?

For now, my wife and I have decided not to think about the bigger picture, at least not until the end of the spring, when Patty wraps up her academic year as a Tulane professor. In the meantime, this battered, waterlogged sinkhole continues to hit me with small reminders of why I stuck it out here for 20 years. One of them came on a night in mid-December, at Little People's Place, a hole-in-the-wall club in the impoverished but famously musical neighborhood called Treme. That night, I hooked up with composer Bruce Bennett (Reed '90) to see a new band called "Davis," named for front man Davis Rogan (also Reed '90), a hometown piano player with a raunchy but genius lyric wit.

A crowd of about 14 people—black and white, young and not-so-young—filled the joint. Strangers bought rounds of beers for the band, and for other strangers. Rogan served everybody red beans and rice. He let his sax player strut his formidable chops. The drummer went to town. Rogan improvised some hilarious Katrina lyrics and everyone danced. I still can't fathom how three Reedies ended up in a deep groove at the tattered edge of civilization in a mostly vacant neighborhood in a ruined city.

But I know it could only happen in New Orleans.

Appendix 2

Thirteen Unique Journalists

This journey into the minds of journalists began with a series of profiles of the thirteen journalists interviewed for this project. Their insights appear in two forms in this book. First, they are joined with insights from other journalists in chapters 1–8, and their observations are grouped around the themes of those chapters. Second, their observations are part of each of the following profiles, which show the uniqueness of each journalist. Each of these journalists emphasizes different aspects of the challenges confronting reporters, editors, producers, and news anchors, although they are responding to a similar set of questions, which look at such areas as the lure of journalism, the so-called "priesthood of journalists," worldviews, theory and ethics, journalists' ideologies and faith, how some journalists cope with being a celebrity, and other vexing issues confronting them today. These observations are gleaned from their many years in the news business and, in some cases, from the years following that, years spent teaching university and researching aspects of journalism. Indeed, some of these journalists have moved on to teaching the craft, while others remain fighting in the trenches of daily journalism. These journalists represent the worlds of print, broadcast, and even online journalism and come from both large and smaller media markets. They also represent different ages, genders, races, and political and religious ideologies. They all strive to keep their personal beliefs separate from their reporting, and they probably all realize how difficult that is at times. They all share a passion for telling stories accurately and engagingly and for making a positive difference in the world through good reporting and editing. These interviews were conducted during 2007, as each reporter took time from his or her busy schedule to reflect on the mind of a journalist.

Curiosity Pays Off With a Pulitzer

Barry Bearak

Foreign Correspondent, *The New York Times*

From Los Angeles to the Texas Panhandle to New York City and Afghanistan, Barry Bearak has covered an unbelievable range of stories in his career thus far. As a foreign correspondent for *The New York Times*, Bearak won a Pulitzer Prize for international reporting in 2002, and, in early 2008, he was headed to Johannesburg to codirect the South African Bureau of the *Times*.

It was this intense curiosity and desire to accumulate experiences from different spheres of life that drew Bearak into the news business in the first place. He has an offbeat way of framing that motivation, too.

"I suppose the opposite of original sin is original virtue, and I wish I could claim that I had some indomitable moral compass that pointed me toward journalism in order to right the wrongs of the world," Bearak says. "But my altruistic impulses—and I think I have plenty—mostly strengthened me over time. The original impulse was a yearning for experience—to see events and people up close—and to write about them for a living."

When thinking about reporters for *The New York Times, Miami Herald*, or the *Los Angeles Times*, all of which the Chicago native has reported for, the adjective "shy" does not readily jump to mind. Yet that is how Bearak has always felt about himself.

"I'm shy, and journalism has a way of compelling you out of your shyness," he confides. "Reporting is like a free pass into forbidden worlds, and deadlines are the whip that forces you to use the free pass. So journalism was a good fit for me. And, of course, you get paid to do it, which solves the problem of how to handle the bills."

After graduating from Knox College in Galesburg, Illinois, Bearak found he wasn't very career oriented, but he did understand that a person had to work for a living. So he took odd jobs, sorting mail at the Evanston post office and writing press releases for a life insurance association.

"Those weren't very fulfilling jobs," he recalls. "Newspaper work seemed so much more romantic than anything else that came to mind, but how do you get started? I was facing a skills deficit. I could write okay, using prose that tried to imitate the styles of Joseph Heller, Kenneth Patchen, Gay Talese, and a few other favorites. But, at the time, I couldn't write or report anything that resembled a clear-eyed newspaper story, so I did something very conventional, trading the good grades I had in college for a scholarship to the journalism school at the University of Illinois. That got me started."

Bearak has done so many interesting and fascinating stories over more than three decades, it's easy to lose track of some. One story that won a National Newspaper Writing Award was called "Visions of Holiness" and focused on a young woman named Theresa Werner in Lubbock, Texas, who was convinced she had experienced a personal encounter with God. She heard His voice loud and clear, and the occurrence changed her life and caused an uproar for the Catholic Church in this West Texas outpost.

This story serves as an appropriate springboard into Bearak's thoughts about attachment and detachment from reporting assignments and about his views on covering matters of faith. Bearak found himself face to face with both issues when, as a Jewish reporter covering the Catholic community in Lubbock, he also had to decide how close to get to the sources for that story, most notably Theresa herself.

As a young reporter, I often wanted to befriend sources I liked or admired. That's a dangerous trap. It's pretty obvious you shouldn't be writing about your friends, but it's just as dangerous to be writing about people you'd like to recruit as your friends. Over time, that problem sorted itself out. I simply drew the line: sources over here, friends over there.

As for other emotional attachments, that's an interesting thing. While I try very hard not to allow my personal beliefs—political or otherwise—to color my reporting, I don't curb my emotions. To the contrary, I think my visceral responses work to my benefit. I want to ramp them up, not tamp them down. I want to feel things as strongly as I can. My empathy is the road map to readers' empathy. If someone's hunger or pain or loss is bringing me to tears, I can use that emotion to make the reader feel the same thing.

Emotional attachment is not the only kind of connection that Bearak wrestles with, however. He has thought a lot about *professional* detachment, and he has come to a conclusion about it.

Your use of the word "detachment" makes me think of something else. Some reporters seem to put professional detachment on some sort of pedestal. I've heard the question asked, "If a man is dying at your feet, do you try to save his life or note the color of his lips?" Some journalists would say your job is to let the person die and record the death accurately. Not me. If I had to make that choice, I'd put my notebook away and try to save the life.

Fortunately, I've never had to make that kind of split-second decision. But I've many times come across people who are sick or injured, and I was their best hope for help. At those times, I've always found that I could have it both ways. I was able to report my story *and* get them medical assistance.

When journalists report on the subject of religion, Bearak feels they can find issues that connect with many readers, and they should not be shy about tackling these issues. He refers to them as "crossroads events" and calls them important.

"I don't know that journalists are tone deaf to religion, but they certainly have trouble playing the tune in newspapers," he says. "Daily newspapers aren't so good at the day-to-day things that pack most of the meaning into life. That would include religion, but it also includes love and family and friendship. I've always thought newspapers ought to do more with the cross-roads events in everyday lives: the day we had to put Mom in a nursing home; the day Joe quit the factory and opened a bait and tackle shop; the day Jack and Jill dropped their kid off at college; the day Bill decided to become a priest and the day Bill yielded to his doubts and dropped out of seminary. The joys and pains of everyday life."

Bearak says these are stories that should not be ignored: "These are really great stories, but, like most great stories, they're hard to do well. They need time and space. They need reporters and editors with talent and editors with patience."

To some degree, covering religion may be easier or harder depending on a journalist's location or beat, Bearak believes.

Religion, I think, is an easier topic for foreign correspondents. Like other beat reporters, foreign correspondents are at the mercy of news events. Wars, disasters, elections all have to be covered, but, during the course of a foreign posting (which usually lasts three or four years), correspondents are also expected to paint a mosaic of how the people in a region live. You could make a checklist of things to include in the mosaic. There are major social issues like schools, courts, police, healthcare, housing, and the like. At the same time, the mosaic ought to show what people are eating, reading, watching on TV, what their weddings and funeral are like. Religion is an obvious part of the mosaic.

As a foreign correspondent, Bearak is on the front lines reporting on international issues. He won a Pulitzer Prize for his reporting in Afghanistan and Pakistan in 2002, and he was back in that region again in 2007, producing front-page stories for the *Times*. So how does he see the popularity—or lack of it—of foreign news? "I like the quote from the movie *Spider Man*, when Peter Parker's uncle tells him, 'With great power comes great responsibility,'" Bearak says.

America has so much power that you'd hope its people would feel more of an obligation to be informed about international events. I can't overstate this: The world is depending on the United States for leadership, and the American people, through their willful ignorance, fail to take on this responsibility. And, of course, looking at an example like the invasion of Iraq, we hurt ourselves along with everyone else.

So how can foreign correspondents do a better job of "selling" the public on the importance of their stories? I think the best thing they can do is write the hell out of them, make them compelling so that a broader audience is swept into the words. But is that enough to cure what ails us? I don't think so. Part of life is a civics lesson, and Americans are flunking the course. If 9/11 wasn't enough of a wake-up call, one wonders what kind of noise needs to emerge from the alarm clock.

Does a reporter's personal political orientation enter into what gets reported or how it gets reported? Once again, Bearak provides an offbeat but insightful response:

One of the biggest biases among journalists is the bias toward the bigger story. If you have 100 reporters who are Democrats, and you gave them a choice of uncovering the corruption of a Democratic governor or a Republican lieutenant governor, 100 out of 100 would go after the Democrat. The bias is always to catch the bigger fish.

Of course, this hypothetical is artificial in the sense that journalists look under rocks for wrongdoing, and a Democratic reporter may be more likely to suspect that something is amiss under the Republican rocks. So that colors things too. As for pushing for change, I think liberals and conservatives equally push—just in different directions.

Some reporters worry that daily journalism puts too much focus on distinct events and neglects the larger picture. Others worry about the opposite. How does Bearak feel about this debate?

"When I think of daily journalism, I think of newspapers," he says "But even though a daily newspaper is likely to contain a lot of stories written in a mad scramble an hour before deadline, it may also contain articles that have been months in the works. Besides, large truths often come in small formats. Some stories are done by beat reporters who bring years of expertise to a subject, and daily stories sometimes have elements of brilliant crystallization."

The veteran reporter is impressed with so much of what he has seen in print, stories that represent both the smaller and larger elements of truth.

"I keep a file that I've labeled 'GWF' for the 'Great Writing File.' It's full of newspaper and magazine stories," he says. "There are some wonderful features in that folder—some of them done in a day—[features] that hold up over time because they contain larger truths about the human condition. Some of these stories are 30 years old and, like wonderful poems, they're as worth reading now as when they were published."

Good reporting should always have an ethical underpinning to it. Readers and viewers hope that journalists spend a lot of time considering ethical concerns and talking about ethics in their newsroom conversations. Bearak, however, gives journalism mixed grades on this, but he finds his own way of handling ethical dilemmas.

Gossip seems to run far ahead of ethics when it comes to newsroom conversations, but I'm the wrong one to ask. Though I've been a newspaper reporter for 30 years, I've spent very little time in newsrooms. Most often, I've worked in small bureaus, including one where I was the one and only reporter. When I run into an ethical conundrum, I usually thrash it out with my wife, Celia Dugger, who is one of the best journalists I know.

And I also have a network of close friends in the profession who are good to consult with. As far as journalists in general, I think the public is used to seeing a lot of scummy behavior on the part of reporters portrayed in movies and TV. In actuality, I think the behavior is pretty good. Reporters for the better publications hew to a pretty high standard.

According to this veteran journalist, the most difficult challenge that reporters face on a daily basis is being accurate and fair. One thinks of what Joseph Pulitzer had to say about journalism when he turned away from the era of yellow journalism, which he "cofounded" in the 1890s with William Randolph Hearst, and converted to more serious reporting. Pulitzer would advise reporters that there are only three things they need to worry about: "Accuracy, accuracy, and accuracy!" Part of Pulitzer's legacy is the graduate journalism school at Columbia University where a cornerstone is ethics.

"Ethical issues—things like the use of anonymous sources—are great topics for journalism schools, but the hardest thing about journalism is to get the facts right and to tell the story fairly," Bearak (who has been a visiting journalism professor at Columbia) says. "To me, that's the essence of the journalist's ethical challenge, and it's that responsibility that keeps me awake at night virtually every time I'm ready to publish a story. Beyond that, other ethical concerns aren't usually so immediate and compelling, nor hard to sort out."

It's at this point in the interview that Bearak's social conscience projects most vividly and touches upon an interesting ethical issue that doesn't get much attention in journalism textbooks. The following passages also reveal how this journalist finds a way to be a good journalist and a good human being at the same time.

Are there some ethical matters that keep recurring? I suppose so. One involves giving money to the desperately poor or ill. A reporter needs to be strict about not paying for information. But what happens when you come in contact with a child who can be bought out of bondage or some sickly old woman who desperately needs medication or some family that is living on the margins of starvation? I think reporters can scrupulously indulge their impulses for charity. When I want to give money to someone who might appear in my story, I wait until the reporting is absolutely finished. If possible, I'll leave and send the money back with someone reliable.

Another matter that keeps recurring is whether to use the name of a willing source when I suspect that such use might harm them. A lot of people don't understand the power of a big newspaper. They'll tell you it's okay to use their name even after you tell them about possible consequences like the loss of a job or humiliation for their families. Sometimes, even when someone gives me the go-ahead, I'll override their judgment.

So, after his more than thirty years of reporting, which of Bearak's professional expectations have been met in the news business and which have gone unfulfilled?

I didn't get into journalism in order to change the world, but, as I experienced more and more of the world and observed the people who ran it, I increasingly thought change was fairly urgent. And reporters are better positioned than most to grab people by the lapels, shake them up, and say, "Hey you! Things are a mess. Fix it!" For nearly fifteen years as a roving national correspondent for the *Los Angeles Times*, I had one of the best newspaper jobs imaginable. I was given huge chunks of time and huge amounts of space to write whatever stories caught my eye.

I used the opportunity to dig into social issues—most every topic on the poverty hit parade: housing, drugs, AIDS, racism, corporate greed. I suppose I had hopes that my stories would force people to think in a more compassionate way. And, on rare occasions, I probably hoped to force lawmakers to rewrite laws. Did those expectations go unfulfilled? I think the stories were good enough to make people think, and there's some evidence that some appropriate brainwaves were provoked."

As time went on, Bearak came to the conclusion that, if he really wanted to make a more significant difference, he might have to have a bigger megaphone.

As for changing policy, I'd come away disappointed. Actually, that was one of the things that led me to *The New York Times*. It had a more powerful audience and that meant more influence, and I think that has proven to be true to some degree. But I still usually come away disappointed. I haven't stopped trying to change the world, but I have decidedly diminished expectations.

Fighting for Better Journalism

Jim Redmond

Former Anchor/Reporter, KUSA-TV, Denver

Jim Redmond is unique among his former colleagues in television journalism in several ways. For one, he is openly critical of what he sees as deepseated flaws in the way television does journalism. He is even more unique in that, while he was still in the prime of his anchoring career in Denver, he was planning his escape to a much lower paying (but hopefully more rewarding) career in teaching.

Today, he may be the only major-market, prime-time television anchor who managed to pick up a PhD during his off-hours from the nightly anchor desk.

"I was in the news business 22 years, 18 of those in Denver," Redmond recalls. "While in Denver, I saw deterioration of journalism ethics—all kinds of cases of the steady erosion of truth, justice, and the American way and the rise of consultants, along with the crumbling of the wall between the sales side and the news side. It was a slow kind of dissolve that just kept turning legitimate journalism organizations into kind of wordsmithing bordellos."

Strong words, and they reveal Redmond's discontent with the growing emphasis on the word *business* in the phrase "the news business."

"By the mid 1980s, I knew that, while I loved being a reporter, and still do believe in the importance of ethical journalism, those days were gone," Redmond laments. "That's when I decided to go back to graduate school."

At the time, the Montana native had the top job at the Denver station, anchoring the 5 and 10 p.m. evening newscasts and making the kind of money that anchors enjoy in the nation's top 25 markets. But he was driven by ideals more than by money, so he began taking classes at the University of Colorado in nearby Boulder to pursue a master's degree. That was in 1986, and he didn't stop until he had become Colorado's first doctoral graduate in journalism in 1993.

That's when Redmond moved to Memphis to begin his teaching career at the University of Memphis. By the year 2000, he was chairing the department.

As a college professor, he works to find a balance between championing the best in television journalism and leveling with students about the sobering and frustrating realities of that business.

Although many journalists enter the business according to a well-conceived plan, perhaps after preparing themselves for a career of exposing corruption and righting society's wrongs, Redmond's motivation was somewhat different.

"When I got in the business it was by accident," Redmond says. "I got out of the army and needed a job. There was a recession on, and I didn't want to work construction again. I'd put myself through college as a hod carrier and apprentice stone mason. But I had a degree in English literature and wanted to try to do something to use that."

That translated into taking a job at a small radio station in Billings, Montana. Although going to work for a low-rated station that played religious and elevator music might seem like an inauspicious career start, Redmond is glad he did it.

"I took the radio job because it sounded like fun, and they were really nice people. It was the best decision I ever made. They didn't have any news department, but, after I was there a couple of weeks, the program director told me that I could make $50 a month extra as a stringer for UPI if I wanted to cover news. He gave me a two-hour break on my morning shift to go run the city and county government beat, and we did a little 15-minute noon newscast. I just took to it. It was a blast. I'd cover the stories, phone them up to the UPI bureau in Helena, and, when I got back to the station, my newscast was already written on the wire. So a career took off."

Redmond's first television job was with KGVO-TV in Missoula, which also had an AM radio station. The position proved a great training ground for Redmond's move into the Portland and Denver markets, which would follow.

"It was a three-man news department. I wrote and anchored the newscasts and shot and edited the film for the other reporter too," Redmond says. "The third guy was the news director who did all radio, except the late-night roundup at 11. I did that after I did the TV newscast from 10–10:30. He taught me a lot about delivery, especially on radio, and it was a great experience. In retrospect, he was the only real journalist I can say I had as a news director. The rest were all, to one degree or another, somewhere in that netherworld between legitimate journalists and sell-outs to the business side."

Once into news, Redmond embraced it and all its ideals. "When I got into news I guess the motivation was the sense of doing something more important and contributing to the social good," Redmond says.

I was idealistic, and I was never driven by the celebrity or the money. It was the sense that I could work in a job, covering the day's events, and then help boil those down to help people who had to do other things all day understand their world.

I had a great sense of being of service, of doing something important, and there was, too, the luxury of being able to learn something new every day. As a journalist, you really are a student of the world, its peoples, and its affairs. It was having a job where you were paid to learn things and find out what was going on, every day. For a romantic idealist, it was great.

Eventually, however, the vivid colors of the ideal would fade to the muted grays of reality, and Redmond saw a profession that was taking a different direction from the one he had in mind.

Later, particularly after the consultants took over the business by about 1975, all that [idealism] was gone. It was just about money, and I started running into the ethical things. In Portland, we had a Jewish program director who put together a deal with a Jewish organization to pay for one of our crews (the reporter was also Jewish) to go to Israel and do some travelogue pieces stripped as a series during the rating book.

So, when it aired, I put up a super on the first night (I was then the anchor and producer of the 11 p.m.) that said, "Trip paid for by Jewish Defense League." The stuff hit the fan. I was fairly innocent. The "super" was true, and I thought, as a journalism organization, we should be open about that. But clearly neither the sponsor nor its station agent had that intent.

Then, in the middle of the week, a Jewish settlement was attacked by Palestinians, and our crew did some stories and air shipped them back. Gee, I guess they didn't want our coverage to appear like PR coverage by a crew paid for by an organization obviously aligned with Israel. So I was told no "trip paid for" supers. A few weeks later, I was taken off the 11 p.m. news and made a straight general assignment reporter. It took a few months, but I fairly quickly got a new job in Denver.

A year before the completion of his doctoral work, Redmond was offered a job anchoring the 5 p.m. newscast in Dallas, the sixth largest television market in the country. He was tempted, but he decided instead to stay in Colorado and finish his degree. The die had been cast; his career path was about to take a major turn to a minor salary level.

"I'd always had a little doubt about going into academics," Redmond says. " It cost me more than 75 percent of my annual income, and I sort of felt like I was cheating my wife and kids out of a better life. But she just smiled at me, told me she loved me and that she was happier than she'd ever been in TV. We were all so much better off without the insanity of TV, the stress, and the night shift. We're both highly ethical people. TV just isn't that kind of place anymore. It's just another kind of game show."

Redmond says the downslide of television news is noticed not just by television journalists who are dedicated to comprehensive and accurate reporting but also by the television viewing audience itself, and he points to research that underscores that point.

"Television news just keeps getting worse. The audience continues to abandon it in droves," he says. "That's being caused by both a combination of new technology being available to the audience and a lot of outright rejection too. The latest PEW studies show continuous decline in audience believability, credence, and trust in TV news. It's mostly a lot of hustle, gloss, and bluster now with increasingly less of any serious content or context. The vacuous superficiality of TV news is quickly killing the golden goose, and the egg that came with it."

Redmond explains that "Ed Murrow's famous 1958 RTNDA [Radio and Television News Directors Association] speech echoes in its perceptive truth," and he goes on to quote a portion of that famous speech:

> One of the basic troubles with radio and television news is that both instruments have grown up as an incompatible combination of show business, advertising and news. Each of the three is a rather bizarre and demanding profession. And when you get all three under one roof, the dust never settles.
>
> The top management of the networks, with a few notable exceptions, has been trained in advertising, research, or show business. But by the nature of the corporate structure, they also make the final and crucial decisions having to do with news and public affairs. Frequently they have neither the time nor the competence to do this. I began by saying that our history will be what we make it. If we go on as we are, then history will take its revenge, and retribution will not limp in catching up with us.[1]

"And so 1958 evolved to 2007," Redmond continues. "What was once somewhat respectable is now more of a current events side show of market-driven news where the stories of the day are decided based on audience research studies of what people say they want. And there is a hollow echo left by the footsteps of what they need retreating daily from what is served up as news but has been rendered to mere infotainment."

Where does it go from here? Redmond foresees a death by the "syphilis of market-driven news" where there is only a "vacuum" in store for journalists who really care about good reporting, followed by a time when the media will use every kind of content imaginable to try to fill that void.

"Eventually, as profits continue to decline (though still way above any normal business) new journalistic entrepreneurs will be attracted and create things of substance to fill the void. There will be more wrenching, more sappy attempts to pander to the lowest common denominator with "solution" news, "community" news, and other grasping. And, eventually, serious news consumers will just create their own news products, as they are doing already via the Internet or in other new ways we can't imagine. And the dinosaur of the 20th century, mass medium of news will devolve into something very different."

If this were a Shakespearean play, Redmond would call it a tragedy. In fact, he does say that, if he were writing a book about his career in television journalism, he would call it *Death of a Dream*.

> The tragedy is that already most people are disengaged, and we no longer have as much of a central, binding thread of daily news and information to tie us together. The destruction of legitimate news is a process of tearing apart the tapestry that once helped unify our culture.

> The big three networks now only reach about a quarter of Americans. Rush Limbaugh's weekly talk radio audience is about 15 million. I have conservative friends who say they only watch FOX, discounting the others as liberals. The college kids watch Jon Stewart's *The Daily Show*, which is a comedy show making fun of news events, but that means they get their current events through the lens of satire, not balanced coverage. And I've found that, when I go to Europe, I can actually find news worth watching on the BBC and elsewhere that hasn't been so eroded in content or professionalism.

> Across America, there is little news on the air any more; [it's] mostly replaced by agenda-driven ranters like Nancy Grace or Glenn Beck or phony news on the local level with irrelevant series about nothing and no serious coverage of governmental affairs. Indeed, few newspapers or TV news operations are providing serious coverage to the courts or government, in most markets eliminating those beats or combining them to have one reporter cover what a half dozen used to cover. Increasingly, if it is news, it's news to those who formerly could be relied upon to recognize it. And, as the University of Minnesota 2005 VNR [video news release] study indicated, about three-quarters of it is PR-generated fluff that isn't edited at all but passed off as the station's own reporting.

What would the framers of the U.S. Constitution think of today's television journalism? Is this the press they had in mind as a protecting influence when they crafted the First Amendment? Redmond is dubious.

"There is an open question whether the framers would ever write the free press clause the way they did if they could come back and see what has happened. The implication that between the lines of the First Amendment was invisibly etched a sense of responsibility to the society is now cast off out of hand by the money people who see news as just another bucket of bolts to peddle down the street."

Leading the Charge for Newsroom Diversity

Arlene Notoro Morgan

Former Assistant Managing Editor, *The Philadelphia Inquirer*

Arlene Notoro Morgan has been driven by at least three passions in her illustrious career as veteran journalist with *The Philadelphia Inquirer* and associate dean of the Columbia University Graduate School of Journalism. Those passions are excellence in journalism, the racial and ethnic diversity of journalists, and the credibility of journalism to readers.

In 1995, Morgan was honored with the first Knight Ridder Excellence in Diversity Award for her work to diversify the *Inquirer*'s staff and for her leadership in fostering a diverse content and workforce throughout Knight Ridder newspapers. (Knight Ridder was then the corporate owner of the *Inquirer*.) A graduate of Temple University in Philadelphia, Morgan was a fellow in 1996–1997 at the Freedom Forum's Media Studies Center, where she coedited the book *The Authentic Voice: The Best Reporting on Race and Ethnicity*.

Morgan, who spent 31 years at the *Inquirer* and rose there to the position of assistant managing editor, believes that all three of these qualities—excellence, diversity, and credibility—must exist in American journalism if it is to achieve the level of truthfulness and effectiveness it should. Two common threads seem to run through Morgan's three passions: honesty and fairness. It was her belief in fairness, in fact, that motivated her to become a journalist in the first place.

"I grew up during the 60s when the civil rights movement, the Kennedy and King assassinations, and the Vietnam War were converging," Morgan says. "The work of Edward R. Murrow, the coverage of political conventions, and the Kennedy election—along with the civil rights marches and riots in the South—had a major impact on me to pursue this as a career."

So, early in her life, Morgan embraced the highest ideals of American journalism and discovered she couldn't think of becoming anything other than a journalist, even though there weren't that many women in the business then.

"When I think back about it, I cannot remember a time when I did not want to be a newspaper reporter," she says. "I actually used to play being a reporter when I was 6 or 7, even though there were few female role models. My uncle used to kid me about being the family's 'Lois Lane.'"

Her love of the profession and her belief in its ideals grew stronger over the years that she worked at the *Inquirer* under some gifted editors.

"I was lucky to work for the majority of my career for Gene Roberts, Gene Foreman, Max King, and Bob Rosenthal, who held steadfast to the value of strong journalism. I left [the *Inquirer*] in the summer of 2000, first because I would get the chance to write a book on the coverage of race . . . and second because I had lost faith in the *Inquirer* publisher and Knight Ridder executives [corporate owner representatives]—that they knew what they were doing about rowing the paper, particularly when it came to reaching out to new immigrants."

Morgan says that more than 100,000 Russian immigrants had settled in Philadelphia over a ten-year period, and the *Inquirer* management was doing nothing to embrace them as readers.

"The entire approach was to cut and snip in order to make more money, rather than to grow and experiment," she says.

Morgan chafes at journalism that strives to make money instead of focusing on achieving its highest potential as provider of needed information to readers. She recalls another instance of this happening early in her career at the *Delaware County Daily / Sunday Times.*

"The new publisher, who had been the ad director, shut down an investigative project into political corruption because the Republican powers in the county triggered an ad boycott by the car dealers," she recalls. "Four of us, including the city editor, quit. That was a sad day but also one of my proudest days since I only had 18 months experience and no job. That's when I was hired by the *Inquirer*, and six months later Knight bought the paper."

In assessing the status of American journalism today, Morgan sees some things being done right in the profession, but she also sees room for improvement. Not surprisingly, given her passions, she counts diversity as one deficiency in journalism.

"I think newspapers have to bring more voices into their stories. So many stories are still framed around the institutions that we are covering, rather than by the people those institutions are serving," she says. "I also think the news media have to figure out how to better reflect a multiple number of communities who live in the coverage areas. I think, if they are to grow, they must move beyond the 'us' (most often white) vs. 'them' (immigrants, people of color) treatment, which to a large extent represents a class issue."

Nevertheless, she seems proud of the way most of the major media conduct themselves today, in terms of providing news and information of value to the public.

I think mainstream is still doing public service watchdog journalism better than any other media in a consistent way. Yes, magazines and TV news—the *New Yorker* or *Frontline* for instance—do occasional "wow 'em" pieces, but nothing in comparison to the work *The Wall Street Journal* did last year in China, the *Los Angeles Times*'s "Altered Oceans" on the environment, or *The Washington Post*'s examination of what was going on at Walter Reed Hospital.

I think newspapers still can be depended on to give us information and stories that we don't know we need or want. They continue to surprise us, dig beneath the surface, and help a community change. Over the past decade, newspapers have also become easier to use, and they now produce Web sites that can link you to almost every piece of information you need to live your life, not only in the community but the world. That is an enormous public service.

Morgan says she has not altered her views over the years about journalists remaining detached from their sources ("not being in bed with your sources or carrying out your own agenda," as she states it). She believes reporters must be better prepared to understand their sources, however, especially before beginning interviews.

"Parachute journalism does not do anyone much good," she quips. "Beat reporters, in particular, should constantly be improving their knowledge through self-education, workshops, and just getting out on the streets to meet the real people their stories affect."

And again, the topic of diversity enters into her thinking: "I believe that multiple perspectives are now more required to make a story fair and complete than the traditional, 'he said, she said' formula."

What does Morgan think about the newer forms of online and blog reporting?

"While I appreciate the insights that a blog can bring to a story, I am still wary about personal involvement and what it can do to a reporter's credibility. I look at what (CNN's) Lou Dobbs has done on the immigration story and just shudder. In my eyes, he is an anti-immigration advocate, not a journalist, on the issue."

Although she believes a reporter should remain detached and not personally involved with sources, Morgan doesn't necessarily decry a journalist who becomes involved with a cause that he or she is not reporting on. She uses a personal example to explain.

When I was in Philadelphia, I was one of the few editors who was active in a cause. I was a director of a Quaker hospital for the mentally ill. [Editor Gene] Roberts allowed me to do it because he knew it was a passion based on issues in my own family and because I agreed that I would never cover the hospital.

But the work I did at the hospital allowed me to learn a great deal about management issues and certainly about the field of mental health, parity for patients, and issues surrounding story ideas that came out of the mental health field. I was able to give others at the paper my insights and led them to sources and ideas that they would have never thought about otherwise.

I always felt the need to disclose my advocacy. When I had my hospital hat on, I was also very careful to speak up when I thought my integrity as a journalist could be compromised. It was a very tender line to walk. I am glad I did it because it was important to me to feel that I was making a difference, in a very tangible way, for the mentally ill.

Morgan says her own ethnic background has helped her to understand the issues she has covered over her years as a journalist from the perspectives of the different ethnic groups involved.

> I think growing up as an Italian American in South Philadelphia and attending Catholic schools there gave me an understanding about community reporting that an outside person could never bring to the table. At one point, when we were trying to hone neighborhood coverage, Roberts sent me out to do about three months of reporting on how the paper was perceived by Italian American readers.

> I interviewed people from a congressman to relatives. Doors opened for me that would have never opened to anyone else. I think the paper learned a great deal from my being "out there," and Roberts was smart enough to use me as a sounding board. He also did that with several other staffers including Acel Moore in the black community, for instance.

Morgan finds herself at odds with the latest round of "emotional reporting," which has cropped up especially on television news at the local level but also at the level of cable network news programs such as *Lou Dobbs Tonight* or *AC 360°* with Anderson Cooper. "I am not comfortable with this approach," Morgan says.

> I think you let your sources show the anger and that this emotionalism, to my mind, is being used instead of bringing various voices on to debate the issue. I don't watch CNN that much. Anderson's personal style clearly appeals to younger audiences, and, while I think he is more emotional than network anchors, I don't think he crosses the line that often. Dobbs, on the other hand, is obviously appealing to a segment of society who fears that immigrants are taking away their jobs, and I rarely hear the other side in any measured way.

> I think there is a big difference between Dobbs and Cooper in that Cooper is still out there reporting while Dobbs is issuing his opinion but with not much that I can see in reporting all the sides to this complicated issue.

In looking at how a journalist might go about reporting on the spiritual or religious aspects of stories, Morgan finds an area of interest that she doesn't think journalists should discount. Although journalists mostly cover the here and now of the secular world, should they be exclusively secular in their own worldviews? Do professionals trained in objectivity steer away from matters of faith, which cannot be verified in the same way as many secular events can?

"I think this is a fascinating question," Morgan responds, "especially pertaining to issues of racial and ethnic intolerance and how religious beliefs enter into those discussions. I actually think journalists are much more spiritual, if not religious, than most understand." She continues,

> At the *Inquirer*, one of our managing editors was a lay minister in the Catholic Church; one of our editorial board editors was a very strict Jew. The list goes on and on about how many of our reporters and editors were religious and actually brought that perspective to their reporting in terms of looking for that perspective in their stories.
>
> As we have seen over the past years, religious convictions permeate almost every aspect of life and policy, from stem cell to Islamic fanaticism. I strongly believe that reporters should learn all they can about how spiritual and religious convictions can impact one's decision making. Perhaps, had we been more in tune to the rise of Islam in the world, we would not have had to struggle so much to understand the context of what happened on 9/11.

If journalists are so committed to the profession of making objective observations to the world and exposing corruption and sham, why do so many leave the profession and move into business, politics, public relations, and advertising—the very professions most journalists would say fuel manipulation and obfuscation?

"Actually," Morgan responds, "I do not agree that every journalist comes into the business to be objective or to expose corruption and sham. That might be 20–30 percent of the profession. And I have not seen many of the journalists who are committed to those ideals leave the business." Morgan thinks other motives are responsible for journalists joining and then leaving the profession:

> You have to acknowledge that some people come into it for their own glory and ego. And I have known a lot of journalists—they are human after all—who are not always objective. Just look at TV journalist Lou Dobbs right now. He's certainly not objective about immigration, but he is getting good numbers out there. So, obviously, people may not care as much about so-called objectivity as they do [about] finding someone who will confirm their views.
>
> I think objectivity is an ideal that, sadly, is not always reached. The best we can ask for these days is that every journalist does work that is fair.
>
> As for leaving the business to pursue financial, political, or other goals, I think again that it is human nature to seek what you think is best for you. I would not want to stereotype anyone who leaves the business for financial gain because so many news jobs just don't pay enough to meet the living standards required to raise a family and have a decent life. So I am not going to condemn anyone for taking a job outside of journalism as long as they do that job with integrity and are not corrupted.

Serving as the Eyes and Ears for Others

Peter Bhatia

Executive Editor, *The Oregonian*

From a primitive neighborhood newspaper that a young adolescent produced, with help from his dad, using a Ditto master to Oregon's largest daily and the executive editor position, Peter Bhatia has seen it all as a journalist.

And he still loves it all.

"It is the same today as it was when I was a teenager," Bhatia says about his motivation to become a journalist. "I loved writing stories, I loved being the eyes and ears for others, and I very much wanted the opportunity to do something that had a social purpose."

About that neighborhood paper he produced at age 11, Bhatia jokes, "No copies survive—which is a good thing. But, from there, it was off to the high school paper, the college paper, and the real world."

Bhatia came to *The Oregonian* as managing editor in 1993, rising to his current rank of executive editor in 1998. During his leadership tenure, the newspaper has won four Pulitzer Prizes. Before moving to Portland, he served as executive editor of *The Fresno Bee* and managing editor of the *Sacramento Bee,* to name just two of his previous newspapers. He has also taken on industry-wide leadership posts as president of the American Society of Newspaper Editors and past chair of the ASNE Ethics and Values Committee, where he helped lead the group's groundbreaking credibility project.

The Stanford University graduate says he has not seen any perceptible shift in the motivations of those individuals wanting to become journalists.

"I don't think there has been a monumental shift. There are certainly more reporters who have come into the business with a set notion of what they want to cover and how they want to do it," he says. "For example, many young minority journalists want to cover minority issues. Not all, to be sure, but the early-on focus may be sharper among young journalists than it was when I came into the business."

One motivator, he notes, is still very strong among young journalists. "I do think the social purpose—wanting to report on issues, educate the public, and to be a force for positive change—is still very strong," he says, although he has detected what he calls a "generational shift."

There has been some generational shift in the business that is common throughout society: the boomers were raised on the principle of "work hard and you will be rewarded." So we paid our dues working nights, weekends, and split days off to get better assignments. The kids of boomers weren't necessarily raised with the same attitude.

Which of his own professional expectations have been met in the news business?

Working in newspapers has fulfilled my career expectations. I wanted to do meaningful work, have the opportunity to be a witness to history, have an opportunity to make a difference through the work we do in newsrooms.

Early on, leadership wasn't among my goals or expectations. But that came surprisingly early in my career and has been a dominant part of it; most of my expectations have been met. Again, it is about making a difference, helping others to be successful, leading our work and the changes that have been necessary over the years.

And which expectations have gone unmet? Peter Bhatia is not one to dwell on them, and seems to prefer making lemonade out of the sour fruit.

"My frustrations come from not being able to always get to where I believe we need to be," he says. "Of course, expectations continue to evolve, especially given today's rapidly changing media landscape. There are new aspirations and expectations—such as figuring out how newspapers survive in an Internet-driven world. My expectation is that we will figure it out and that I can help us get there."

Bhatia has mostly held to his beliefs that journalists should remain detached from the stories they are working on and from the sources they deal with to get those stories.

"They [his beliefs] haven't changed much," he confides. "Even in an era where closeness to sources is more common due to the burst of excellent, narrative writing in newspapers, I think the cautions and distance remain important. Balancing that remains a great test for reporters and editors, and it will always be so, I think."

How does he define "distance"?

"Distance does not mean in writing or voice necessarily," he explains. "That's something we have figured out in recent years. That is, our reporting and writing can be intimate, but we can still maintain an appropriate distance from our sources. The simple equation is to remember our obligation to the reader, to be fair, honest, truthful, and complete in our work. Those old values are still good values."

In assessing how a journalist's own political ideology might affect his or her zeal for chasing certain issues and exposing wrongdoing in government and business, Bhatia finds a complex issue lurking. Certainly, all surveys of journalists nationwide show there are more who describe themselves as politically independent or liberal than conservative. Is there any correlation between a journalist's political ideology and his or her interest in exposing corruption? "This is a very complicated issue," a thoughtful Bhatia muses. "One that is prone to simplistic answers from journalists and our critics."

The notion of the liberal media is way overblown. And, if you live in a town like Portland, you get it from both sides anyway. The liberals are as vicious as the conservatives.

But the nature of people who go into journalism is they want to make things better; they want to do work that will cause positive change. This is not a political orientation; it is a social orientation. And this is exactly where the liberal media notion becomes an imprecise one. I will not argue for a minute against the fact that most journalists favor liberal political causes.

What are some of those causes, and does a certain "social orientation" affect how a journalist writes a story?

"Most journalists support abortion rights, gay marriage, and they vote for Democrats," he explains. "But our critics forget that most journalists are people of tremendous integrity, and we are trained to set aside our personal feelings to cover whatever is in front of us. The vast majority of newspaper stories are straightforward and honest. The critics may not believe that—especially these days when they want journalism to suit their ideology as compared to being factual. Are newspapers without bias? Of course not. There is no such thing as an unbiased human being. We can do better at confronting some of our biases that flow from the descriptions above as to who we are. But the bottom line is American journalism has never been better, even in the face of the economic crisis we face today."

Is it the job of daily journalism to just get the facts straight and spit them out to show what is happening here and now, or is there a "larger-truth" responsibility of journalists to put the here and now into a wider and more meaningful context? One essayist, Roger Rosenblatt, once wrote in *Time* magazine years ago that the "larger truth" is outside the bounds of daily journalism. "That sells short the role of journalists in today's society," Bhatia counters.

> Certainly, no one should totally depend on us or any other media for their total view of things. My 21-year-old daughter, for example, likes going to the BBC site to get a different view of world events. But I think the role of the daily journalists is much larger than just "dribbling in place" to overdo the basketball analogy. Rather, it is to explain, put in context, provide a larger frame for news, especially in print.
>
> After all, pretty much all breaking news is migrating to the Web. That handily leaves the world of understanding (as compared to just what happened) to the next day's print product. That is a good place for us to live, given the depth of expertise, quality of writing, and commitment to depth that lives in newspaper newsrooms.

Along with media bias, the idea of unethical journalism has been a rallying cry for critics of the press. Nevertheless, ethics is a subject that is written about a lot in journalism's professional publications, and journalists often discuss ethical quandaries among themselves. Is there enough emphasis on ethical journalism?

"We can always have more conversations about ethics," Bhatia believes. "But I think the events of the past few years . . . have reignited the passion around ethics that perhaps had faded into the routine somewhat or no longer was top of mind. In our newsroom, the newsroom-wide conversations have ramped up in recent months, thanks to having a managing editor for whom that is an important part of her job. All this is good. But it has also served to remind us that ethics is a dynamic process."

How does he define that dynamic aspect of ethics, and what does it mean for the journalist who works at *The Oregonian*?

> We believe, for example, that being a journalist requires us to forfeit some of our rights as citizens. We should not, for example, contribute to campaigns, sign petitions, participate in marches for causes, or have lawn signs for candidates.

For many of us, that is and has been a no-brainer. But there are always some who disagree. Donation lists are public, of course. We weren't happy to find one of our reporters recently contributed to a campaign.

Regardless, the conversations need to be regular and out in the open. More often than not, they are situational and between a reporter and an editor. But more often, the outcomes of these conversations need to be shared with the rest of the staff and our readers. Many in the public are surprised and pleased to find we have ethical standards that we take seriously.

Bhatia points to an example of a tough ethical issue an *Oregonian* reporter faced recently in discerning how much information to divulge in a story about a teacher's aide.

There are always ones that stand out, such as a recent story we did on a teacher's aide who had a criminal record that likely would have prevented her from being hired, but the district didn't check. He [the reporter] wrote the story [after a tip] named her; she was very forthcoming, and people rallied around her. Really interesting, difficult story and ethical case.

Most ethical cases revolve around naming people who may not have wanted to be named in the paper and around anonymity of sources. We generally favor the former—naming—and discourage the latter—granting anonymity. But every case needs to be looked at individually. The facts and circumstances may well lead us against our preferred practice in many cases.

Going back to the idea of journalism covering the here and now, Bhatia comments on where he believes that leaves the coverage of the spiritual aspects of people's lives and of religion itself.

Actually, I think the form of daily journalism is changing rapidly, thanks to the Internet. More and more breaking news is going to the Web. As a result, more and more of newspaper space is being devoted to enterprise reporting and [to] news you can only get from a newspaper because of the depth and context we can offer. That bodes well for specialty topic areas such as religion, especially since it is an area on which there is discussion and a need for more explanation.

As for the coverage, there are some excellent religion writers in the country. Personally, I think the reporting could stand to be less about institutions and more about how faith plays out for people in their daily life.

How about how faith plays out in the lives and jobs of elected officeholders in government? For example, Jimmy Carter once said in a National Public Radio interview that, as president, he had to sometimes make policy decisions that ran counter to his own personal moral or religious beliefs. But Arkansas Governor Mike Huckabee, who ran for the 2008 Republican presidential nomination, said that the public cannot expect their government leaders to separate their own personal beliefs from the policy decisions they make for people.

Bhatia believes reporters should take an all-encompassing perspective when reporting on political candidates.

"We elect people to office, and every person is influenced by his or her beliefs, be they religious, moral, or otherwise," he notes. "It is our job to cover those people in the fullest possible way and to illuminate the influences that make them the people and leaders and officeholders they are."

Right-Brain, Left-Brain Reporting

Penny Owen

Features Reporter, *The Oklahoman*

For six years, Penny Owen was working on one and only one major story: the bombing of the Alfred P. Murrah Federal Building in Oklahoma City and its aftermath. From April 19, 1995, when Timothy McVeigh lit the fuse that reduced the federal building to rubble, to June of 2001, when McVeigh met his death via lethal injection in an Indiana prison, Owen was there covering it all.

She began at *The Oklahoman* in 1992 as an intern and then moved to become the newspaper's police reporter for several years. The contacts she developed on that beat helped her in reporting on the bombing later, and working that beat also introduced her to covering a steady stream of violent stories.

"I think, as a woman, it takes longer to gain the cops' respect," she says. "Maybe, after that, they are a bit more open. Also, they don't perceive women as being threats, like they might with men."

The police beat exposes reporters to a lot of violent death. For some, the emotional strain is hard; others get used to it.

"I could certainly separate emotions from the job while I was in the working mode," she says. "It's like a right-brain, left-brain thing. I'm busy gathering information, figuring out quotes, sources, leads, etc. So I don't really have time to internalize it much. Sometimes the emotions would come, but not often. The internationalization came after the fact, if at all."

So did she find it fairly easy to walk away from the story at the end of the day? "Yes, most of the time I did," she says.

> A couple stories still stand out in my head, though. Like two teens who jumped from a building. I just remember images of them lying on the ground, dead. It was pretty gruesome. Then talking to their families, who were hostile to the press. It never got easier calling families who were in raw grief.
>
> I often told them I was sorry to hear what happened. I have no qualms about that. It was sincere. I'd usually then say that "I've been assigned" to do the story about your son's or daughter's death.

Owen is a reporter who generally keeps her emotions in check until she is ready to reveal them on her own terms. But she does often find herself caring about her stories and the people in them. And that brings up another question: Is caring about your story the same thing as caring about the people in those stories? "Good question," she responds.

> It's a mixture of both. I tend to keep a healthy distance from the people I write about, but I do try to capture the emotions, which also means empathizing with the people. My story comes first, but not at the expense of damaging the person I am interviewing.
>
> I think the passion in print comes through in telling a compelling story. We can do this even better than TV, I think, because we can provide details and words that convey images for the reader. If we tell a story with grace and restraint, it allows the readers to draw on their own conclusions, which I think helps them internalize the story more themselves. It is a way of trusting the reader.
>
> But we have to be great storytellers to do that, which means we must feel the story to some degree ourselves. And that isn't always the case. Sometimes it is forced, and that shows.

Does she feel that the reporter should be allowed to tell the story in any way he or she sees fit, regardless of traditional conventions in the way news stories are told?

"Yes, I do," she says. "And the inverted pyramid is rarely mentioned in newsrooms today. I think most journalists know that a great story needs a narrative: a beginning, middle, and end."

Was there a story that challenged her to the point of changing her reporting style?

> I think the first time I got a call from a family of a crime victim lambasting me for not calling them about a story I wrote on their loved one made me braver in calling future families.

> And the bombing started a whole new reality of dealing with victims and survivors. It meant getting to know them over years rather than just a couple of weeks on the cop beat. It does change the dynamics when covering victims over the long term. For me, some self-preservation kicked in. It was tempting to get close to these people I got to know. But to do that meant risking the story, i.e., clouding my judgment, etc., not to mention the emotional toll it could take. It was already emotional, so why make it more so?

> I know other journalists said they kept in touch with long-term victims with cards and so forth, but I didn't do that.

Owen has done a lot of work with the Dart Center for Journalists and Trauma, a nonprofit organization geared toward the study of how covering tragedies produces emotional effects in the journalists doing the stories. She is president of the Dart Society and a member of the Executive Committee for the Dart Center.

"Many journalists, seasoned and otherwise, are opening up to the toll that covering trauma takes on them. It's almost a watershed moment. Studies have been done that show journalists are amazingly resilient. But they succumb to the same symptoms as others like sleeplessness, irritability, and depression."

What about the analogy linking reporters and police or firefighters, in the sense that all are exposed to the same kinds of tragedies?

> The cop-journo-firefighter analogy is very accurate. But cops and firefighters are way ahead on recognizing the trauma within their ranks. I think news management is recognizing some need for counseling or at least some recognition of what the journalists' experience is, which is sometimes all that is needed.

> "I've heard of some terribly insensitive things done to reporters in the field. One bureau reporter in Iraq, for instance, was awakened in the middle of the night and asked to get some quotes to go with a story about a beheading of someone she knew. You can bet that reporter didn't get any sleep that night and for some nights after.

Another reporter in Afghanistan who was embedded with the Marines felt terribly isolated and would call his newsroom for some normal conversation.

Freelancers have a particularly tough time because they have no safety net of a newsroom, even though a newsroom isn't always as compassionate as it should be.

What about covering stories about emotions? Is it okay for a reporter to let herself or himself feel in those cases? And is it ethical to inject those personal feelings into stories?

I think feeling the emotions to the point of understanding them well enough to convey to readers is important. I've written many stories through tears. But I also felt a tug that pulled me back, helping me resist getting too immersed into their horror.

Of course my situation was a bit different. When you have so many victims, you'd be a wreck if you took all of their emotions personally. Also, there was a real ebb and flow to it. Some days I was numb; I felt nothing, and that was disturbing. Then someone would say something or something would happen to snap me back into the emotion of the story, which was a good thing. My stories are better when I feel the emotion behind them.

My biggest struggle in the "full-of-emotion" situation is finding the right words and avoiding clichés. So I try to show it instead of tell it.

Many reporters feel more comfortable socializing with journalists than with non-journalists who might not understand their work or mission, and who may even bash journalism and journalists at times. How does Owen feel about this?

I've been in situations where friends or colleagues—some in the navy [where Owen is a Reserve officer]—are bashing journalists, and it does bother me. I hate hearing about how negatively the press reports this Iraq War. Those sorts of encounters make me realize that there must be a big divide between what journalists do and how we perceive the news and what readers or viewers see and how they view it.

I do think what we do is somewhat of a mission. I don't think it wise to adopt a cause or anything, however. I'd call it a truth mission. But then we have the Sabbath gasbags spewing opinions every week while reporting the news, so I can see how things get blurred.

What keeps her from becoming burned out with the business of reporting?

Taking a short break helped some. I'm not sure I'm over my burnout I experienced. I miss my early enthusiasm. But I also miss journalism terribly when I'm not doing it. Creativity helps. Camaraderie helps. Journalists are an interesting breed. I feel entirely comfortable with them, which isn't true of everyone. They're a bit rebellious, always curious, intolerant of small talk. I like that.

How did she finally get off the long series of assignments on the Oklahoma City bombing? "I was on it until McVeigh was executed in 2001," Owen responds. "I didn't ask to get off of it. I guess it did just naturally fade away. I'm glad it did, frankly."

Why was she glad to see the end of the story? "I don't know," she says. "Maybe I have a short attention span. Maybe I think other things have come along that are bigger than what happened there and for us to still write about it is too much. I interviewed McVeigh's father when I went to Terre Haute for the execution. That was a great story. But Bill McVeigh is not a talker, so, yes, it was a hard interview. Plus it was quite sensitive because I was asking him about the last time he'd see his son. So it was emotional."

Finding the Music in Writing

Michael Walker

Author of *Laurel Canyon* and Former Reporter, the *Los Angeles Times* and *The New York Times*

Journalism is music to the ears of Michael Walker.

This former writer for both *The New York Times* and the *Los Angeles Times* decided in the 1990s to leave the newspaper world and turn his attention to writing books, specifically a book about his passion: rock and roll. The result is the nonfiction bestseller *Laurel Canyon: The Inside Story of Rock and Roll's Legendary Neighborhood*.

As Walker spent months interviewing and writing about the legends of the 1960s and 1970s rock scene in Southern California, he found he was living the dream that lured him into journalism in the first place: "What got me interested in journalism was good writing," Walker explains.

> My father used to read my brother and me James Thurber short stories as bedtime stories; plus both parents were avid readers of the *Chicago Daily News* in the 70s when it still had Mike Royko and others. Also I was deeply influenced by *Rolling Stone* and the writings of Joe Eszterhas, Hunter Thompson, and Timothy Crouse.
>
> They were such good writers; they made me want to write and report as well as they did. So I took the shortest route I could think of, and, since I liked rock and played in a band, I started writing concert reviews for my high school paper. Stuff like Jethro Tull, Elton John, the Faces, etc. All the big shows that came through Chicago.

Walker, who graduated from Drake University in 1979, says he was a little too young to really experience the "pure 60s stuff" that he writes about in *Laurel Canyon*. But he still had an avid interest in that period.

"I was lucky to grow up in a very small town of 350 people near Chicago, and so I was hanging around guys who were 18 when I was 11, and they turned me on to all their favorite artists, so I was absorbing pretty sophisticated stuff when I was still in grade school."

Was he also into the protests that the music of the time gave voice to? Did he become a journalist to somehow strike back at what he viewed as a mean or wrongheaded system? Not really, he says.

> "I wasn't angry, but I was definitely an outsider. All my friends were. We didn't participate at all in the high school infrastructure. Nobody was on the football team or worked the school paper or even student council.
>
> The town I grew up in was about 50 miles west of Chicago, and, in those days, it was countryside, I viewed the world as a pretty friendly place as I grew up with the same people. My whole life, nobody moved. It was pretty protected. I walked to school until I was 13. We had to take buses to the nearest large city, Elgin, to go to junior high and senior high school.
>
> That changed my worldview, as Elgin was then a decaying industrial town with a lot of racial tensions in the school. There were race-related disturbances at both my schools. Also, as I got older, I was of course absorbing the crisis in the Nixon White House, the Vietnam War. My friends and I had discussions about whether or not we'd go if we got drafted. But, overall, I

looked at the world as exciting and inviting. I couldn't wait to get out of high school and get into it.

Walker's entry into the world of for-pay journalism came during college, and, again, his love of music factored into that experience.

"My sophomore year, I was staying the summer instead of going home, working unloading semis at a tire warehouse, and I started stringing for a little music paper out of Peoria, Illinois," he recalls. "I was their Des Moines correspondent and covered all the local music scene and the big bands coming through town."

After graduation, Walker joined an alternative newspaper in Des Moines called *The Daily Planet,* and he loved the experience of working for a start-up newspaper. Then he joined the Meredith Corporation, a media and marketing company based in Des Moines that publishes several magazines. Walker was a copy editor, and the company moved him to their New York offices as a senior editor. He remained in that job until the mid-1980s when he quit to freelance for magazines. At that time, *The New York Times* owned a number of magazines that he worked for, so he eventually moved to the *Times* business section as a copy editor. He moved to the arts and leisure desk next, editing and writing stories on the arts. Walker became a freelancer after his next move, which was to Los Angeles, where, after a while, he joined the Sunday magazine of the *Los Angeles Times.*

The *L.A. Times* was, by comparison, a sloppily edited newspaper outside of its A section. There were some very talented writers and reporters, but the editing overall was inconsistent and sometimes nonexistent, especially in the cultural coverage. Also this was . . . when walls between business and editorial were supposed to come down, which ran counter to everything I'd been taught and believed in, at least when it came to newspapers.

Finally, the paper was cutting back in lots of counterproductive ways. The Sunday magazine, for example was left out of the national edition of the paper. My colleagues and I were doing a lot of really good work that was only being seen in Southern California. It scared me that my future as a journalist and writer was being presented through the prism of this newspaper that wasn't taken very seriously even in its hometown, so I got out.

Since then, life has taken Walker back into the world of freelancing and now into the book-publishing world as an author of a popular bestseller. But he has always considered himself a journalist. He realizes that covering his passion—rock and roll and its legendary leaders from the 1960s and 70s—moves him emotionally closer to the subject than some journalists think appropriate. But he sees value in feeling that passion.

"Interesting. That's what also made the Katrina coverage so compelling," he says. "The only danger I see in getting too close is this: Someone without experience, I would find less trustworthy in telling the story. There's a danger in pandering."

Laurel Canyon, however, is an incisive study of a singularly important era in American musical and cultural history. A review of the book says it this way:

> In *Laurel Canyon*, journalist Michael Walker tells the inside story of this unprecedented gathering of some of the baby boom's leading musical lights—including Joni Mitchell; Jim Morrison; Crosby, Stills & Nash; John Mayall; the Mamas and the Papas; Carole King; the Eagles; and Frank Zappa, to name just a few—who turned Los Angeles into the music capital of the world and forever changed the way popular music is recorded, marketed, and consumed. It was Brigadoon meets the Brill building, and the reverberations from the unprecedented music being made—and the sex, drugs, and rock and roll lifestyle it created—profoundly shaped the attitudes and expectations of an entire generation.
>
> In new interviews with Graham Nash, the Byrds' Chris Hillman, the Turtles' Mark Volman, Gail Zappa, the groupie legend Pamela Des Barres and other insiders, Walker traces Laurel Canyon's transformation from a countercultural paradise in the Sixties, when a song written on a redwood deck could enter pop culture's permanent collection within weeks, to the dark decadence of the Seventies, when fame, fortune, sex, cocaine, and, finally, sadistic murder, finally shook the flowers out of everyone's hair.[2]

For Michael Walker, some of his expectations about journalism failed to materialize in a sustained way. But other expectations were exceeded. From a shaky journalistic start writing music reviews for his high school paper in Elgin, Illinois, to international publication of his rock and roll history book *Laurel Canyon*, Michael Walker is definitely living his dream.

Honoring the Contract with Readers

Jim Robertson

Managing Editor, *Columbia Daily Tribune*

Any college journalism major who has come through the University of Missouri's venerable School of Journalism, always named among the elite of

the country's training grounds for reporters, knows about the *Columbia Daily Tribune*. This is the crosstown rival of the journalism school's own *Columbia Missourian*, and its staff is peppered with U of M grads who often go on to major metropolitan dailies.

The *Tribune* has long been seen as one of the nation's top small dailies. Serving a college town of about 60,000 people, the newspaper has been among the country's small town leaders in design, editing, and reporting. Many University of Missouri student reporters for the *Columbia Missourian* have chafed at getting beaten on a story by a more seasoned *Tribune* reporter.

Jim Robertson is managing editor of the *Tribune,* and he is no stranger to the concept of community journalism.

"I got my first byline in our community weekly paper at about age 10," Robertson says. "It was an account of a 4-H camping trip, and I instinctively used storytelling technique. The positive feedback was a revelation. I led a team in high school that established a weekly community alternative newspaper. During that time in the late 1960s and early 1970s, the power of newspaper journalism took on a new tone for me as I read reports from Vietnam and Watergate—unprecedented war coverage."

What he discovered was that a kind of unwritten contract exists between the journalist and the reader when it comes to newspaper journalism.

"I started to understand the intimate connection between readers and their newspapers," he explains, "and the fact that readers expect not only information but leadership. Tremendous potential to be a progressive force. The mix of ego and altruism hooked me early and sustained me through high school and college."

Contrary to a popular view that it helps if a person wanting to enter journalism is a loner, Robertson believes it helps to be a joiner.

"In fact, the joiner probably has an advantage over the loner as a reporter," he explains. "He or she is more comfortable interacting with all kinds of people and can more easily interview in a flowing, non-threatening way. Journalism is not a solitary endeavor. The 'calling' finds motivation within—the proverbial fire in the belly—and not from external separation."

Has he seen that passion in the young journalists he has hired in recent years, or are there other motivations crowding out the fire in the belly?

"Considering the fashionable pummeling of the 'mainstream media,' it's a wonder newsrooms can still attract the talented, committed young journalists we do," he says. "Almost universally, they come from homes in which newspapers and their role in democracy are important. It seems to me they're motivated by many of the same reasons I was at their age."

Among the motivations Robertson lists are these two:

- People see the potential for journalists to do good.
- The nontraditional lifestyle and creative cachet connected with writing appeal to them.

Does he believe that reporters who lean toward the liberal political view are better meant for uncovering wrongdoing, or is it a bad rap for conservatives to say they're less inclined to go after corruption in government?

A good friend wrote recently about the differences in the two dominant political parties, and his explanation struck me as a pretty good description of why journalists might lean toward the more liberal end. At the risk of oversimplifying . . . Republicans tend to be oriented toward creation and protection of capital—which they believe drives prosperity—and Democrats are more concerned with basic questions about the welfare of the people.

The legislative friction between the two ideologies is essential to the success of American democracy. That concern about people and their conflicts and struggles is what informs and motivates many journalists. It's what makes good stories. That's about as clear a link as I can see between journalists and progressive politics.

And is part of uncovering wrongdoing going for the "larger truth" of a situation or issue, or is such a macro-exploration beyond the pale of daily journalism? "It's the job of reporters and their editors to tell readers 'where the ball is' with enough background and perspective to fully inform," Robertson says.

> The editorialists and columnists take over after that to offer their version of a "larger truth." Add to their voices the op-ed writers, the letter writers, bloggers, and anonymous call-ins, and the larger truth begins to emerge.

> It's probably hubris to believe we can detect a larger truth during the snapshot of time we report on people and events.

How do ethics factor into that search for the truth, at either the micro or macro levels, and are journalists paying enough attention to ethical issues today?

> By the time they get to our newsroom, young journalists have a pretty good awareness of ethical issues. They recognize when a situation arises that we should discuss. They recognize, and I continually emphasize, that our credibility is the currency of the realm and that an ethical slip can do damage that might be out of proportion to the sin.

> It's my impression there's very little discussion about hypothetical situations. Most of the conversations have to do with specific questions that arise during the reporting and writing of stories.

In cataloguing the key ethical issues that confront him and his journalists on a regular basis, Robertson says daily reporting is full of ethical dilemmas, and some of them just keep reappearing.

> Pretty basic stuff, really. For example, what do you do when you've identified yourself as a reporter and after a long Q&A session the source says, "It's all off the record"? Another example: Should we always identify ourselves, or is an "undercover" role acceptable? What if we're contacted by someone who trusts us who is a suspect in a crime?

> We discuss these questions, consult resources such as Poynter [Poynter Institute of Media Studies], including professionals we know and respect who might have encountered similar issues. We weigh our role and the potential damage to others affected by our decisions. Then we decide.

Do any of those ethical considerations involve how close or how far away a reporter should get to his or her story or sources? Have Robertson's thoughts on this kind of emotional attachment changed over the years? To answer this question, he separates the notion of detachment from the concept of balance.

> If a reporter is emotionally detached from a story, the story probably won't have much impact. Detachment isn't important, but balance is. I subscribed to that principle early on. Readers have abandoned newspapers in droves in favor of platforms and story forms that better match the way they live and see the world. We don't have to abandon our principles to be a force in this new universe.

> We must, however, stand back and recognize what draws readers to a story. Emotion creates a powerful pull, and you can't write it if you don't feel it.

What about matters of spiritual faith? Are stories involving them beyond the pale of daily journalism, and should reporters try to keep their own faith—or lack of it—separate from their work or their assessment of the situations they cover?

"Our coverage, like that in many newspapers, is event based," Robertson says, echoing a long-held truism in journalism. "We mainstream our coverage—mostly wire service produced—of big events such as debate about gay clergy, papal visits and pronouncements, etc. It's probably not terribly satisfying for those whose faith is a large part of their lives." He continues,

> Journalism and religion is a tough mix. Religion depends on faith, and journalism demands proof.

What about coverage of the spiritual faith of political candidates and office-holders? Important? Not important? Should journalists be looking for how separate the politicians keep their personal faith from their public decisions?

"They've got to be separate in the making of public policy," Robertson says. "The alternative is theocracy, and you'll be hard pressed to find widespread support for that. We should be totally tolerant of personal beliefs, but when our representatives press their beliefs on others in the form of public policy, we should throw the rascals out."

Republican presidential candidate Mike Huckabee once said that he would "consider it an extraordinarily shallow faith that does not really impact the way we think about other human beings and the way we respond to them." Robertson has a mixed reaction to that thought, especially when it comes to journalists' personal faith.

That's the tough part for some reporters I've worked with. One young reporter, very involved in his fundamentalist church, refused to write about things his church found repugnant. I let it slide with the first refused assignment and discussed our responsibility to report fairly about things we might find uncomfortable. I asked him to rethink his career decision if he found that impossible.

After the second refusal, we agreed to end his employment. I have to believe it's possible to practice journalism at the highest standards of balance and fairness and still retain a religious faith. But it takes effort and accommodation. Like voters, newspaper readers come in all sizes, shapes, colors, and ideologies, and our coverage should reflect the richness of that mixture.

Searching for Balance

Gretchen Dworznik

Former Reporter, WNWO-TV, Toledo

Gretchen Dworznik, a graduate of Ashland University, was looking to strike a balance between attachment and detachment when she worked as a reporter for the Toledo television station WNWO. But she was having a hard time of it. The search proved so frustrating that, after a few years, she decided to leave the daily practice of journalism.

"My decision to leave the news business had a lot to do with the issue of detachment," she says. "I didn't like to be too detached, but it became hard to handle the attachment as well after the fact. So I was in a kind of Catch-22 situation. Do I care? Do I not care? So I told myself maybe this dilemma is telling me perhaps I should get out now."

Dworznik was voicing the problem a lot of journalists face when they try to decide how much to let themselves feel for the people and the issues they cover. While traditional journalism is founded upon detachment, the reality that reporters are human beings and not robots is always present. Added to that reality is the fact that readers and viewers like to know a reporter cares about the story he or she is covering. And the broadcast medium brings the audience closer to its reporters' emotional responses. Watching a televised report, rather than reading a print story, gives people a better sense of how much reporters care, which may be one big reason that survey respondents usually say they trust TV news more than newspapers. Dworznik notes:

> The visuals allow a viewer to feel like they have more input into what they're seeing. They can see the reporter's face and tell if that person is honest, or [they] have a sense that "I can see the picture, so this must be true."

Dworznik cares so much about this issue of emotional attachment vs. detachment that she has made it the centerpiece of her doctoral dissertation at Kent State University where she is pursuing a PhD in mass communication. The thesis is an analysis of the emotional aspects of journalism and the lingering psychological effects that some stories can have on the journalists covering them.

> There are several studies showing that the relationship between what journalists do and police or firefighters do and see is very similar. Actually the reactions are pretty identical. Journalists talk to the same victims and eyewitnesses that the cops and firemen do, and they can be affected in the same way.

> It's a very fine line [detachment vs. attachment]. If you go overboard and so immerse yourself in a story that you can't see the forest for the trees, then you're wrong.

A couple of stories stand out from Dworznik's memory as examples of this last point.

Two cases that I can remember when this happened. I did a story about a woman whose landlord had turned off her heat and water because she supposedly wasn't paying the bills. She went on and on about her babies being cold and unclean and how the landlord refused to fix the place up. She also said that she had paid the landlord. I was pretty green at the time, and it didn't occur to me to get the landlord's side. I did this big piece about her, and it turns out she was lying. She wasn't paying her bills, and she was the one who had destroyed the house. I felt really dumb.

Another time, I interviewed the son of an elderly woman who'd been attacked in her home and killed. The guy cried and cried, and I did this warm and fuzzy piece about this nice old lady whose son was so sad that she was dead. Turns out he killed her. Fortunately for my ego, three other stations had been fooled too.

In time, Dworznik grew weary of being tricked by people she was trying to help.

"That fact—that even regular people would try to manipulate me really bummed me out. But I just learned to be very skeptical. It's funny, even now that I'm not reporting, it's a little hard to turn off. I am routinely skeptical of grieving people. In my head, I'm always thinking, "Are they really sincere about this? Or are they just putting on a show?""

Dworznik says that the emotional punch of journalism was one aspect of the job she was not prepared for when she entered the field following graduation in 1998 and a brief four-month stint in public relations.

"There was never any mention of a journalist's emotional state in school, and, at first in the business, many reporters would discount it too," she says. "So my first reaction when I began reporting was to cut myself off from the emotions and try to erect a wall."

She said this became difficult to do, especially because she was the police reporter for NBC 24 in Toledo and she covered a lot of traumatic stories involving death.

"Once I covered four deaths in just one week," she recalls. "It can get to you."

Dworznik thinks the first story that pierced her emotional wall was one involving the death of a woman's husband who had been shot. She was assigned to interview the widow and could not prevent herself from feeling deeply for the woman's plight.

"I was unprepared for it," she explains, "and I stumbled through the interview asking the 'how-do-you-feel' thing, which was totally wrong. I learned later to ask that question in different ways like, 'What was your reaction when you discovered . . .' and to ease into the question more slowly."

Dworznik agrees it is easier for print reporters to let those emotional reactions surface in an interview because they are not pressed for time; for television reporters, however, the camera is rolling and deadlines are quicker. Television loves emotional reactions on camera, she notes, and, sometimes, reporters feel they must go right for the emotional jugular.

Her biggest traumatic stories were interviews with victims' families.

"I would become very sad just like it was my own loss. But you have to pull back some because you have to get through it and do your job."

How does she view "the world out there?" With suspicion? A glass half empty or half full?

I think, by nature, I tend to always want to look on the bright side and give people the benefit of the doubt. I tend to see the good in people and assume that they are being truthful and honest. That has gotten me into trouble several times in everyday life and was a huge challenge for me as a reporter. With politicians it was easy—I never trusted what they said and repeatedly questioned everything they told me. Most of them weren't very covert, and their attempted manipulation was so easy to spot it was almost sad.

However, I was not so quick to distrust victims and their families when I spoke to them. I would always think, "How can you be skeptical of this person when they are grieving like this?" It was a back-and-forth battle I fought continuously, but, after I was lied to a few times, it became easier and easier to question everybody, grieving or not.

How did she show her passion for a story?

"Just in the way I wrote it; in the bites I chose. And I became less clinical if I allowed myself to care a little bit. Otherwise, it's just a series of facts. He went here, she did this, he said this. I could also be a little more poetic if I let myself care."

Dworznik says she had the luxury of having producers who knew she could write very well. So they gave her latitude in the way she told her stories. They found she could have all the facts in the story but still make it artistic and entertaining too. "They let me run with whatever I got," she recalls.

Over the years, she developed many other skills as well. Here's how she describes the method television journalists use in handling people who want to talk but don't want to do it on camera: "Sometimes we ask, 'Well can we just show parts of you without showing your face? Can we show your hands, for instance?'"

She says that this strategy enables the camera to pick up on someone's nonverbal communication, especially if a person is being expressive with hand gestures or even with his or her feet, tapping toes in a nervous reaction, for example. And sometimes the person is silhouetted, too.

What got Dworznik into the news business in the first place? Curiosity about the world, in a nutshell.

"I'd always loved the news, and I got most of it from television news shows. Also, Mom was a magazine freak, and I'd read her *Time* and *Newsweek* magazines and even cut out articles on major stories like the Challenger disaster and Pan Am 103. Not out of morbidity, but just out of interest."

A popular student at Ashland University, Dworznik decided to major in communication arts with a television emphasis. It clicked, she loved it, and she was hooked.

But there was another motivating factor: Dworznik loves novelty in her days and avoids routines as much as possible. She likes each day to be different, and she felt that the news business would offer the kind of variety she was seeking. In that sense, the reality of television matched her expectation of it.

Were there any realities that didn't match her expectations?

> For the most part, the realities matched my expectations. There were two things that I didn't expect, however. One was that there was more of "Let's just get a story because we need to fill the time." Sometimes, a producer wouldn't even care if it was a good story idea or not; we just need to fill the time. Second, there was a lot more stress on my emotional well-being than I thought there would be. I wasn't prepared for that. I so desperately wanted everyone to like me, and I wasn't prepared for the reactions I would get sometimes. Some people didn't like me because I was the media, and I just wanted to say, "But I'm still Gretchen!"

Another frustration for her was to see how many of her family and friends didn't really understand what she did or really know much about the importance of journalism.

> Some of them would try to bash the media, and it became very frustrating. Most journalists are into the passion of journalism. There is a certain love for news and for all things media, and for "Look at what I did!"

In that sense, journalism is more of a mission or calling than a job, Dworznik believes. So it made the bashing of her business frustrating, and she found herself hanging out more with journalists than non-journalists.

"I don't think a lot of students today get it," she said, referring to the passion of journalism and its mission. "A few of them do, and you can see it in them and in their work. But most of them are into it because they think TV is cool, and you get to wear make-up and wear nice clothes and be on camera."

There is also some confusion as to what journalism and journalists actually are because of all the pseudo news shows and pseudo journalists.

"And some students just don't like the news itself because they think it's all slanted or boring. Those are the ones who won't make it in this business."

Dworznik says her favorite compliment would be a thank-you note from a victim's family because she covered a lot of crime and cared deeply about being accurate but also about being sensitive to the innocents, the victims, and their families. "A note just might say 'Thank you for caring and for doing such a nice story for us,'" she explains.

When questioned about dealing with the celebrity factor that confronts television journalists, she said that she remembers only two times when it got in the way of a story. One was when she covered a story about pickets. Before she showed up with the cameraman, the picketers were just sitting around. But, upon her arrival, they jumped to their feet, starting marching, and one guy started banging a drum. She got after the picketers later and said she didn't want them changing things just because she was there.

She dealt a lot with the fairness issue: "After I screwed up a story or two, I got very worried about fairness. But sometimes it's really hard to be fair, especially when only one side will talk and the other won't."

Once, when Dworznik covered a dispute between two families, the victim's family set two Dobermans on her. She left and went to interview the other family, who did talk. Then the first family came back to her after the story was done and critiqued her for not getting their side. "But you set your dogs on me!" she replied. She then tried again to get their side, but they said they didn't want to talk.

In other situations as well, reporters find it difficult to be balanced and fair. For example, journalists often seem to be confronted by the dilemma of projecting their own worldviews and religious beliefs onto the picture appearing in front of them as they piece together a story. How has Dworznik handled that dissonance, or is it something journalists should worry about?

What should a journalist do with her or his own worldview when going into a story?

You have to set your own beliefs aside. I believe in God, but I am not an openly religious person. In fact, openly religious people, those who are overzealous about it, tend to make me really uncomfortable. As a result, I've never volunteered for any story that had even the slightest religious tones. Even those silly ones where people see Jesus in an apple pie. I just knew I wouldn't believe that it was Jesus, or see it, so what was the point? The only stories I ever did that involved religion were abortion issues. And even then, I did not use bites that spoke about God's will and whatever. I don't know that it was because those claims couldn't be proven, but I think it was because I knew those religious-based comments would cause a stir, and I didn't want the phone calls. I still got some anyway for not including the religious angle, but I think it would have been worse if I had.

And what of a reporter's political beliefs? Same thought there? "This is a hard question to answer because I worked only in local news at a station that did very few investigative pieces—political or otherwise," she says.

However, I will say this. There were several reporters whom I worked with who had very strong political beliefs. But I never saw any evidence of that affecting how they did a story or what stories they pitched. Our government reporter loved all facets of government and routinely did stories critical of both the Republicans and Democrats in office.

I know there is all this talk about the liberal bias in the media, and maybe, at the national level, there is. But, on a local level, I never saw it. We did the stories we were told to do, whether we agreed with them or not. Maybe those stories that were in line with our own political beliefs turned out to be better pieces, but I think something like that happens on a more subconscious level. Purposely changing the way we did a story for whatever reason would have brought to us much more grief than we were interested in enduring.

Dworznik has given some thought to why dedicated journalists often leave the profession to pursue careers in business, public relations, or advertising—the very institutions they were skeptical of as journalists.

I think this happens for two reasons. First, compared to television, all of those professions are so much easier. It's kind of the, "If you can't beat them, join them" idea. You get so tired of fighting the power that you just give up and join it. Being skeptical and challenging all the time can be exhausting. It's much easier to be the person trying to fool the media than it is to be the media person trying to figure out whose fooling them.

Second, I think that television experience tends to make people very marketable to those in the non-TV world. TV journalists tend to stand out from the pack when that pack is full of just the average Joe. So I think they move into those professions because it's so easy to get jobs in them. You make contacts while you're still reporting, and, as soon as you say you want out, chances are some of those contacts will get you a job.

In her own case, after only about five years as a full-time television reporter, Dworznik decided it was time to leave and to turn instead to teaching the news business in a college setting. She picked up her MA at Ashland and is now finishing her PhD at Kent. She has just been hired as an assistant professor of communication arts at Ashland University.

"I talk about the emotional aspect of journalism with my students now," she says. "But, for me, it just wasn't fun any more as a reporter. I was doing that battle [between attachment and detachment] every day."

A Flood of Memories, A New Idea of Objectivity

Michael Perlstein, *The Times-Picayune*

Twenty years on the same newspaper, reporting on the same city day after day, would seem to leave a journalist little room for surprise. Not so for Michael Perlstein or his colleagues on the New Orleans *Times-Picayune*, who were to face an event beyond their imaginations in 2005.

It was, to quote Perlstein, a time "when it actually seemed plausible that my home for the past 20 years would become the next Atlantis." It was a time that came to be known in New Orleans as simply "the storm" and "the flood."

To the rest of the world, it was Hurricane Katrina.

Perlstein, who reported from the New Orleans area throughout this tragedy, has regained his ability to crack a smile and even crack a joke, and he has moved on in a number of other ways following Katrina. He and his family are rebuilding their lives, and he has left newspaper reporting for the halls of higher education, specifically, Loyola University of New Orleans, where he teaches journalism. He is obviously well respected by his colleagues and students, and, in a gathering at a local restaurant in 2007, two referred to Perlstein and his *Times-Picayune* colleagues as "heroes." After hearing the story of their flood coverage, it is easy to see why.

The Loyola campus is next door to Tulane where Michael's wife Patty teaches. But, like many New Orleanians, theirs is a rebuilding job in progress, and the reminders of devastation are still there as they walk the streets of the Crescent City.

"For local journalists, there was no way to cover the story as a dispassionate outsider," Perlstein says.

> While reporting and writing about flooding, lawlessness, separation from family, bungled government response, and the mounting death toll, most of us were experiencing a combination of those hardships in a direct and personal way.
>
> More than half of us at *The Times-Picayune* lost homes to flooding. While working feverishly in the first week to write and publish stories, we somehow found time to canoe into our flooded homes, rescue pets, ferry neighbors to safety, and check on the homes of friends and colleagues. All the while, for those of us in New Orleans, getting in touch with family was impossible for several days and difficult even then.

The memories seem to flood back to Perlstein, reminiscent of the way the waters swept through New Orleans following the cave-in of the city's levees.

> We saw looting on a mass scale, such as inside the Tchoupitoulas Street Super Wal-Mart, and became victims on a smaller scale if our homes or cars were hit. My car, parked high and dry on an overpass and surrounded by a moat of water, was nevertheless looted of a radio, CDs, baby car seat, and golf clubs.
>
> On a more tragic level, most of us knew people who perished, including a popular New Orleans police public information officer and a prominent physician who was the brother of a veteran *T-P* writer. At the very least, those who

reported the disaster from New Orleans confronted dead and bloated bodies for a solid 10 days after the levees breached. Throughout the ordeal, we worked despite intense feelings of sadness, anger, frustration, disorientation, grief, and anxiety about the future. As I said at the time, adrenalin is a powerful drug, and it was critical in keeping us going during those first harrowing weeks.

Perlstein's wife and three young children—four-year-old Max and one-year-old twins Eli and Jackie—were among those lucky enough to evacuate the city, albeit in bumper-to-bumper traffic. Their destination was Milwaukee, a thousand miles north where they could take refuge with family. Mike stayed on with nine other *T-P* staffers to cover the tragedy of a city and many of its inhabitants drowning in water.

The Times-Picayune itself had to be published on ground safer than New Orleans provided, and the paper moved to Baton Rouge and Houma, leaving Perlstein and his colleagues in what came, ironically, to be known as the paper's "New Orleans Bureau." From the whole experience, Perlstein and other reporters developed a new idea of journalistic objectivity.

> Objective reporting quickly gave way to subjectivity (and even advocacy) in the storm's aftermath, and the immense scale of the calamity and our personal immersion also gave rise to another level of journalism that I have coined "hyper-objectivity." Those of us in the floodwaters also were fueled heavily by reporting instincts, journalistic training, sense of duty to get the story out, loyalty to our newspaper, and the realization that this was "the big one," the story of a lifetime in which our words carried immediate weight and urgency and [which], eventually, would become the first draft of this history of tragedy.

> Amid this intense reporting experience, we quickly became aware of how easy it was to get the story wrong. We saw false information come from the mouths of top officials, from the governor down to the mayor and police chief. We saw some of the bogus information repeated in news reports, from sensational TV accounts to AP updates. We saw veteran journalists of major newspapers and magazines miss the mark because they didn't understand New Orleans, strived too hard to capture the hopelessly complex aftermath into a made-for-deadline epic.

> Clarity slowed us down—made sure we got it right, understood the complexity of New Orleans, knew the landscape, [were] informed enough not to fall for easy stereotypes.

Perlstein is like the many journalists in New Orleans and beyond who have experienced tragedies first hand. These experiences change reporters professionally and personally and often leave them facing the question of whether they would exchange the biggest story of their lives for a rewritten past in which a particular tragedy or disaster never happened at all. Perlstein has already found his answer to that question.

As he wrote for the magazine of his alma mater, Reed College, "If I had a chance to give it all back—the plaudits from peers, the national media appearances (I did CNN, MSNBC, NPR, and others), the gratitude from citizens—I would forgo every byline, every life-altering moment, in exchange for the pre-Katrina New Orleans."[3]

How Faith Enters the Picture

Terry Mattingly

Religion Columnist, Scripps Howard News Service

Terry Mattingly is a veteran religion news columnist for the Scripps Howard News Service. He is also a conservative who dislikes the word because he thinks "conservative"—like "liberal"—has lost its meaning in a sea of broad usages. He feels the same way about the words "evolution" and "creationism," by the way.

"Those words are very unevenly defined," he says. "I believe newspapers are more libertarian than liberal or conservative. And the single thing about journalism that ticks me off the most is that [in the debate over the world's origin] we only use two words: 'evolution' and 'creationism.' The press just doesn't catch the different gradations and possible meanings of each of those words."

Mattingly admits that's a tall order, especially for the time- and attention-conscious broadcast media.

"I don't know how you do it in the broadcast media," he says. "How do you get that kind of depth into four-second sound bites? It's easier to do it in the print world."

Still, Mattingly believes precise meanings are too often missing from today's world of journalism, he thinks they are vitally important, and he prizes such accuracy even more than objectivity.

Mattingly is also director of the Washington Journalism Center (funded by the Council for Christian Colleges and Universities), and he has a simple rule he passes on to the college journalism students who come there to learn. It sounds strangely familiar.

"I just tell them to report unto others as you would have them report unto you," he says.

The third professional hat he wears is editor of the Web site, GetReligion.org, whose founding editor is Douglas LeBlanc, associate editor of *Christianity Today* magazine. When added to his other two jobs, writing for this site gives Mattingly three ways to deliver his message about the importance of covering religion better.

Religion has always factored into Mattingly's journalism. Although he originally became a journalism major at Baylor University because he wanted to write about music (a music major seemed doubtful without requisite talent on the piano first), his motivation morphed in the spring semester of his sophomore year.

> I became interested in how the media largely ignored religion. [A professor] told me that other students on the college newspaper's staff have already picked up that religion is the worst covered subject in the entire American mainstream press. Then he asked me, "Do you want to do anything about that?" That's when my interest in covering religion really intensified.

Mattingly completed his BA in journalism and then picked up an MA in an interdisciplinary Baylor program mixing religion, government, and law. He later got a second master's degree in journalism from the University of Illinois. While in Urbana, he began writing some religion news for a local paper. Then he moved to North Carolina and became a religion reporter for the *Charlotte Observer* and later for the *Rocky Mountain News* in Denver. The *News* was part of the Scripps newspaper chain, and it was there that Mattingly began writing a syndicated column called "On Religion" for the Scripps Howard News Service.

Today, 18 years and counting, that column appears in some 300 dailies and another 600 smaller newspapers around the country.

Much of Mattingly's thinking about the lax coverage of religious news can be found on the GetReligion.org Web site. Here, in part, is his explanation of what he and his colleagues aim to accomplish and why they think it is important:

> Day after day, millions of Americans who frequent pews see ghosts when they pick up their newspapers or turn on television news. They read stories that are important to their lives, yet they seem to catch fleeting glimpses of other characters or other plots between the lines. There seem to be other ideas or influences hiding there.
>
> One minute they are there. The next they are gone. There are ghosts in there, hiding in the ink and the pixels. Something is missing in the basic facts or perhaps most of the key facts are there, yet some are twisted. Perhaps there are sins of omission, rather than commission. A lot of these ghosts are, well, holy ghosts. They are facts and stories and faces linked to the power of religious faith. Now you see them. Now you don't. In fact, a whole lot of the time you don't get to see them. But that doesn't mean they aren't there.[4]

Mattingly has also taught in theological seminaries, and he enjoys mixing writing and religion. That is controversial territory for many journalists, but Mattingly believes it can be negotiated by paying attention to a few guidelines.

> It's false that a reporter can unplug his ideology and somehow become neutral. Objectivity should be more of a methodology thing. Balance is a better word than objectivity.
>
> Editors need to produce a paper that's fair to the audience they are trying to reach. If you have a large section of your readership that says your abortion coverage is unbalanced, and if one side is saying their views are being distorted, then the editor must take that seriously.

Mattingly believes that journalists can solve many of the problems endemic to covering religion simply by applying good journalistic principles.

"The answer to journalistic problems is almost always journalistic solutions," he says. "Journalists get into trouble in covering religion news by applying non-journalistic solutions. Just do more religion coverage, and use a wide array of sources."

When it comes to advocacy journalism or pushing for a particular conclusion in a news story, Mattingly draws the line. "Advocacy and commentary are fine as long as they are clearly labeled as that," he says.

Still, he believes diversity dictates that all sides of issues are covered equally well. Mattingly recalls the late David Shaw of the *Los Angeles Times* taking the media—including his own paper—to task for presenting only one worldview on the abortion debate. And he cites *New York Times* Editor William Keller as saying that even his newspaper can do a better job when it comes to understanding alternative political viewpoints and that its reporting on religion and the military needs improvement. And finally, he cites veteran journalist Bill Moyers as saying that so many journalists "are tone deaf to the music of religion."

How does he advise young journalists of faith to steer the waters of objectivity? Does he believe journalists should propagate their own worldviews through their reporting? How would that work?

"You have to be aware first of what your own ideology is so that you can see if it is unfairly creeping into your stories or distorting facts," he says. "And it's not so much what beliefs are in the journalists' heads as it is that others believe their views are being covered accurately."

It is interesting that Mattingly fits his answers to these questions under the journalistic value of diversity. Reiterating that journalists cannot "unplug" themselves from their ideologies and magically become neutral, Mattingly calls upon editors to extend newsroom diversity beyond race and gender to include journalists of faith as well as nonbelievers.

"Diversity of newsrooms is important," he says. "People's information and beliefs must be covered accurately. If more young Christians were committed to the basics of journalism, they would add to the diversity of the newsroom. I'm comfortable that every reporter has his or her own lens."

Covering the Bases in the New South

Otis Sanford

Editor for Opinions and Editorials and Former Managing Editor,
The Commercial Appeal

For many years, Otis Sanford and Memphis journalism have been virtually synonymous. Now editor for editorials and opinions of *The Commercial Appeal*, Sanford has been interested in journalism since becoming a regular

newspaper reader at age 8. While other kids his age were finding various ways to spend their leisure time, one of Sanford's favorite pastimes was sitting down and reading the news.

"My father subscribed to *The Commercial Appeal* six days a week and also occasionally brought home the afternoon Jackson [Mississippi] *Daily News*," Sanford recalls. "He asked me to read them, mainly to keep up with sports, but I soaked up everything about the paper and became an avid newspaper reader. I also loved to write, and, after I wrote my first story for the high school newspaper, while still in the seventh grade, I was hooked on being a reporter."

In the city where Martin Luther King was assassinated, the same city that has experienced so much racial divide over the twentieth century, Sanford was the first African American to become managing editor of the city's largest newspaper, and he is now its editor for opinions and editorials. No small feat, and one that speaks to his strong journalistic credentials and suggests others find him a voice of reason and reconciliation in a city that has needed one badly over the years.

That opinion seems shared by the Associated Press Managing Editors (AMPE) organization, which has named Sanford to its leadership ladder, putting him in line to become president of the APME in 2011. He has also chaired the Mid-America Press Institute.

Sanford began his reporting career at *The Clarion-Ledger* in Jackson, MI. He joined *The Commercial Appeal* in 1977, leaving 10 years later to become assistant city editor at the *Pittsburgh Press*. In 1992, he was named deputy city editor of the *Detroit Free Press,* returning to Memphis and *The Commercial Appeal* in 1994 as the paper's deputy managing editor. He was promoted to managing editor in 2002. He has also taught journalism at the University of Memphis and at the University of Mississippi.

Sanford realizes that any young person who is a joiner might have difficulty taking on journalism as a profession because it can separate a journalist from friends and social situations.

I think the difficulty is mainly in the fact that, to be a really good journalist as a college student, you have to devote most—if not all—of your time to it. If you are a joiner with scores of other interests, it will be difficult for you to put in the time necessary to be the best you can as a journalist. It is much harder for a joiner to be in this business.

Honestly, however, for the journalists I come in contact with the most, I have not seen any downward shift in motivation. Of course, that could be because I seldom talk to the marginal students who have no motivation to be good reporters. My contact is with students who have a strong desire to be in this business. They are the ones seeking internships and wanting to soak up everything when I visit with classes and journalism groups. The two most dominant motivators for young journalists these days seem to be a desire to work at a larger newspaper and to get plum assignments.

What were the key expectations of this veteran journalist when he entered the profession, and have they been met during his years in the news business?

"My number one professional expectation early on was to be a good writer and to eventually write columns and opinion pieces, and that has been met," he says. "I also wanted, after several years as a reporter, to see how high I could possibly go in newspaper management, and that expectation has—for the most part—been met. What has gone unfulfilled so far has been the opportunity to be the top editor of a newspaper. I also would love to win a major journalism prize, but basically all of my goals as a journalist have been met."

Many of Sanford's views on journalism—such as the need for reporters to remain detached from the stories they are working on—have remained intact over the years. He does, however, grant some leeway when it comes to a reporter's emotional attachment to stories.

"I can't say that my views have changed that much," he explains. "I still believe reporters should not get so close to a story that it compromises them ethically. However, I don't have a problem with an emotional attachment to a story if it means that the reporter will dig even deeper to uncover information they do not ordinarily get. Just as long as the decisions are ethical, I am okay with it."

As to the issue of a reporter's political ideology affecting his or her zeal for exposing corruption, Sanford has an interesting view. He understands that many more journalists define themselves as politically independent or liberal than as conservative, and he knows it has been suggested by some that conservatives are slower to accept change while liberals have a strong desire to push for change.

"I think, in many respects, the premise of this question is true. I believe that most journalists who want to effect change have more independent or liberal views," he says. "Most journalists want to watch out for the have-nots in society, to be a watchdog on government, to uncover mistreatment of people who cannot fight for themselves. My personal view is that, in order to push for real change, you have to have an independent political philosophy that shades slightly left of center."

He understands why many journalists are frustrated about not having more resources to present the "larger truth" of a story, but he says the most resourceful of those reporters usually find a way to do it anyway.

> I think that we in daily journalism are confined too often to reporting where the ball is because of a lack of time and resources do anything else. The superior journalists working for daily publications find a way to do both: report the daily news but also seek out the larger truths or the perspectives and deeper meanings of issues.

Sanford would like to see more time spent on ethical discussions in the newsroom, however.

> We don't spend nearly enough time discussing ethical issues. That is one of my passions. I am viewed as the chief of the ethics police in my shop because I preach ethics all the time. We have those discussions, but not nearly enough. We do have them when issues arise, but I would like to see ongoing dialogues on ethics.

> One issue is political affiliation and the difficulty some reporters have in being totally neutral during political campaigns, particularly at the national level. I am not sure I know how to go about resolving that. We cannot legislate a person's political beliefs, but we do ask them to keep their views to themselves and, whenever possible, we make sure our reporters who cover politics remain as impartial as possible.

Sanford's passion for sound ethical behavior is documented in his newspaper columns. For example, on August 5, 2007, he wrote an impassioned plea for more ethics in government. In part, the column read as follows:

It's not every day in Memphis that you get honesty from a politician, particularly during an election year.

So imagine the elation that Memphis Rotary Club members felt last week as we listened to refreshing political candor delivered by someone who has never received a single vote in Tennessee.

Arkansas Gov. Mike Beebe was the featured Rotary speaker Tuesday. During his brief talk and a question-and-answer session, Beebe deftly touched on everything from ethics in government to Hillary Clinton's popularity in the state she once called home.

But his overall message was this: Public confidence in elected officials is sputtering on empty. And not enough good people are running for office. His stirring comments should have been recorded, turned into Politics 101 and used as a required short course for everyone seeking elected office in Memphis this year.

Of course you could argue that Beebe, elected governor last year to replace Mike Huckabee, can easily afford to be straightforward in downtown Memphis. He doesn't have to shop for votes on the east side of the Mississippi River.

Still, his clarion call for cynicism about the political process to end and for office seekers to reconnect with the electorate was on target. And it resonated with those of us who are weary of polarizing politicians who care more about posturing and protecting their own interests than serving the public.

In essence, politics these days has a serious image problem, leaving in its wake two sets of voters—the ones who are moved to act through anger and those who, for various reasons, have simply tuned out and may not vote at all.[5]

Turning from politics to religion, Sanford is proud of the way *The Commercial Appeal* has reported on this field over the years, and he sees much value in covering the spiritual aspects of life.

Speaking only for what we do here, I believe we have covered religion very well over the last ten or more years. In fact, one of our best writers for years had a "Faith Matters" column that was extremely well received. He is no longer on the staff, but he set the tone for religion and faith coverage here that . . . is still very strong. Some senior editors also understand the importance that religion plays in the lives of people in this community, so we try not to shortchange it.

Overall, though, I don't think there is enough broad understanding of religious concepts by many reporters, so what you get is very shallow stuff.

Does covering faith issues translate into looking at how well—or poorly—political candidates keep their own religious beliefs separate from or integrated with their elected roles? Should journalists expect office-holders to separate their personal views from their governmental decisions?

"I do think you bring your background to your job," Sanford says. "But there are instances when decisions must be made that run somewhat counter to personal beliefs. They may not be on a grand scale because, in those instances, you should do what is morally and religiously correct. I think you can, on occasion, separate the two."

Does the same hold true for journalists separating their own religious views from their work? What should journalists do with their faith when they go out to report on the world?

"I do think that journalists are called to write about issues and even to go into places that they wouldn't ordinarily go because of their faith. But, in those instances, I think it is still possible to separate your religious beliefs from your job."

The Trauma of Reporting

Joe Hight

Director of Information and Development, *The Oklahoman*

As a managing editor at Oklahoma's largest daily newspaper, Joe Hight knows something about the trauma reporters and editors experience when covering tragedies. Hight's paper, *The Oklahoman*, is located in Oklahoma City and was the first metro daily to respond to the bombing of the Alfred C. Murrah Federal Building on April 19, 1995.

It was also the last to leave.

The newspaper's intense coverage of that story, which involved nearly every reporter and editor from *The Oklahoman* over the weeks, months, and years following the bombing, left its scars, and Hight worries about his fellow journalists. His concern led him to serve two terms as president of the Dart Center for Trauma and Journalism, an international organization based at the University of Washington with offices in London and Melbourne.

Hight, who is responsible for supervising feature stories, research, and development at his paper, has also coauthored the booklets *Tragedies and Journalists: A Guide for More Effective Coverage* and the upcoming *First Responders*. Hight explains that emotional empathy is important to the journalist, even though it can be dangerous:

> The best reporters in the coverage of tragedy are usually ones who are most sensitive to people and their emotions. It's unrealistic for editors and/or management to think that their reporters will be totally unattached in the coverage of people affected by tragedy, in their midst, in their community.

> Children, especially. I think journalists overcome their own emotions to cover a story effectively, realizing that the people and the community are more than numbers—are more than the perpetrators or natural occurrence that caused it.

And that kind of emotional attachment can drain any journalist, especially after time.

"In my years of being connected to the Dart Center for Journalism and Trauma, I've talked to several, perhaps many, reporters who were thinking about leaving the profession because we cover so much tragedy in our lifetimes," Hight says. "I remember one instance at another newsroom in which a reporter told her editor that she had to leave because she couldn't cover the tragedy during the day and then go home at night to deal with her own tragedy."

At least two reporters from *The Oklahoman* were assigned almost exclusively to the Oklahoma City bombing story for a period of two years. A lot of trauma can get stored up over that period of time, even for the steeliest of reporters.

At the newspaper, Hight was the victims team leader for the Oklahoma City bombing coverage that won two national awards from the Society of Professional Journalists, a national Dart Award for Excellence in Coverage of Violence, and many others.

Hight's deep concern for helping others was a prime reason he became a journalist in the first place, and he discovered that many people could be helped simply by learning the truth of situations in the world. He majored in journalism at the University of Central Oklahoma and has spent nearly 30 years in the profession since.

"Idealistically, I wanted to make a difference in people's lives," Hight says. "Early on, when I worked at a campus newspaper, I learned that the media have a significant effect on people and how they react to news and events that affect their lives. I also found that, because of the First Amendment, journalists were vital to our democracy. Those two factors, and my instructors and fellow journalism students in college, motivated me."

So he wasn't in it simply to strike back at what he deemed an unfair or wicked world?

"I've always tried to look at the world optimistically, but I never saw the total of it as friendly," he explains. "In journalism, you quickly learn that people react to you differently, sometimes just because you're a journalist. Or they want to use you for their own personal or political means. I am realistic in that sense, but I do think that journalism can make the world a much better place, especially our country where these freedoms are guaranteed."

Hight has a particular set of motivations he looks for when hiring young reporters, and he likes what he sees in many of the candidates he interviews.

> I look for enthusiasm, drive, and curiosity—the willingness to ask questions about what makes your newspaper work. Show me that you've researched us. Show me that you can ask questions, because that's what you'll be doing. Red flags would be someone who's failed to research who I am and, most importantly, what the newspaper is.

> I also look for people who are willing to learn more. Learning more about writing, copyediting, multimedia skills. Learning doesn't stop when you graduate from college. Those skills must be honed for the rest of your life. It saddens me and frustrates me when I see a young journalist failing to attend training sessions that can help improve him or her.

The quest for learning is definitely high on this editor's agenda when he is looking over prospective hires at *The Oklahoman*. He also likes his reporters to crave challenge and to stretch themselves.

> I've taught and attended hundreds, maybe thousands, of workshops and have always learned something from them. Someone who tells me that he or she is comfortable with the job might as well retire because they're not willing to learn any more that can improve them in the future.

I also look for people who like to do a variety of jobs because that is what it will take to survive in this profession. I understand "finding your niche" or being an expert in a certain area, but that doesn't mean you shouldn't explore new ways to do your job better or explore areas that may expand your "expertise."

As for a reporter's zeal in uncovering wrongdoing being connected to his or her own political ideology, Hight sees little correlation between the two.

"No, as a journalist, I hope there is no correlation," he says. "The desire to uncover wrongdoing in government and/or business should cross political boundaries."

Turning from political leanings to a reporter's spiritual faith, or lack of it, the editor again feels there should be little correlation between religious belief and the story a reporter covers. But he does make allowance for a reporter's personal evaluation of a tragedy when he or she is finished with the story.

"In your own personal time, you have to try to make sense of it through your faith," he says. "However, when you're reporting, you must understand that people have different values than you, and you must be as fair and balanced with them as you would with people of your own faith."

Since journalists cover mostly the here and now of the secular world, should they be exclusively secular in their worldview? Do journalists tend to steer away from matters of faith that cannot be verified? Should they look for spiritual motivations when considering how people react to crises?

"In the United States, the First Amendment defines rights for all of its citizens, which includes journalists," Hight responds. "Journalists should have every right to practice their religion but should be wary about any causes that might seem political in nature. With the advent of religion sections in newspapers, I think journalists are taking more serious looks at how religion and spirituality affect people's lives. It's something that we, as journalists, should not ignore."

But he issues a warning to those reporters who might be tempted to inject their religious beliefs into their reporting.

You can't preach to people and report at the same time. I've witnessed reporters who tried, and it never works and tends to turn off people. It also borders on being unethical. I've resisted signing petitions at my church or in my community because I know that people's perceptions of my fairness to them can depend on it. One time, a person in my church attacked me for it. I felt bad, but it didn't cause me to back down and sign his petition.

The pressure that journalism can exact in asking reporters to separate themselves from civic activities is oppressive for many would-be journalists.

It can also put a dent in a journalist's social life at times. Still, according to Hight, a reporter can remain involved with the world and fair.

> I don't think being a journalist should preclude you from ever being involved in anything. It does, however, require journalists to know their boundaries. For example, a journalist should use his or her right to vote but be careful not to participate in any political campaigns or donate to a cause that would be deemed political.

> Also, they should participate in community and/or school activities but be careful not to participate directly in fundraising. Every future journalist should take an ethics course in college and then seek to work for organizations that have ethical guidelines or defined ethical practices.

Hight believes that there are some serious ethical concerns in journalism today, and he wholeheartedly feels reporters need to pay attention to just ways of resolving the ethical dilemmas they face. One of those dilemmas deals with the separation of fact from opinion in news and feature stories.

"It's always tough to keep your own personal opinion, politics, or faith from your stories," he says. "I think we fight that—and lose—many times."

He also warns against "victimizing" a person who has already been a victim, simply by reporting a story about him or her unfairly or insensitively.

"I'm of the feeling that certain journalists trample on people's lives in the quest to be number one with a story," he explains. "In every major tragedy there are instances in which this occurs. I think the journalists, especially those who are inexperienced or lack basic ethical values, feel pressure to do anything possible to get an exclusive. Many of these are stories no one remembers a year later, except those victims or family members who were further harmed by it."

Hight is frustrated by journalists who see the First Amendment as granting some sort of unlimited hunting license that can be used to hurt innocent people at times.

> Gosh, I wish journalists would realize that the First Amendment provides journalists with many rights, but it does not give us the right to trample on the lives of innocent people. Idealistically, that's what I got into journalism for in the first place: to help the innocent, not harm them.

Clearly, Joe Hight is making a lifelong career out of a profession he loves and still believes in. How does he interpret the decisions of those journalists who decide to leave journalism and enter into professions such as public relations or advertising—professions that, as journalists, they were cynical of?

Money, recognition, power, working conditions, and the nature of what we cover [violence, tragedy, corruption, etc.] are among the reasons that I think journalists migrate to other professions. We shouldn't be surprised that this is happening either, because we cover those areas like public relations, politics, and business consistently and have constant exposure to people in those professions.

Changes in career paths also are becoming more commonplace and, thus, are affecting journalism even more. I would think that most journalists have thought about making changes at some point in their lives. Sometimes the temptations are too much and too hard to resist.

A Matter of Faith

David Waters, *The Washington Post*

Question: What is one of the most important topics, which matters to almost everyone, including its detractors, yet which reporters seem hesitant to touch as a news story?

Answer: Religion.

That is the view of David Waters, former award-winning religion editor of the Memphis *Commercial Appeal* who now produces the On Faith Web site for the online edition of *The Washington Post*. The site is a joint project of the *Post* and its sister publication *Newsweek*, and it aims to encourage online conversations about the intersection of faith and the secular institutions of politics, government, business, and education.

"This [reporting religion] is a subject near and dear to my heart," says Waters. "I could write for hours about it. Generally, I think religion confounds and maybe even scares most reporters. It's so subjective and emotional and visceral and experiential and theoretical and so on. It's not an easy or comfortable subject to cover. So most reporters either ignore it or treat it as any other subject—by gathering quotes through interviews, reading reports or other documents, attending events and meetings, etc."

In short, there is little of what reporters and editors call "enterprise reporting" or "investigative reporting" when it comes to religion, despite its importance in the lives of just about everyone, he says.

"Religion is the most important topic out there. It matters to nearly everyone, even to atheists and agnostics," Waters argues. "It affects nearly everything—from how we raise and educate our kids, to how we make and spend our money, to how we run corporations, communities, and even countries."

Waters first started covering religion as if it were any other beat. He attended meetings and events, talked to leaders, read documents, and looked for trends. He soon realized, however, something was missing in the way he was approaching the subject.

"It wasn't going well. I kept looking for a focal point—like a mayor, a CEO, a team, a building, etc.—but there wasn't one, or so I thought," he explains.

Things were about to change for Waters and his approach, however.

> Then I found the focal point. I decided I shouldn't be covering religion. I should be covering God (or god). I should cover, in the words of Rabbi Harold Kushner, "the difference God makes in the way we live." The whole beat opened up to me, and I realized that I could and should cover "the difference God makes" in the way we live, work, worship, play, pray, eat, vote, wage war, help others, etc. It's the best beat there is.

What should a journalist out on a reporting assignment do with his or her faith? How much should faith be held in check? "Depends on the assignment," Waters responds.

> If I'm a Methodist and I'm reporting on the Methodist quadrennial meeting, I need to check my personal experiences and beliefs at the door and just report what happens, regardless of how I feel about it. If I'm a Methodist covering a

Democratic convention, my faith isn't going to be an issue, although my politics might be. So then I need to check my politics at the door and just report.

Our personal faith deeply affects who we are and what we believe, but it doesn't always have to affect what we do. Far as I know, only one person of faith in the history of the world always practiced what he believed. He would have made a lousy reporter and an even worse politician.

In terms of the debate about whether journalists should seek to present insights into some greater truth, Waters sides with what writer Roger Rosenblatt once wrote in an essay for *Time* magazine: people have come to expect too much from daily journalism if they are looking for "the larger truth." Rosenblatt thinks that the job of the reporter is to report where the ball is at the moment and not where it is not. "I totally agree," Waters reacts.

We can't handle the truth. There is more truth in fiction than in nonfiction. We can point toward the truth. Give people a glimpse of it, a sense of it. I do think that daily journalists either aim too high or too low. We either try to be instant historians or court reporters. Daily journalism is information—useful, relevant, interesting, important information.

But that information should be delivered with as much *context* as possible. That's the value of daily journalism. We tell you what happened, but we also tell you why and why it matters."

This brings journalists into the realm of practicing good ethics, and accurate context setting is one of these ethical practices. But there are many others. Waters believes journalists spend a fair amount of time thinking about the ethical implications of their work.

"It's rare for entire newsroom staffs to have to take the time to discuss ethical issues. Those conversations usually happen on the fly and among two, three, or four people," Waters explains. "Not to say that editors and reporters don't take time every now and then to mull ethical issues or dilemmas. We do. But ethics in daily journalism is practiced on deadline and on a case-by-case basis. We have guidelines, and we know what they are, but they are not and cannot be commandments."

Why not? For one thing, the details of ethical dilemmas often change from one news situation to another, and small changes in details can mean big changes in the way stories are handled. What major ethical issue bothers Waters the most? "The biggest ethical issue in daily journalism today is the ever more difficult effort to provide a public service at a ridiculous profit," he laments.

That tension affects nearly everything we do: staff size and allocation, the time and space we devote to stories, the kinds of stories we pursue and don't, the beats we keep and those we abandon, the level of experience in the newsroom, and the product we put out every day.

Unrealistic profit pressures are reducing the breadth and depth and sophistication of daily journalism. The public and the Republic will suffer because of that.

Although it may surprise those people who believe newspapers are a dying medium, profits for daily newspapers remain high overall. Some observers, such as Dr. Joe Misiewicz, chair of the Department of Telecommunications at Ball State University, estimate those profits at 35 percent, which contrasts considerably with the profits of retail giants like Wal-Mart, who net 3 to 5 percent.

A central ethical concern of many journalists is the concept of objectivity and how well it is—or isn't—practiced in the media. Part and parcel of objectivity is the concept of whether attachment or detachment is the proper stance for reporters when they cover people, issues, and events. Like a lot of veteran journalists, Waters has given these ideas a lot of thought and has even changed his mind somewhat about them.

They have changed. At first I thought objectivity was the goal and actually possible. It's not possible. But it is possible to be neutral and present a fair and balanced report, despite your own personal feelings.

I also thought at first that it was best to remain emotionally detached from sources and stories. That's not possible, nor useful. If I don't feel something or care about something when I'm reporting or writing a story, how can I expect readers to feel or care about it? Just the facts aren't enough. To get closer to the truth of most stories, you need to use your head and your gut and your heart.

Now I think a reporter's emotional attachment to a story almost always produces a more accurate story, especially when that story is dealing with human beings and the human experience.

How do a journalist's political leanings or ideologies fit into this concept of objectivity, assuming they do at all? And do they spur or impede the search for wrongdoing in society?

"I haven't seen any correlation," Waters responds. "I've known liberal reporters and editors who could not have cared less about exposing wrongdoings, and I've known conservative reporters and editors who lived for that. I think a reporter's zeal has more to do with idealism than ideology, more to do with a journalist's character and temperament and talent than a journalist's politics."

Waters majored in political science in college. Did politics factor into his initial motivation to become a reporter? To some degree, he suggests. When asked what motivated him to become a journalist, he answers in this way:

Richard Nixon, Jerry Springer, and my wife. I was thinking of going into politics until Watergate happened. After I saw *All the President's Men*, I shifted gears and starting thinking about going into journalism. I took my first news writing course my sophomore year in college. I was failing "the inverted pyramid" class until my last assignment: writing a profile on the mayor of Cincinnati, then Jerry Springer.

After the interview, I told him I was failing the class. He told me to forget the rules and write the way I wanted to write. I did. Got an A, pulled my grade up to a C. And the professor recommended that I work for the student newspaper.

Despite Springer's advice, I still was majoring in political science, but my heart was in journalism. My future wife persuaded me to follow my heart. I did. Here I am, still married to her and still in journalism.

Is it harder for a college student who is a "joiner" on campus, who might be popular, and who loves his or her friendships to enter a career sometimes described as a mission or a kind of professional priesthood? "Generally, yes," Waters responds.

I'm sure there are exceptions. But I think a commitment to journalism requires a certain detachment and neutrality in what's going on around you. You have to remain, for the most part, on the outside looking in on the world. Joiners get involved, get attached, and often—though not always—lose the neutrality required to gather and tell the truth.

I've never joined a political party. I joined a church, but only before I began covering religion. I'll never join another. I'm a paper member of the PTA, but I never attend meetings or events. That's one of the "sacrifices" you make as a journalist, in order to maintain at least the appearance of neutrality. Not objectivity. Again, no one can remain perfectly objective about important matters and beliefs. But you can practice and achieve neutrality and be fair and impartial in your reporting.

What motivates younger journalists coming into the business today? Any differences from when he began?

"Same as it ever was," he says. "Generally speaking, people who go into print journalism want to write for a living, and they want to find out and explain how things really work. Some of that is idealistic: they want people to know the truth about politics, government, business, and so on. But more of it is just sort of a general curiosity about the world. They want to find out and let others know how politics, government, business really work. It's more realism than idealism."

So how has David Water's own idealism about the journalism profession held up over the years? For the most part, fairly well, he says.

Nearly all of my expectations have been met and exceeded. I wanted my work to be useful and meaningful, and it is and has been. I wanted to be engaged, challenged, pushed to be creative, and given the room to try. I have been and continue to be. I also wanted to be able to earn a living and support a family. So far, so good.

Lately, however, my hopes and expectations for daily journalism are being challenged and even put in jeopardy, mostly by greed. Wall Street is killing daily journalism, and no one seems too upset about it.

Notes

1. Edward R. Murrow, "Lights and Wires in a Box" (speech, Radio-Television News Directors Association Convention, Chicago, IL, October 15, 1958).

2. Rich Lynch and Laura Lynch, "Laurel Canyon: Molded by Music . . . and Manson," *Kweevak.com Music Magazine*, http://www.kweevak.com/files-articles/rd_art_2006_05_30_laurel_canyon.php (accessed April 21, 2009).

3. Michael Perlstein, "Covering Katrina: On Taking It Personally," *Reed Magazine*, Winter 2006, http://www.reed.edu/reed_magazine/winter06/features/covering_katrina/perlstein1.html.

4. Terry Mattingly, "What We Do, Why We Do It," *GetReligion.org* [online posting], February 1, 2004.

5. Otis L. Sanford, "Gov Beebe Delivers Straight Talk on Politics," *The Commercial Appeal*, August 6, 2007.

Selected Bibliography

Boorstin, Daniel J. *The Image: A Guide to Pseudo-Events in America.* New York: Atheneum, 1985.

Bradlee, Ben. *A Good Life: Newspapering and Other Adventures.* New York: Simon and Schuster, 1996.

Cooper, Anderson. *Dispatches From the Edge.* New York: HarperCollins, 2006.

Cottle, Simon. *News, Public Relations, and Power.* Thousand Oaks: Sage, 2003.

Craft, Christine. *An Anchorwoman's Story.* Santa Barbara: Capra, 1986.

Craft, Christine. *Too Old, Too Ugly, Not Deferential Enough to Men.* New York: St. Martins, 1986.

Cronkite, Walter. *A Reporter's Life.* New York: Knopf, 1996.

Darton, Kate, Kayee Freed Jennings, and Lynn Sherr, eds. *A Reporter's Life: Peter Jennings.* New York: Public Affairs/Perseus, 2007.

Emery, Michael, Edwin Emery, and Nancy L. Roberts. *The Press and America: An Interpretive History of the Mass Media.* 9th ed. Boston: Allyn & Bacon, 2000.

Entman, Robert M. *Projections of Power: Framing News, Public Opinion, and U.S. Foreign Policy.* Chicago: University of Chicago, 2003.

Franklin, Bob, ed. *Social Policy, the Media, and Misrepresentation.* London: Routledge, 1999.

Fuller, Jack. *News Values: Ideas for an Information Age.* Chicago: University of Chicago Press, 1996.

Gans, Herbert J. *Deciding What's News.* New York: Vantage, 1980.

Gibbs, Nancy, and Michael Duffy. *The Preacher and the Presidents: Billy Graham in the White House.* New York: Center Street, 2007.

Gilens, Martin. *Why Americans Hate Welfare: Race, Media, and the Politics of Antipoverty Policy.* Chicago: University of Chicago, 2000.

Ginneken, Jaap van. *Understanding Global News: A Critical Introduction.* London: Sage Ltd, 1998.

Graham, Katharine. *A Personal History.* New York: Vintage, 1996.

Hausman, Carl. *The Decision Making Process in Journalism.* Chicago: Nelson-Hall, 1987.

Jamieson, Kathleen Hall, and Paul Waldman. *The Press Effect: Politicians, Journalists, and the Stories That Shape the Political World.* New York: Oxford University Press, 2003.

Kessler, Lauren. *The Dissident Press: Alternative Journalism in American History.* Beverly Hills, CA: Sage, 1984.

Kurtz, Howard. *Reality Show: Inside the Last Great Television News War.* New York: Free Press, 2007.

Liebling, A. J. *The Press.* 2nd ed. New York: Random House, 1975.

Lippmann, Walter. *Public Opinion.* New York: Macmillan, 1922.

Newman, Jay. *The Journalist in Plato's Cave.* Rutherford, NJ: Fairleigh Dickinson University Press, 1989.

Rather, Dan, with Mickey Herskowitz. *The Camera Never Blinks.* New York: Morrow, 1977.

Robinson, Piers. *The CNN Effect: The Myth of News Media, Foreign Policy and Intervention.* London: Routledge, 2002.

Ryan, John, and William M. Wentworth. *Media and Society: The Production of Culture in the Mass Media.* Boston: Allyn & Bacon, 1999.

Snyder, Louis L., and Richard B. Morris, eds. *A Treasury of Great Reporting.* New York: Simon and Schuster, 1962.

Sparks, Glenn G. *Media Effects Research: A Basic Overview.* 2nd ed. Belmont: Thomson, 2006.

Sperber, A.M. *Murrow: His Life and Times.* New York: Fordham University Press, 1998.

Willis, Jim. *The Human Journalist: Reporters, Perspectives, and Emotions.* Westport: Praeger, 2003.

Willis, Jim. *Reporting on Risks: The Practice and Ethics of Health and Safety Communication.* Westport: Praeger, 1997.

Willis, Jim. *The Shadow World: Life Between the News Media and Reality.* Westport: Praeger, 1990.

Woodward, Bob, and Carl Bernstein. *All the President's Men.* New York: Pocket Books, 2005.

Index

About the Author

Jim Willis is a veteran journalist for *The Oklahoman* and *The Dallas Morning News* and is now chair and professor of communication studies at Azusa Pacific University in Southern California. His reporting assignments have included the Oklahoma City bombing, the F5 tornado that struck Oklahoma City, and the tenth anniversary of the fall of the Berlin Wall. He has taught at the universities of Missouri, Oklahoma, and Memphis, and chaired the Communication Department at Boston College. He has authored ten books on journalists and the media, and he lectures widely in Europe on the American news media. He holds a PhD in journalism from the University of Missouri and a BA from the University of Oklahoma. He is married and has two sons and three stepdaughters.

Supporting researchers for more than 40 years

Research methods have always been at the core of SAGE's publishing program. Founder Sara Miller McCune published SAGE's first methods book, *Public Policy Evaluation*, in 1970. Soon after, she launched the *Quantitative Applications in the Social Sciences* series—affectionately known as the "little green books."

Always at the forefront of developing and supporting new approaches in methods, SAGE published early groundbreaking texts and journals in the fields of qualitative methods and evaluation.

Today, more than 40 years and two million little green books later, SAGE continues to push the boundaries with a growing list of more than 1,200 research methods books, journals, and reference works across the social, behavioral, and health sciences. Its imprints—Pine Forge Press, home of innovative textbooks in sociology, and Corwin, publisher of PreK–12 resources for teachers and administrators—broaden SAGE's range of offerings in methods. SAGE further extended its impact in 2008 when it acquired CQ Press and its best-selling and highly respected political science research methods list.

From qualitative, quantitative, and mixed methods to evaluation, SAGE is the essential resource for academics and practitioners looking for the latest methods by leading scholars.

For more information, visit **www.sagepub.com**.